Heinemann IGCSE

ICT

Roger Crawford

WANG·YUCHEN

BELLA

www.pearsonis.com

Free online support
Useful weblinks
24 hour online ordering

Heinemann

Heinemann is an imprint of Pearson Education Limited, a company incorporated in England and Wales, having its registered office at Edinburgh Gate, Harlow, Essex, CM20 2JE. Registered company number: 872828.

www.pearsonschoolsandfecolleges.co.uk

Heinemann is a registered trademark of Pearson Education Limited

Text © Pearson Education Limited 2010

First published 2010

14 13 12 11
10 9 8 7 6 5 4 3 2

ISBN 978 0 435966 87 4

Edited by Matthew Strawbridge
Designed by Tony Richardson
Typeset by Tech-Set Ltd
Original illustrations © Pearson Education Limited 2010
Illustrated by Tech-Set Ltd
Cover design by Creative Monkey
Picture research by Joanne Forrest Smith
Indexed by Martin Brooks
Cover photo © Benelux/Corbis
Printed in Malaysia, CTP-KHL

Acknowledgements
The author and publisher would like to thank the following individuals and organisations for permission to reproduce photographs:

Alamy/Anthony Hatley p.8c, picturesbyrob p.10, Editorial Image LLC p.11, fStop p.14, Oliver Leedham p.18b, Mitja Mladkovic p.82c, Corbis RF p.28cr, Art Directors & Trip p.30, Eddie Gerald p.32c, Johnny Stockshooter p.203, Gautier Stephane/Sagaphoto.com p.236, Shenval p.293, Alex Segre p.296, Mark Bassett p.301, Tetra Images p.309, Paul Thompson Images p.312, StephenBarnes Technology and Engineering p.314; Brand X Pictures/Joe Atlas p.98; Comstock Images p.16; Corbis/David Sailors p.297, 324 (D); Getty Images/Lester Lefkowitz p.244, B2M Productions p.248, Alistair Berg p.284, Charlie Schuck p.283; iStockphoto.com p.6, 7c, 7b, 8t, 11b, 12, 32b, 128, 234, 324 (A), (B); Pearson Education Ltd/Gareth Boden p.1 (main), 18cl, Ian Wedgewood p.1, 40, 57, 165, 300, Naki Kouyioumtzis p.7t, Studio p.8, Clark Wiseman p.13, Lord and Leverett p.267, Mark Bassett p.318, 324 (C&E); Photodisc/ C Squared Studios p.5, 18cr, 25, 28b, 232, Kim Steele p.242, Brofsky Studio Inc. p.295, Life File/Michael Evans p.304; Photolibrary/ James Hardy p.46b, Creatas p.289, 305; Science Photo Library/Will & Deni McIntyre p.310

Image of the BBC Radio homepage reproduced with the written permission of the British Broadcasting Corporation. © BBC 2009. Screenshot of University of Cambridge International Examinations (CIE) public website reproduced by permission of the University of Cambridge Local Examinations Syndicate. Screenshot of Yahoo websites reproduced with permission of Yahoo! Inc. © 2010 Yahoo! Inc. YAHOO! and the YAHOO! logo are registered trademarks of Yahoo! Screenshot of the first direct website reproduced with permission. Microsoft, Excel, Powerpoint, Outlook, Access and Windows are either registered trademarks or trademarks of Miscrosoft Corporation in the United States and/or other countries.

All other trademarks are property of their respective owners.

Every effort has been made to contact copyright holders of material reproduced in this book. Any omissions will be rectified in subsequent printings if notice is given to the publishers.

Websites
The websites used in this book were correct and up to date at the time of publication. It is essential for tutors to preview each website before using it in class so as to ensure that the URL is still accurate, relevant and appropriate. We suggest that tutors bookmark useful websites and consider enabling students to access them through the school/college intranet.

Author's Preface

Throughout this book the emphasis is on preparation for assessment for IGCSE Information and Communication Technology (ICT). The book will be useful in extending theoretical knowledge and understanding, as the practical skills needed to do coursework are developed. The text should be read with the Cambridge IGCSE ICT specification, specimen papers and other support materials provided by the awarding body at hand, and these can be obtained from University of Cambridge International Examinations (CIE).

In writing this book I have valued the help and advice given to me both directly and indirectly. My thanks go to editorial staff at Pearson and others who made useful comments at different stages of the development of this book. In particular, Matthew Strawbridge edited the original manuscript that referred throughout to Office 2003 running on XP so that it now refers to Office 2007. I am grateful to colleagues at Rhodesway School, Bradford and at Queensbury School, Bradford for their help and inspiration while I was employed at each school. I am particularly grateful for the assistance given to me by the School of Education and Professional Development at the University of Huddersfield where I am now employed as a Senior Lecturer in Education coordinating the PGCE teacher training course in ICT. My wife, Jennie, has patiently tolerated the long hours I have spent writing this textbook. Without the support of colleagues, friends and family this book would not have been written.

This book is based on an original work written by Roland Birbal and Joseph Blair to help students cover the CSEC Information Technology Technical Proficiency syllabus. It has been extensively edited and adapted.

Roger Crawford

Contents

Chapter 1

Hardware

Information and Communication Technology (ICT) systems based on computers are commonplace. From the moment you wake, ICT affects you every day. In many cities, ICT systems control the power supply. Computers also print your electricity and telephone bills and many others. The milk you use at breakfast comes in a package marked with a bar code. The pattern of bars represents the identification number for the contents of the package. The checkout at the supermarket serves as an electronic point-of-sale machine, reading the pattern and recognising the number. The computer then knows which item has been purchased, and what its price should be. So the computer affects your breakfast! And computers are used to design and test many parts of the car, bus or bicycle that you use. The effects of ICT systems can be seen everywhere.

Input, output, processing and storage

A common feature of every computer is that its user always has some information to be processed. The user may type in the **data** (unprocessed information), then press a key or perform some other action so the processing can take place. When the job is complete, the answer is produced. So we have three stages: input, processing and output.

◀ **Figure 1.1**
Computers are now part of our everyday lives

Storing data

A **computer** *is an electronic machine that can follow a set of instructions to input, process, store and output data.*

Let's look at each part of that sentence.

- **ELECTRONIC** – Computers are electronic devices. They use tiny electric currents, flowing through circuits, to do their operations.

- **MACHINE** – This is a device to do work easily.

- **INSTRUCTIONS** – The computer must have a sequence of instructions, given in a **program**. The computer will follow this sequence, so the program is essential in getting the computer to do its job.

- **INPUT** – is when data is typed in or otherwise entered into the computer.

- **PROCESS** – The computer processes data, just as you could process your ingredients to get a tasty cooked meal. Think of the computer program as a recipe with instructions to follow. Raw food goes in as input and, after processing, out comes the well-baked dish!

- **STORE** – A computer not only processes data, but can store or save it too.

- **OUTPUT** – This is when the computer displays text or graphics on the screen, prints, plays sounds or otherwise communicates to the user.

- **DATA** – This is the raw information to be processed – just like the raw food.

A computer is a *programmable* machine. Basically it can do whatever it is programmed to do. And notice carefully that it is just a machine. It cannot think. It automatically follows the set of codes or instructions given in a program.

What is the difference between data and information? **Data** means raw, unprocessed information. It could be numbers, or words and letters. **Information** is data that people understand. In order to understand *data*, you may have to interpret it.

For example:
The number 10092004 is data.

This can be interpreted as:

- A date 10/09/2004
- A sum of money $100,920.04

The interpreted data is information. That is, the date or the sum of money is information.

We need to be careful how we interpret data as it can mean quite different things when it is information.

Typically, a computer inputs data, processes it following program instructions, and outputs information. This is often a cyclical process with the user inputting data, viewing the output, and responding to the output by inputting more data. While the data is being processed, data can be retrieved from backing storage or saved on it. This is interactive processing and it provides the user with an immediate response. This can be like an active two-way conversation between the user and the computer.

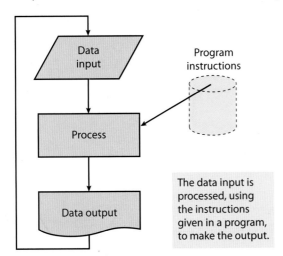

The data input is processed, using the instructions given in a program, to make the output.

◀ **Figure 1.2**
Flow of data

What is hardware?

Computer hardware is the equipment that makes up the physical ICT system. Components such as the **keyboard**, the **monitor** screen, the **system unit** and everything inside it, and other devices that might be attached externally, such as a **printer**. Usually, the monitor, keyboard and other devices will be connected to the system unit.

- The **keyboard** has keys that enable you to enter individual alphabetic characters and numbers. There are extra keys that perform special functions.

- The **monitor** screen will let you see what you are doing as you work (or play) on the computer.

- The **mouse** is your pointing device. As you move the mouse on its pad, a pointer on the monitor screen moves in the same direction as the mouse does. You use the mouse to position the pointer on the screen, and you click the mouse buttons to select and activate items.

- The **system unit** is the box where all the processing takes place. All the other devices are installed in it or connected to it.

- The **microprocessor** or **Central Processing Unit (CPU)** is the heart of the computer, and is inside the system unit.

A computer system may also include a **scanner**, a **modem**, **speakers**, a **DVD drive** and other hardware devices temporarily attached to it, such as a smart phone or an external hard disk.

An **input device** is for 'putting in' information to the machine. The keyboard is an input device; you type characters in using the keyboard.

Look for these keys on your keyboard:
- Space bar
- Alt
- Ctrl
- Del
- Shift
- Caps Lock
- Tab
- Enter
- Backspace
- Numeric keypad

The mouse is another input device. The monitor is an **output device**. Your computer uses it to display things to you. Another output device is the printer.

Look at Figure 1.3. The arrows show the direction of data flow. The keyboard sends information *in* to the system, hence the direction of the arrow from the keyboard to the system unit. Copy this diagram and draw in the arrows that are missing from the other lines. The big circles are for you to name some additional devices. Then draw in the arrows for those devices too.

Figure 1.3 ▶
Common computer devices

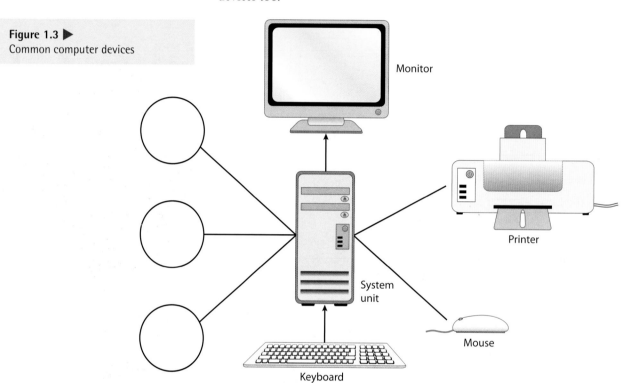

Types of computer

At first, computers were very large, but today a complex circuit can fit on a single chip the size of your fingernail. This means that computers can now be small and yet very powerful. It also means that if someone today builds a large computer, that machine will be really powerful. A computer just as powerful as the original machines can now fit easily into a schoolbag.

Computers can be grouped into microcomputers, minicomputers and mainframe computers:

- A **microcomputer** is usually for individual use, and so it is also called a **personal computer (PC)**.

- A **mainframe computer** is a large expensive computer, with huge processing power. It will be used by many people at the same time, and to carry out intensive tasks.

- A **minicomputer** is a smaller version of a mainframe computer.

- A **supercomputer** is a very large mainframe.

Different types of PC

A **desktop** PC usually has these basic components: a monitor, a keyboard, a system unit and a mouse.

Individual microcomputers

System units

A **laptop** computer is about the size of an A4 file. Laptops are increasingly becoming lighter and more portable (see Figure 1.5).

- A **tablet** computer is a laptop computer with a sensitive touch screen that can be used instead of the keyboard.

- A **notebook** computer is a small laptop computer that is about as big as an oversized book. A notebook computer is likely to be half the size of a laptop and is light and easy to carry.

- A **hand-held** computer or **Personal Digital Assistant (PDA)** or **palmtop** can fit in one hand or in your pocket, but it is too small for general work. A PDA has a touch-sensitive screen. Although PDAs can be temporarily attached to a keyboard, you cannot comfortably type a long document into a PDA. A **smart phone** is a mobile phone with the functions of a PDA. Handheld computing devices can perform a range of activities such as personal record-keeping and satellite navigation.

▲ **Figure 1.5**
A laptop computer

Figure 1.6 ▶
A hand-held computer attached to a larger keyboard

Exercise 1.1

1. Describe three ways your daily life is influenced by ICT systems. *entertainment*

2. Describe the similarities and differences between data and information.

3. Explain what is meant by hardware.

4. Draw a labelled diagram of a desktop computer system showing the range of hardware devices that could be attached to it.

5. Describe the similarities and differences between a desktop computer and a laptop computer.

6. Describe the similarities and differences between a desktop computer and a hand-held computer.

7. Describe the differences between the system unit and the microprocessor.

8. Explain how a PDA user can benefit from having an external keyboard.

9. Mainframe computers are not mass-produced. Give reasons for this.

10. Figure 1.2 shows the flow of data through the input–output process. If the input was the intake of pupils into a school, describe what would represent the 'PROCESS', the 'INSTRUCTIONS' and the 'FINAL OUTPUT'. See Figure 1.7.

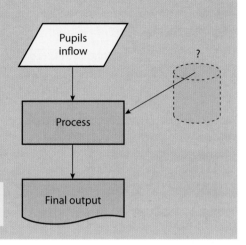

Figure 1.7 ▶
Another form of data flow

Input and output devices

There are many devices for putting information into a computer, and for displaying the information that is output. Essentially, the **peripheral** devices attached to a computer system are for input, output or storage.

Input devices

Input devices accept data signals, and translate them for usage and storage in the computer system.

Keyboards

The most widely used input device is a keyboard. There are different types of keyboard and of these the QWERTY keyboard (see Figure 1.8) is the most popular.

Advantages of keyboards:

- Keyboards are almost always available as an input device. They are widely used at work.

- Many people know how to use a QWERTY keyboard, so help is usually available.

Disadvantages of keyboards:

- To use a keyboard efficiently, you need to know the layout and be able to touch-type.

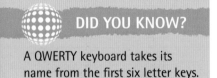

DID YOU KNOW?

A QWERTY keyboard takes its name from the first six letter keys.

Figure 1.8 ▶
A QWERTY keyboard

The **concept keyboard** is useful in some circumstances. A concept keyboard has a flat touch-sensitive surface. A plastic overlay is placed over this surface and different regions of the surface are programmed to act as keys. This can be useful where especially large keys are needed for use by people with disabilities. A similar arrangement is useful where there is a risk of dirt getting in the keyboard, such as at supermarket checkouts and cashpoints.

Numeric keyboards only have keys to input numbers and a few special characters. A QWERTY keyboard may have a numeric keyboard built into the right-hand side. Some devices have only a numeric keypad – for example, an automated teller machine (ATM), also known as a cashpoint.

▲ **Figure 1.9**
An automated teller machine (ATM) or cashpoint showing the numeric keypad

Pointing devices

There are many other input devices, including **pointing devices** that are used specifically for pointing to (and selecting) objects that are displayed on the monitor screen.

- The **mouse** is the most widely used pointing device. Some have a ball underneath that moves when you move the mouse, resulting in a similar movement of the pointer on the screen. An optical mouse detects movement using light instead of a ball.

- A **joystick** is a lever that gives you similar control to a mouse but its behaviour is slightly different. Joysticks can be used separately or can be built into game pads, where there are often two simple joysticks, one for each thumb (see Figure 1.10). Suppose you are playing a computer game, where you control a 'car' on the screen. The forward speed of the car may depend on how far forward you push the joystick. Moving the joystick left and right can determine the tightness of your steering turn. Some separate joystick have handles that can be twisted, and some have 'throttle' buttons as well or these features can be built into a game pad. All of these features can have different effects, depending on the program being used. So the joystick or game pad can be more than just a pointing device.

▲ **Figure 1.10**
A game pad with joysticks built in

- A mouse may have a ball underneath it which rolls as you move the mouse. If you turn it over, you can roll the ball with your index finger. A **tracker ball** (see Figure 1.11) is like an upside-down mouse. The ball is on the top of the device and you move it with your thumb.

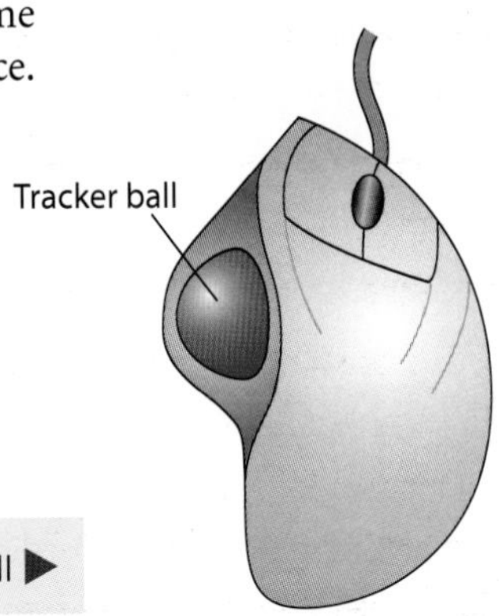

Tracker ball

Figure 1.11 A tracker ball ▶

- A **TrackPoint** (see Figure 1.12) is a small rubber cap in the middle of the keyboard, like a pencil eraser. Push it forward and the mouse pointer goes forward. A TrackPoint does not actually move like a joystick; but the harder you push it, the faster the pointer moves, since it is sensitive to the force upon it. A TrackPoint can work in conjunction with two buttons on the keyboard, below the space bar.

▲ **Figure 1.12**
The IBM TrackPoint II™, sitting between the keys of a notebook computer

- A **trackpad** (see Figure 1.13) is a small, flat, square pad below the space bar. As you move your finger across the trackpad's surface, the pointer moves across the screen.

- A **graphics tablet** (see Figure 1.14) or graphics pad is a flat rectangular pad between 6 and 30 inches (15 and 76 cm) wide. It works with a stylus, which you move along the surface of the pad to produce drawings in the computer. There are several types of stylus. One, the puck, is a small rounded device with cross-hairs for tracing lines accurately and with a number of buttons. The stylus can also be pen-shaped. A graphics tablet is used mainly for computer-aided design and drawing.

Figure 1.14 ▶
Graphics tablet and puck being used to trace a drawing

Advantages of pointing devices:

- Many people find it easier to point and click than to use a keyboard.

- It is usually easier to access most of the features of the software being used.

Disadvantages of pointing devices:

- A pointing device is not useful unless a graphical user interface is being used.

- Some people find it difficult to control the on-screen pointer using a pointing device.

- It can be much harder to input text with a pointing device than with a keyboard.

Scanners

A scanner reads printed data, usually a picture, into the computer. A number of different devices are referred to as scanners:

- A **hand-held scanner** reads in the picture while being dragged over it.

- In the case of a **flatbed scanner**, the picture is laid flat on the scanner's surface, and is captured in a similar manner to that of a photocopy machine.

- A **sheet-fed scanner** feeds the picture in through rollers. The scanner reads the picture as the paper goes through. The picture must be printed on a flexible sheet of paper.

There are also systems where the scanner reads a particular type of picture, and the computer tries to interpret it as something meaningful. In this case, there needs to be a program to analyse the picture. A bar code reader is an example of such a system. This reads a pattern of bars representing the code number of the item on which it is printed. The bar code reader usually passes a small laser beam over the pattern and reads in the pattern of reflected light. Bar code readers may be hand-held, but some are built into the surface of a supermarket checkout counter. Many other devices can scan information that has been printed or encoded in some way.

Advantages of scanners:

- Scanners quickly convert printed pictures on paper to electronic form.

Disadvantages of scanners:

- The accuracy of the data input is unlikely to be verified.

▲ **Figure 1.15**
A bar code

Light Pen

A **light pen** (or wand) is an input device shaped like a pen that can be used to draw on a computer screen or to point at objects. It is generally used like a mouse; for example, to select from a menu. When the tip of the light pen touches the screen it sends a signal back to the computer giving the X–Y coordinates of the point. Light pens work with cathode ray tube (CRT) monitors but not with liquid crystal display (LCD) screens. Light pens were moderately popular until LCDs displaced CRTs as the most popular computer monitor technology but are now rarely used.

The term **light pen** is also used to describe hand-held bar code readers and other hand-held scanners.

Optical Mark Recognition (OMR)

OMR technology is used to interpret pencil marks on a piece of paper. An OMR reader can recognise the position of a mark or set of marks on paper, because the mark is darker than an unmarked area. The computer then records the mark's position and can analyse it to determine the meaning of the data. Marks made on this kind of form must be very clear, or they may not be properly recognised.

Advantages of OMR:

- There is no requirement to type in the information written on the paper form. Because of this, input is faster and less expensive.

- The person who fills in the form is responsible for the accuracy of the information on it.

Disadvantages of OMR:

- OMR forms must be printed very accurately because the position of the mark on the paper affects the accuracy of the input. Because of this, printing costs more.

- Verification checks on the input are unlikely to be carried out, so mistakes inputting the data are less likely to be detected.

▲ **Figure 1.16**
A UK National Lottery form. An OMR reader is used to input the information on the form

Optical Character Recognition (OCR)

OCR is the identification of printed or written text characters by a computer. Printed text is scanned and input to the computer, which attempts to recognise the characters in it. These are then stored as text that can be word-processed. OCR can also be used to read handwriting. OCR software is often included when you purchase a scanner, so that any office with a scanner has OCR capabilities.

A similar process of character recognition is used to interpret handwriting on the screen of a PDA or tablet computer. PDAs and tablet computers have touch-sensitive screens that accept handwriting as input and have character recognition software that can convert it to text characters that can be word processed.

Advantages of OCR:

- Text printed on paper can be converted to electronic form and edited. This is especially useful for creating electronic versions of books printed before computers were available.

Disadvantages of OCR:

- Character recognition is not always accurate and the electronic text has to be checked carefully.

Magnetic ink character recognition

Magnetic ink character recognition (**MICR**) identifies data printed using a special magnetic ink. Instead of relying on reflected light to detect a character, it depends on the magnetic behaviour of the ink, which is activated by a magnetic field that can be detected by a MICR reader. Specially shaped magnetic ink characters are used to speed up recognition.

Do you notice the similarity between OCR and MICR? One difference is that one technology uses reflected light, while the other uses magnetic field patterns produced by the characters. Another important difference is that OCR systems can recognise handwriting and different types of text, but MICR needs specially shaped characters.

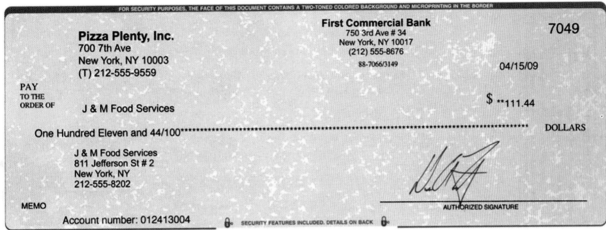

Figure 1.17
MICR uses uniquely shaped characters, printed in magnetic ink

Advantages of MICR:

- Forms can be pre-printed with data which can be read by a computer. This can save time as otherwise all the data on the form would have to be typed in using a keyboard.

Disadvantages of MICR:

- MICR characters have to be printed in magnetic ink and this is more expensive.

- Characters printed in ordinary ink are not detected.

Magnetic stripe card reader

A **magnetic stripe card reader** reads information from a magnetic stripe on the surface of a plastic card (see Figure 1.18) when it is swiped through the reader.

Stripe cards can be used to control access to buildings. For example, to gain access to a building or to leave it, a stripe card is passed through a reader that controls whether a door opens or closes. If the identification number on the card is recognised by the ICT system, the door will open; if not, the door remains closed. As a result, the ICT system knows who is in the building. Such a system could be used for registering school pupils; however, when large numbers of pupils enter a school at the same time, some may not bother to swipe their card through the reader. The ICT system can only know if a particular card is in the building and some pupils will give their cards to others to swipe for them. Such difficulties suggest countermeasures such as turnstiles or very careful supervision but these are often impractical as they can lead to long queues, disorder and the expense of employing supervisors.

Figure 1.18
A magnetic stripe card

Magnetic stripe cards are also widely used as bank or credit cards. In addition to being able to read the magnetic stripe, some devices can also write information to it. The stripe can store a permanent value, such as an account number, or a value that could change, such as the amount of cash you are allowed to withdraw from a cashpoint.

Advantages of magnetic stripe cards:

- They are often used as a form of identification that is small and light and can be carried at all times.
- The data recorded on the magnetic stripe is in electronic form and can be input directly into a computer.

Disadvantages of magnetic stripe cards:

- The data recorded on the magnetic stripe can be affected by electromagnetic radiation, such as that from televisions and computers.
- The data recorded on the magnetic stripe can be copied or edited. This is an opportunity for determined criminals to commit identity theft and fraud.

Smart cards

▲ **Figure 1.19**
A smart card showing the microprocessor chip embedded in it

A **smart card** is similar in shape and size to a magnetic stripe card, but has a microprocessor chip embedded in it (see Figure 1.19). The chip can do some processing, as well as storing information. Special devices can communicate with the chip to read and write information on the card. Security features can be programmed into the chip.

Bank and credit cards used to be magnetic stripe cards but are now more usually smart cards or **Chip and PIN** (personal identification number) cards. In most European countries, these cards can be used to withdraw cash at a cashpoint. Cashpoints are specialised computer terminals with a small screen, numeric keyboard and smart card reader. The customer puts their card in the reader and is prompted to enter their four-digit PIN. If the PIN entered on the keyboard matches the PIN read from the card, the customer can proceed; if not, the card is either confiscated or returned to the customer. Most ATMs will dispense cash and display the balance in the customer's bank account. In a similar way, bank and credit cards can also be used to pay for goods in retail stores such as supermarkets.

A Chip and PIN card provides very secure access to a bank or credit card account. The customer should remember their PIN (it should not be written down), and no one else should know it. For this reason, the numeric keyboard is shielded so that it is difficult for anyone other than the person entering their PIN to see what number is entered.

An Oyster® card is an electronic smart card that can be used to pay for travel, as well as in shops, theatres and restaurants and for entry to tourist attractions. It is used very much like a bank or credit card except that it is preloaded with cash credits. This can be done on the Web or in a manner similar to withdrawing cash from a cashpoint. As a result, payments can be made without online access at the time. Payment is made by touching the Oyster card on a reader and the payment is automatically deducted. This speeds up payment. Oyster cards are in widespread use in London.

Advantages of smart cards:

- Often used as a form of identification that is small and light and can be carried at all times.
- The data recorded on the chip is in electronic form and can be input directly into a computer.

- The data recorded on the chip is more secure than data recorded on a magnetic stripe.

- The data recorded on the chip can be updated during transactions.

Disadvantages of smart cards:

- The data recorded on the chip can be affected by electromagnetic radiation; for example, from televisions and computers.

- The data recorded on the chip can be copied or edited by very determined criminals and used for fraud.

Digital cameras, digital video cameras and webcams

Digital cameras store pictures on a memory card in a format suitable for saving and displaying on a computer. Pictures can be transferred from the camera to the computer where they can be edited and enhanced in graphics software or viewed on screen. The pictures can be transferred to a computer directly by connecting the camera to the computer, or the memory card can be removed and read using a memory card reader, which may be built into the computer or connected to it. Television sets can also have memory card readers built in or connected so that several people can view the pictures together on a large screen.

The picture made by a digital camera (as for a printer or a monitor) is formed by a mass of very small dots of different colours, merging to form a picture. The picture quality is related to the density (or closeness) of the dots making the picture, the accurate placement of the dots and the correctness of the colours being displayed. Thus an 'eight mega-pixel' camera uses eight million dots (the **pixels**) to form a picture, and so would usually produce better output than a 'two mega-pixel' camera.

Digital cameras may have a traditional viewfinder but more usually have a small LCD screen or both. The advantage of having both is that the viewfinder can be used if bright sunlight makes the LCD screen unclear.

A digital video camera or camcorder has similar functions to a digital camera but records moving images with sound. Camcorders can save recordings on a memory card but may also use DVD, miniDV tape or a built-in hard disk. All these formats are transferable to a computer for editing and storage and are likely to be playable on a home entertainment system.

A **webcam** is a type of digital video camera where the image captured is viewed using a computer. Recordings can be made but this is not always done. A webcam can be used to view a remote location. The computer connects to the webcam over the Web and the image is displayed on the computer screen. This has a variety of different uses:

- You could see if the weather is suitable for skiing by viewing the webcam in the mountains above Grindelwald in Switzerland.

- You could install a webcam at home for security and view this when you are out at work.

▲ **Figure 1.20**
A digital camera

- You could attach a webcam to your computer and contact a friend who has a webcam so that you could both see each other while you are talking. You could use VoIP (Voice over Internet Protocol) software to do this. You could use a similar arrangement to practise speaking a foreign language.

- You could set up a webcam in a classroom and listen to a teacher from another school. This might be useful if you were learning to speak English and could not find a teacher locally.

Simple webcams have a fixed position and can see only one view; however, some webcams allow the user to turn them so that many different views can be seen.

Advantages:

- Photos and video can be recorded in a digital form that can be saved on a computer. This makes backup easier, more reliable and more extensive.

- Digital photos and video can be displayed on a wide variety of devices, such as smart phones and television screens. This allows access in a wider range of locations and by several people at the same time.

- Digital photos and video can be sent by e-mail.

- Digital video can be broadcast over the Internet so that TV programmes can be available on demand.

Disadvantages:

- Users tend to have more photos and longer videos and this creates a need for more backing storage.

- High-quality photos and videos can be in very large files. When these are sent by e-mail or broadcast over the Internet, this uses bandwidth and slows down the network.

Biometric scanners

A **biometric scanner** is a pattern recognition system which makes a personal identification based on a person's unique physical characteristics. Biometric scanners can use face recognition, fingerprint matching, iris and retinal scans, voice recognition, and hand geometry. Biometric scanners can be built into mobile phones, desktop and laptop computers, and smart cards. They can be used to control entry to buildings, and can even replace keys in cars.

Advantages of biometric scanners:

- There is no need to remember to carry personal identification.

- The person has to be present. This makes identification theft and fraud much less likely.

Disadvantages of biometric scanners:

- Identification using biometric scanners is not yet sufficiently accurate. Permitted users will not be recognised at times, and blocked users will sometimes be permitted.

▲ Figure 1.21
A biometric scanner using finger prints

Sensors

Sensors are used to input data about the environment into a computer. There are many types of sensors. They are available in many different shapes and sizes, and they have a wide variety of uses. For example, sensors can be used to record light intensity, temperature and pressure. Sensors usually produce a low voltage which must be converted to a digital signal for the computer using an analogue-to-digital converter (ADC).

Sensors are used extensively for data logging and control applications. They are essential in applications such as the following: automatic washing machines, automatic cookers, air conditioning controllers, central heating controllers, computer-controlled greenhouses, burglar alarm systems, control of factory production lines, robotics, and for monitoring scientific experiments and remote weather stations.

Advantages of sensors:

- Sensors can be placed in dangerous locations where people would be hurt.

- Sensors can continuously and reliably record data whereas to organise this using people could be much more unreliable and expensive.

- Sensors can record data that people do not sense or do not sense accurately, such as humidity.

- The data recorded by sensors can be automatically recorded in a form that can be processed by a computer.

- Data can be collected by a central computer from sensors in remote locations. People do not need to travel and this saves time and allows data to be collected more frequently.

Disadvantages of sensors:

- Sensors cannot interpret the data.

- Sensors detect a very restricted range of the different types of data.

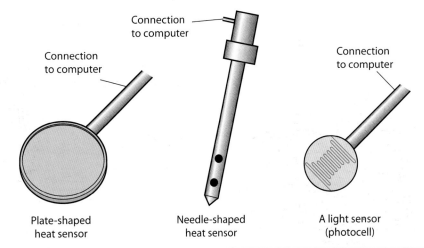

Plate-shaped heat sensor

Needle-shaped heat sensor

A light sensor (photocell)

Audio input devices and technologies

There are various input devices and technologies relating to computer input from sound.

- A **touch-tone telephone** issues a beep whose frequency depends on the button being pressed. A receiving device on the other end of the line can analyse the beep to determine which button is being pressed. So your touch-tone telephone can function as an input device. You may then listen to a voice response on the earpiece.

- A microphone can be used to record sounds and voices, to give voice commands and for voice communication over the Internet.

▲ **Figure 1.22**
Sensors are available in different shapes and sizes

- Your voice carries many tones, all making up the sound that people hear. People can recognise your voice because they can recognise the combination of tones that make up your voice. Computers have also been programmed to do voice recognition. **Voice recognition** software enables the computer to know who is talking but not what has been said.

- **Speech recognition** is often used for **voice command systems**. These require that the voice first be recognised, as above. A microphone is used to input the spoken words, which are then analysed by the program. The sound is compared with other sounds stored in the computer, to find the matching word; this match may be interpreted as a command. This is an unreliable process because a user can make words sound differently at different times, and different users will say the same words differently. As a result, the software may have to be trained to recognise a particular user.

- **Natural language processing** is where a computer processes a sequence of instructions or data given in a natural language – for instance, spoken English. You could use natural language processing to dictate a letter or give instructions to a computer.

Advantages of audio input:

- People speak to the computer and do not have to learn how to operate a keyboard or other input device.

Disadvantages of audio input:

- Voice recognition software has to be trained to recognise human speech. This can be a very lengthy process if the computer needs to recognise the full range of words used.

- Voice recognition is not entirely accurate because people pronounce words differently and speak in a wide range of accents and different tones of voice.

Remote Control

Many devices can be operated using a remote control handset (see Figure 1.23). Here are some examples: televisions, video players and recorders, DVD players and recorders, satellite receivers, hi-fi music systems, multimedia projectors, model cars and airplanes, and garage doors.

The main remote control technology used in the home is infrared. The signals between a remote control handset and the device it is controlling are infrared light pulses, which are invisible to the human eye.

The **transmitter** in the remote control handset sends out a pulse of infrared light when a button is pressed on the handset. A transmitter is often a light-emitting diode (LED) which is built into the pointing end of the remote control handset (see Figure 1.24). The infrared light pulse represents a binary code that corresponds to a command, such as 'power on' or 'volume down'. A **receiver** is built into the device being controlled in a position where it can easily receive the infrared light pulses – for example, it is built into the front of a satellite TV receiver. The receiver passes the code to a microprocessor, which decodes it and carries out the command.

▲ **Figure 1.23**
A remote control handset

The remote control handset will often have two LEDs that light up at the same time when a button is pressed. One LED is the infrared transmitter and the light from this is invisible. The other LED emits a visible light and this is to reassure the user that the remote control is functioning (see Figure 1.24).

Some handsets only work when they are pointing directly at the receiver on the controlled device, while others work when they are pointing generally towards the receiver. This is because the strength of the infrared light pulse varies. A handset with more than one infrared LED or a very powerful LED can produce a stronger, broader signal.

▲ **Figure 1.24**
The LEDs built into a remote control handset

Advantages of remote control:

- Less movement and energy are needed to operate remote controlled devices.

- Inaccessible or hidden devices can be controlled.

Disadvantages of remote control:

- Some devices cannot be operated without the remote control handset. If this is lost or damaged, the device cannot be used.

Output devices

Monitors

Monitors are also known as **visual display units** (**VDUs**). They come in different styles and quality levels. Screen colour quality, resolution and clarity are just some of the features that affect how desirable a particular monitor is to you.

Picture elements

Although the picture on a computer monitor may look sharp and clear, it is made up of many illuminated dots known as **picture elements** or **pixels**. The dots are usually so tiny that you would not normally notice them individually – you just see the whole picture. If you could actually see the picture elements, the picture would look jagged (see Figure 1.25).

The screen itself may perhaps have 1024 screen dots going across the screen, and 768 from top to bottom. In this case the screen is said to have a **resolution** of 1024 by 768. These screen dots are not the same as picture elements, because some software packages use picture elements that are much bigger than the tiny screen dots. For many packages, however, the picture element is as small as the screen dot – this is the smallest possible size for the pixel.

The display card

Also known as the **video card**, the **display card** is housed within the system unit, and controls the signals going to the monitor screen. Higher-quality cards can produce very clear graphics. Some computer games demand advanced display cards and high-quality monitor screens.

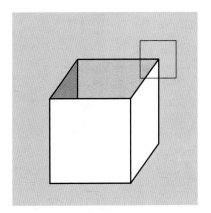

A perfect box

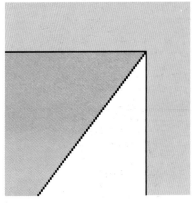

Close-up view of the top right corner, showing the picture elements (pixels)

▲ **Figure 1.25**
Picture elements

Cathode ray tube (CRT) monitors

Cathode ray tube monitors used to be the commonest type of monitor. In a CRT monitor, the inner face of the glass screen is coated with phosphorescent material. A beam of charged particles strikes this, causing it to glow. For a colour display, three different types of particles coat the inner glass of the screen, each supporting a different colour: red, green or blue. They blend to form the full range of colours. The accuracy of the beam and the closeness of the screen coating particles affect the display's clarity. CRT monitors can be relatively bulky (see Figures 1.26 and 1.27).

Liquid crystal display (LCD) monitors

Liquid crystal display technology allows the screen to be flat, instead of bulky as with CRT monitors. LCD screens consume less power than CRT displays. An LCD screen is generally more compact but more expensive than a corresponding CRT display (see Figures 1.26 and 1.27).

Figure 1.26
Front view of an LCD monitor and a CRT monitor ▼

Figure 1.27 ▶
Side view of an LCD monitor and a CRT monitor

Touch screen

A touch screen is not just an output device; it is a two-way user interface. You can interact with the computer by touching pictures or words on the screen. Touch screens are widely used with tablet PCs, PDAs and ATMs.

Multimedia projector

A multimedia projector projects an image that would normally be displayed on a computer screen onto a larger, separate screen. This allows the image on the screen to be shared with an audience in a large room. Multimedia projectors are almost always used when giving a computer-based presentation. They can be found in school classrooms, university lecture theatres and commercial training organisations. Multimedia projectors are also used with home entertainment systems, enabling people to watch TV and DVDs and to play computer games.

Advantages of monitor screens:

- Enables the use of a graphical user interface.
- Interactive, on-screen use of a computer is more natural and intuitive than programming.

Disadvantages of monitor screens:

- Screen size can limit the extent and detail of what can be seen. For example, it is possible to refer to several printed pages at the same time. It could be much more difficult to arrange this on a monitor.
- Screen displays can be difficult to read for people who have impaired sight.

Printers

Printed output is often called a **printout** or **hard copy**. An **impact printer** usually strikes through an inked ribbon, making marks on the paper. A **non-impact printer** uses a non-striking method to form the image on the paper. Examples of non-impact printers are laser printers and inkjet printers.

- **Dot-matrix printers** have a printer head consisting of a matrix of pins which strike a carbon ribbon, each hammer causing a dot to be printed on the paper. The dots combine to form the shapes of letters. Dot-matrix printers are a type of **impact printer**.

- **Inkjet printers** use tiny dots of ink sprayed onto the paper, forming the shapes of characters and pictures. Inkjet printers are much quieter than dot-matrix printers and produce better quality output. They usually produce colour prints, and are very popular for home and small-office use.

- **Laser printers** use laser light to make patterns of ink on a drum. This drum then transfers the ink to the paper, and finally a heating process fuses the ink to the paper. Laser technology gives excellent quality, and prints quickly. Laser printers are widely used but are more expensive than inkjet printers, and often only print in black and white.

- **Thermal printers** use heated wires to mark dots on the surface of a heat-sensitive paper.

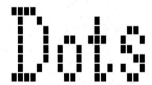

▲ **Figure 1.28**
Enlarged dot-matrix printing showing how the dots form characters

- **Thermal dye transfer printers** use special coloured dyes heated into a gas. This process gives the best quality of colour printing, but is very expensive and requires special paper.

- **Thermal wax transfer printers** use molten wax, forming tiny dots of different colours on the paper. These coloured wax dots blend to produce tones.

Buffers and spooling

Printers (and some other devices) are much slower than the computers and networks that send information to them to be printed. So that the computer does not have to wait for the printer to finish printing, most printers have a **buffer** (a small memory amount of memory) built into them. A document sent to the printer will be quickly saved in the buffer so that the computer can do other tasks while the printer is printing the document.

A buffer will only hold a few short documents, and on large networks many users may be sharing the same printer. To avoid users having to wait, documents are first put into a queue on a server and then sent for printing in turn. This queuing process is known as **spooling**.

Print quality

All these types of printer use very small dots to produce pictures. The smaller the dot, the better the quality of the picture. An important measure of print quality is the number of **dots per inch (dpi)**. The higher the dpi, the better the picture. In addition, for the best-quality output the dots must be accurately placed.

Printers and paper

Printers can use different types of paper.

- Many printers use sheets of A4 paper.

- Some printers have a long stream of **continuous paper** flowing through. Usually the paper is perforated, so that it can be torn easily to produce separate pages of output. There may be several sheets together, either impregnated with carbon or with carbon sheets between them, so that multiple copies are produced at once.

- In pre-printed stationery, certain information – for instance, the name of a company – has already been printed on the paper. This is usually the case with utility bills, which are printed with a high-volume single-coloured printer on forms that already have coloured logos and other symbols printed on them.

Photo-printers

Photo-printers are specially designed to print digital photographs. A memory card storing pictures taken by a digital camera can sometimes be plugged directly into the printer, and the pictures printed. In other cases, the camera can be directly connected to the printer.

Advantages of printers:

- Printed output can be viewed without the need for a computer.

- Many people and organisations still use paper-based communications and similar legacy methods.

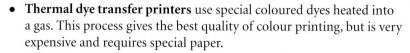
DID YOU KNOW?

You can see this process in action. If you are using a computer with a local printer attached, print a long document then turn off the computer but not the printer. The printer will continue printing and will print that part of the document that is in its buffer.

Disadvantages of printers:

- Printing is slow and expensive compared with electronic communications and storage.

- Paper is bulky and deteriorates in storage.

- Printed materials are more difficult to access and distribute. For example, printed photographs can be viewed by a limited number of people compared with digital photographs displayed on a TV screen, and it is more difficult and expensive to send copies to others.

Plotters

A **plotter** draws lines on paper using differently coloured pens. In a flatbed plotter, the paper is held still while the pen moves. Other plotters have the pen moving from left to right, while the paper goes forwards and backwards. Yet others use wires to draw charged patterns on special paper, then fuse toner onto the electrically charged patterns. If a job essentially consists of lines – for instance, a graph – a plotter will quickly draw the required lines. An upright plotter can also handle very long sheets of paper, because of the way the paper flows, and can produce long continuous lines. Plotters are frequently used in **computer-aided design**.

Advantages of plotters:

- Much larger and longer sheets can be printed.

Disadvantages of plotters:

- Printing is very slow.

- Plotters are usually more expensive than printers.

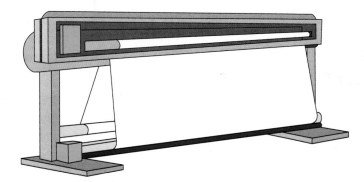

◀ **Figure 1.29**
An upright plotter

Multi-function devices

Printers are now being built in combination with scanners, and sometimes with fax machines. Combining a printer with a scanner produces the effective functionality of a photocopying machine, as well as providing the separate functions of scanning and printing.

Advantages of multi-function devices:

- A multi-function device takes up much less space on the desktop than the individual devices it replaces.

- A multi-function device is usually less expensive to buy than all the individual devices it replaces.

- A multi-function device will be used more before it becomes obsolete.
- A multi-function device can be replaced more frequently, having provided good value, so that more modern technology is available for use.

Disadvantages of multi-function devices:

- If part of the device develops a fault, all the functions may be unavailable.
- Only one person at a time can use a multi-function device.

Speakers

A simple set of two stereo **speakers** makes a range of sounds available. Sound is needed when computers are used for any of the following activities: to play music, to make telephone calls using VoIP, to listen to voicemail, to play video and DVDs for entertainment and education, or to listen to online TV and radio.

Speakers are also needed for **speech synthesis**, where a computer reproduces human speech. The voice need not be a recording – it could be computer-generated. For instance, you can have a text-reading program that takes a word-processed document in electronic form and reads it aloud.

Advantages of speakers:

- They allow computer systems to be used for a wide range of multimedia applications.
- Interaction with a computer using voice recognition and speech synthesis is more natural and intuitive than programming.

Disadvantages of speakers:

- Applications that use speakers can be difficult to operate for people who have impaired hearing.
- Voice recognition systems can be difficult to set up and use.

Actuators

In control applications, computers make events happen using **actuators**. Examples of actuators are valves, heaters, coolers and motors. These can be powered by a range of different sources of energy, including electricity and compressed air. Actuators also include devices such as buzzers and alarms, which can warn us about various events: a burglar has entered through the window, the automatic cooker has finished cooking our pizza, or the microwave oven has defrosted the frozen chicken.

Advantages of actuators:

- Actuators enable a computer to perform physical tasks in the real world. For example, computers can control a central heating system or a mechanical digger.

Disadvantages of actuators:

- Actuators perform physical operations when instructed by a computer. This can be dangerous for people if their presence is not known to the computer.

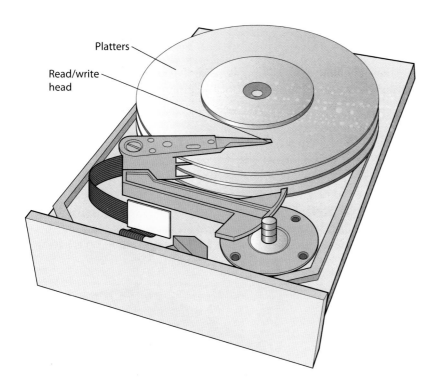

Platters

Read/write
head

Access time

To reach the correct spot on the disk for reading or writing data, the head
must first move to the correct track. Meanwhile, the hard disk spins,
maintaining a constant speed. The byte to be accessed arrives under the
head as the disk turns. On average, it takes half a rotation for the correct
byte to reach the head's position. The total access time on average is then:

$$\text{Time for head movement to the correct track} + \text{Time for half a complete rotation}$$

If the drive needs to access bytes that directly follow each other on a single
track, no further head movement is needed because the head can remain
on that same track. Moreover, if the bytes follow each other, it takes very
little time for each consecutive byte to arrive beneath the head. So the
average access time per byte is far less if a stream of consecutive bytes is
being read than it is for one-off access.

Fixed heads and moving heads

Some types of hard disk have a read/write head permanently stationed
above each track of the disk. Each surface has many fixed heads instead
of a single moving head per surface. This means that no time is needed to
reach the correct track: the respective heads are already in place. So access
is much faster – on average, the time for a half rotation.

RAID (Redundant Array of Inexpensive Drives)

This storage device essentially carries multiple copies of data, on different
hard disk drives. If one fails, the data can still be recovered from the
others.

External hard disks

External hard disks are built into a separate case and are robust, small and lightweight. They can be easily and safely carried around, and can usually be connected to any computer with a USB socket (these are very common on PCs).

Zip drives and disks

A **Zip disk** is a removable hard disk that stores data magnetically. Zip disks can store up to 750 MB. Zip drives can be built into the system unit or an external drive can plug into it. Plug-in Zip drives are portable and can be moved from one computer to the next. They can be used for transferring large graphics files between computers and for backing up personal computers. However, these are now not often used because DVDs have a larger storage capacity and are relatively inexpensive.

▲ **Figure 2.3**
An external hard disk drive

Figure 2.4 ▶
An Iomega® Zip® drive and a Zip disk

CDs, DVDs, HD DVD and Blu-ray

Compact discs (CDs)

A typical compact disc (CD) stores around 700 MB of data on one side of the disc. Access time is slower than a hard disk. Although CDs are easily damaged, they are inexpensive.

A CD is a piece of plastic, about $\frac{4}{100}$ of an inch or 1.2 mm thick. During manufacture, a pattern is etched onto the lower polycarbonate plastic layer. This pattern is a single, continuous, extremely long spiral track of data. This lower layer is covered with a thin, reflective aluminum layer. Then a thin acrylic layer is sprayed over the aluminum to protect it. The CD's label is then printed onto the acrylic. The CD drive has a laser beam in the read/write head, which can read the information on the disk.

▲ **Figure 2.5**
A compact disc

Figure 2.6 ▶
Cross-section of a compact disc

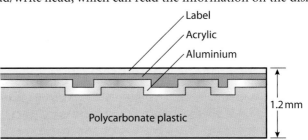

Label
Acrylic
Aluminium
1.2 mm
Polycarbonate plastic

Digital versatile disks (DVDs)

A digital versatile disk (DVD) looks much the same as a CD. A single-sided, single-layer DVD can hold up to 4.7 GB on one side. In contrast, a dual-layer DVD can carry two layers of data on each of its two sides: this means it can hold up to 18 GB of video, audio or other information.

Types of CD and DVD

- Data can be read from but not written to **CD-ROM** and **DVD-ROM**. This type of CD or DVD is used to prevent the deletion or amendment of data. For example, they are used for the distribution of software, music, electronic reference books and encyclopedias. Films are distributed on DVD-ROM.

- **CD-R and DVD-R** allow data to be written to them on one occasion only; after this, the data on them can only be read. This enables you to create your own music CDs and record TV programmes on DVD. CD-R and DVD-R are useful for backing up the hard disk on a computer, because once the data has been written it cannot be deleted or changed.

- **CD-RW and DVD-RW** can be written to repeatedly up to around 1000 times, and can be used for continuously backing up data or archiving. Data recorded on them can be deleted or replaced by more up-to-date data.

- **DVD-RAM** may be sealed inside a cartridge and can be rewritten more than 100 000 times. Data written to DVD-RAM is expected to last at least 30 years. DVD-RAM drives are used in video recorders, camcorders and computers.

- **HD DVD** is an optical disk format for storing digital information, similar to DVD but with sufficient capacity for high-definition video and movies. Its development was supported by a group of manufacturers led by Toshiba. HD DVD was created to succeed DVD but found competition in Blu-ray, which is a rival format. In 2008, HD DVD marketing and development ceased.

- **Blu-ray** is a high-definition DVD format supported by a group of manufacturers led by Sony. It is intended as a replacement for the current range of DVDs and is used for distributing HD material such as movies. A dual-layer Blu-ray disk can store 50 GB, almost 10 times the capacity of a single-sided, single-layer DVD. It is the same size as a CD.

Compatibility problems

There are many different types of CD and DVD. DVDs may also be described as, for example, DVD+R/RW and DVD-R/RW. All these different types of media formats are confusing and there are compatibility problems because a CD, DVD or Blu-ray drive may not play or write all the different formats. In addition, not all drives can read recorded disks. A further problem with music CDs is that not all players will play MP3 files, which is the most common format for music files stored on a computer.

Magnetic tapes

A magnetic tape is wrapped onto a reel and provides a large amount of surface area. This abundance of surface area means that a great quantity of information can be stored on a tape. But tape storage offers only **serial access**. So if you want to access data at the middle of the tape you must start at the beginning, and forward through the tape to reach the part you want. For this reason, accessing data on a tape can be very slow, and so magnetic tape is mostly used for backing up data, not for quick regular access, for which you might use a CD, hard disk or memory stick. Magnetic tape is available in a variety of formats. One of the most common formats used for backing up PCs and servers is the magnetic tape cartridge.

Backup

A **backup** is a copy of a file. You should back up all your files regularly so that you always have up-to-date copies of all your work. A backup is more secure if it is stored separately from the computer.

The data stored on backing storage could be very important to you. For a business, there are costs involved in collecting the data. However, the data could be lost if the media is damaged; for example, because of a hard drive crash, power supply failure or fire. A backup is a way of trying to make sure that you do not lose your data. Ways of doing this can be simple or very elaborate.

Personal backups should be done systematically:

- You could back up a file after every session in which you edit it.
- You could back up every time you create an important piece of work.
- You could back up all your data files every day, week or month.

When making a backup you should:

- Arrange for a backup of all your data files to be done automatically so that you do not forget to do it. Make more than one copy of this backup.
- Save more than one copy of files created or changed between major backups, and keep copies of any data used to change files.
- Keep a backup on hand so that you can conveniently use it if a file is lost.
- Keep a backup on hand in a fireproof safe so that if the building burns down you still have a copy.
- Keep at least one backup in another location so that if all your local backups are destroyed you have a copy elsewhere.

Backing up a home computer

You might back up all the data saved on the hard disk of your home computer onto a DVD-RW every month. If you create any important work in between these major backups, you could save it on the hard disk and make a copy on an external portable hard disk. If you keep the DVDs, eventually you will have copies of your work going back over several months or years. You might store some of these in a safe place away from your home, so that if it burnt down you would still have a copy of your work. A DVD-RW will probably be big enough to store all your work if this is only word-processed documents, spreadsheets and database files. If you start storing pictures and graphics you could use several DVDs or you could compress your files.

If you kept backups in this way, if a file became lost or corrupted you could recover it by looking for a copy on the external portable hard disk, and then on the most recent DVD. If you could not find a good copy then you would work back through the DVDs until you found one. If the backup file was compressed, you would have to decompress it before you could use it.

Backing up a network

Networks can be automatically backed up as frequently as required – it is usual to do this at least once every day. The backup may be a copy of an entire hard disk or of several hard disks. Backups can be made using the network so that a backup can be made locally and saved onto backing storage media attached to the network anywhere in the world. Backup copies are often made onto other hard disks because this speeds up the copying. If the speed at which the backup is made is not important, magnetic tape cartridges are often used as these are cheaper. Some of the backups could be onto backing storage devices and media that are enclosed within containers that are fireproof, waterproof and bombproof.

The software that is used to organise automatic backups will keep track of when they were taken and where they are stored. When a file is lost and needs to be recovered, the backup software will search back through all the copies of the file to find the most up-to-date version. A systematic method of organising backups, called the *ancestral backup system*, is described in Chapter 12.

Memory
Main memory

The computer's **main memory** may be **random-access memory (RAM)** or **read-only memory (ROM)**. Random-access memory can be written to, read from and edited. The data in it can be accessed in any order (hence the use of the word 'random'). Read-only memory can also be accessed in random order, but the data in it cannot be changed. ROM is intended for permanent data, necessary for the operation of the computer system. RAM is **volatile** memory, which means that it is cleared when the computer is switched off; ROM is **non-volatile**, which means that it retains what is stored in it when the computer is turned off. Both ROM and RAM are made in the form of microchips. RAM is now supplied in **modules** comprising a number of chips together on a small board. When the memory of a PC is upgraded, more memory modules are installed in the system unit.

The computer uses RAM to store data and programs in memory while it is running. This is why computer scientists refer to the RAM as the **main memory** (or **primary memory**). Main memory holds the programs currently running, and the data being used by the programs that are running. Memory sticks and hard disks are called **backing storage** (or **secondary memory**).

The term **immediate-access store (IAS)** means the memory immediately available to the CPU – which includes both RAM and ROM.

Types of ROM

Programmable read-only memory (PROM) has no data locked into it when first manufactured. But later, a company using PROM chips to make a computer can put in its own information. The data would then be locked in place, so the memory can no longer be changed. **Erasable programmable read-only memory (EPROM)** gets its original data in the same way as PROM does. But, if necessary, the data can be erased using a special light shining on a 'window' on the chip, or by using a special electric charge (**electrically erasable programmable read-only memory – EEPROM**). This means that the data can be used in read-only mode, but that the memory can also be reset as required.

Flash memory

Flash memory is a type of EPROM. The memory can be reset quickly and easily so that it can be written to, read from and edited. It retains what has been stored without a power source.

A common use of Flash memory is for the **basic input/output system (BIOS)** of your computer. On virtually every PC available, the BIOS makes sure the computer starts up as it should and that all the parts of the computer work together.

Flash memory is often removable. Popular forms are the Compact Flash memory card (see Figure 2.8) and the memory stick. These can be moved easily from one device or computer to another and can be used as backing storage.

Memory cards are removable and are used in video game consoles, digital cameras, mobile phones, PDAs and other portable devices. PCs often have card slots. Memory cards can store up to 32 GB of data. There are many types of memory card, including Compact Flash (CF), Secure Digital (SD), mini and micro SD, xD cards, SmartMedia and MultiMedia cards.

Memory sticks (see Figure 2.9) usually plug into the USB port on a computer. They are lightweight and fit easily into your pocket so that they are a convenient way of moving data from one computer to another. They have a storage capacity of up to 32 GB. They are used by teachers and lecturers to store presentations and other files, because they can be easily moved from one classroom to another. They can be incorporated into other mobile items; for example as a key ring fob. They often have a clip or cord for attaching them to clothing. They are robust and not easily damaged, and are a relatively inexpensive storage medium.

▲ **Figure 2.8**
A Compact Flash memory card

▲ **Figure 2.9**
A memory stick.

Addresses and locations

Memory is divided into many different locations, each of which can store one byte. The computer can find a specific location in memory using its **address**, which is a unique number referring to that location. Having *addressed* a particular location in memory, the computer can read or change its contents.

Words, bits and bytes

A **word** is the amount of data that a computer can directly access at one time. Different computers can access one, two, four or more bytes of data at one time. Each byte is a combination of eight signals, each of which can be either off or on (0 or 1). Each of these signals is a **B**inary dig**IT or bit**, so each byte has eight bits. We say that the computer has a word length of that many bits. The word size is always stated in terms of the number of bits, and not the number of bytes. For example, if the computer reads four bytes at once then its word length is 32 bits.

QUICK QUESTION

- What is the word size in bits if the machine reads one byte at once?
- What is the word size in bits if the machine reads two bytes at once?
- What is the word size in bits if the machine reads eight bytes at once?

Exercise 2.1

1. Write down the number of 250 MB Zip disks that would be needed to store 1 GB.
2. A memory stick stores 16 GB of data. Write down the number of DVDs that would be needed to store this amount of data.
3. Describe the differences between a storage device and a storage medium. Give an example of each.
4. Describe the similarities and differences between a memory stick and a hard disk.
5. Describe the similarities and differences between a DVD and a hard disk.
6. A magnetic tape provides serial access. Explain why this can be a disadvantage. Describe one use for tape.
7. Explain the need for backup procedures. Describe suitable backup procedures for a small business, including how often backups should be taken and where they should be kept.
8. Describe the similarities and differences between main memory and a hard disk.
9. Describe the similarities and differences between main memory and flash memory.
10. Explain the difference between a word, a byte and a bit.

Data representation (extension material)

Data is stored in each memory location as a pattern of bits. These bit patterns can represent different types of data.

Representing numbers

In our normal counting, we use ten digits {0, 1, 2, 3, 4, 5, 6, 7, 8, 9} – so our method of counting is **base ten**. We can use a single digit until we

Counting from 1 to 20 in binary					
Denary number	Binary number				
1					1
2				1	0
3				1	1
4			1	0	0
5			1	0	1
6			1	1	0
7			1	1	1
8		1	0	0	0
9		1	0	0	1
10		1	0	1	0
11		1	0	1	1
12		1	1	0	0
13		1	1	0	1
14		1	1	1	0
15		1	1	1	1
16	1	0	0	0	0
17	1	0	0	0	1
18	1	0	0	1	0
19	1	0	0	1	1
20	1	0	1	0	0

▲ **Figure 2.10:**
Counting to twenty in binary

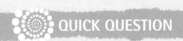

QUICK QUESTION

What is the ASCII code for F?
What is the ASCII code for f?

Figure 2.11 ▶
Examples of ASCII codes

reach 9, after which we must use two or more digits. A computer uses **base two**, and has digits representing values 0 and 1 only. Since the digit can take only two values, it is a **binary** digit. Eight of these digits make a **byte**.

It is useful to be able to count in binary. Notice how the patterns of 0s and 1s are repeated in the binary count (see Figure 2.10). Recognising these patterns will help you remember how to count in binary.

Representing characters

A character is a symbol that can be represented by a computer. For example, characters include A to Z, 0 to 9 and punctuation marks.

American Standard Code for Information Interchange (ASCII)

We have seen that a pattern of bits can represent a number. We can also represent alphabetic letters and other characters as bit patterns. Under the ASCII system, the binary pattern **1000001** represents the capital letter 'A'. The next binary number, **1000010**, represents the letter 'B'. The ASCII representations for lower case letters follow a similar pattern. The ASCII for 'a' is **1100001**. All the upper and lower case letters, punctuation marks, numeric characters and other symbols (including the space character) have ASCII representations. The ASCII system uses the left-hand seven bits of an eight-bit byte, and can represent up to 128 different characters. The range of characters represented is known as the **character set**.

Examples of ASCII codes		
	Character	**ASCII code (7 bit binary)**
	ESC (Escape)	0011011
	Space	0100000
	"(double quote)	0100010
	* (asterisk)	0101010
	/ (forward slash)	0101111
Note that the ASCII code for digits 0 to 9 are similar to, but different from, their binary number representation	0	0110000
	1	0110001
	2	0110010
	3	0110011
	4	0110100
	5	0110101
Note that the ASCII code for capital A is similar to, but different from, the ASCII code for lower case a	A	1000001
	B	1000010
	C	1000011
	D	1000100
	E	1000101
	a	1100001
	b	1100010
	c	1100011
	d	1100100
	e	1100101

Representing graphics

Graphics are the pictures and drawings on your computer. Graphics can be represented as **bitmapped** or **vector** graphics. Graphics are represented as bit patterns stored in memory locations.

Bitmapped graphics

The display on a monitor is made up of tiny dots or picture elements called **pixels**, which are used to make a picture. A monitor can have a display that measures, for example, 1024 by 768 pixels, and each pixel can display a different colour.

A simple black and white bitmapped graphic could have each pixel controlled by one bit. 0 would be white and 1 would be black. The patterns of 0s and 1s would make up a black and white picture. To use colours each pixel could be mapped to a byte (8 bits). A byte can have up to 256 different bit patterns so 256 different colours could be used. If more colours are needed, the pixel could be mapped to several bytes which taken together could have many more different patterns and represent many more colours. Some computers map 24 bits (3 bytes) to a pixel, which gives up to 16 777 216 different colours. This means that a display of 1024 by 768 pixels will need 2 359 296 bytes or 2.25 MB of memory for the monitor display. A small image will occupy much less memory than a large image if bitmapped graphic representation is used as the small image will use fewer pixels.

Bitmapped graphics are used in applications such as photography and scanning where an exact copy of the detail is needed. If a very high resolution is used then bitmapped graphics can provide very clear and detailed images. However, if a low resolution bitmapped image is enlarged, the detail of the image can become unclear. Paint software can be used to create bitmapped images. Common file formats are .gif, .jpg and .bmp.

Bit patterns stored in memory

0	1	0	0	1	0	0	1
1	1	1	0	1	1	0	0

Pattern of pixels displayed on part of the monitor screen

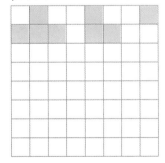

◀ **Figure 2.12**
The pattern produced by simple bitmapped graphics

Vector graphics

Vector graphics are produced using mathematical codes rather than bit patterns. For example, to represent a square on the screen the coordinates of its corners would be stored. One advantage of this method is that if the square is later enlarged this can be done by changing the stored coordinates but no more storage space would be needed. Information about the colours used to produce the image is also stored in a vector graphic file. Vector graphic images can be resized and still retain their original quality and take the same storage space. Drawing software can be used to create vector images. Almost all CAD/CAM systems and animation software use vector graphics.

Representing sound

Sound must be in a digital form for a computer to process it, but sound is analogue. **Sampling** is the process of recording sound waves and converting them from analogue into a digital form. The analogue sound is sampled at regular time intervals. The smaller these intervals are, the better the quality of the sound recording but the bigger the sound file. Ideally, the time between sampling should be so small that we hear a continuous sound without any gaps.

Computers store digital representations of sound in sound files, for example, .wav files. Good-quality sound files can contain a very large amount of data. Audio compression reduces the size of sound files and the time required to transfer and play them, but can lead to the loss of sound quality. Compression techniques, such as MPEG, reduce the file size with little loss of quality.

Representing colour

Red, green and blue (RGB) are the primary colours of visible light. Television and computer monitors create colour using RGB. Different amounts of red, green and blue light are mixed to produce other colours, and combining all three primary colours produces white. RGB is also used by digital cameras and scanners.

Thousands of dots (pixels) make up the images on TVs and monitor screens. Because the dots are very small and close together, we do not see them individually, but see the colours formed by the mixture of RGB light that is combined to produce each dot. Colours often vary slightly from one TV or monitor to another and you can see this when you look at different TVs on display in an electrical appliance store.

Hexadecimal RGB codes

Each colour is made up of the component colours of red, green and blue (RGB). In the hexadecimal RGB code, the strength of each component colour is given as a two-digit hexadecimal number. The smallest two digit hexadecimal number is 00 and the largest is FF; these correspond to the numbers 0 and 255. In this way, the hexadecimal RGB code sets the mix of the component colours and hence the colour displayed.

The two-digit hexadecimal equivalents of the numbers from 0 to 33 are shown in Figure 2.13 to illustrate how to count in hexadecimal, however, a full explanation of hexadecimal is not appropriate here. If you want to know more, ask a Mathematics teacher!

DID YOU KNOW?

An **analogue** signal is one that is continuously variable. A **digital** signal jumps from one value to another without covering all the values in between.

▼ Figure 2.13

Counting in hexadecimal

Number	0	1	2	3	4	5	6	7	8	9	10	11	12	13	14	15	16
Hexadecimal	00	01	02	03	04	05	06	07	08	09	0A	0B	0C	0D	0E	0F	10
Number	17	18	19	20	21	22	23	24	25	26	27	28	29	30	31	32	33
Hexadecimal	11	12	13	14	15	16	17	18	19	1A	1B	1C	1D	1E	1F	20	21

An example of the use of hexadecimal RGB codes

In Hyper Text Mark-up Language (HTML), common colours can be chosen either by their name or by their hexadecimal RGB code. For example, the <**BODY**> tag can be used to set the colour of the background and the colour of the text for a web page.

The tag:

<BODY BGCOLOR="Silver" TEXT="Black">

sets the background colour to silver and the text colour to black, and is equivalent to the tag:

<BODY BGCOLOR="#C0C0C0" TEXT="#000000">

Figure 2.14 shows the name of the colour and the corresponding hexadecimal RGB code for some of the colours that have names.

Hexadecimal RGB code			Colour
Red component	Green component	Blue component	
00	00	00	Black
00	00	FF	Bright blue
00	FF	FF	Bright Cyan
00	FF	00	Bright green
FF	00	00	Bright red
FF	FF	00	Bright yellow
80	80	00	Brown
00	00	80	Dark blue
80	00	00	Dark red
00	80	00	Green
80	80	80	Grey
80	00	80	Indigo
FF	00	FF	Magenta
C0	C0	C0	Silver
00	80	80	Turquoise
FF	FF	FF	White

◀ Figure 2.14
Colour names and the corresponding hexadecimal RGB codes

Exercise 2.2

1. Count in binary from 20 to 25.

2. Write down the ASCII code for K. Write down the ASCII code for k.

3. Write down the binary number 3. Write down the ASCII code for 3.

4. State whether a graphic created using paint software is more likely to be a bitmapped graphic or a vector graphic. Give reasons for your answer.

5. When a low-resolution bitmapped graphic is enlarged, picture quality is degraded. Explain this.

6. When a vector graphic is enlarged there is no loss of picture quality. Explain this.

7. A large bitmapped graphic will have a larger file size than a smaller version of the same bitmapped graphic. However, a large vector graphic will have the same file size as a smaller version of the same vector graphic. Explain this.

8. CD-quality sound needs 16-bit words sampled at 44.1 KHz. Describe the effects of reducing the rate of sampling.

9. Describe the advantages and disadvantages of sound compression to someone using the Internet to download music.

10. Which colour is represented by the hexadecimal RGB code #FF0000?

Summary

1. A byte is 8 bits, each of which can be either 1 or 0 (on or off). The bit pattern represents the piece of data in that byte of storage.

2. 1 kilobyte = 1024 bytes; 1 gigabyte = 1024 kilobytes; 1 terabyte = 1024 gigabytes.

3. You need backing storage (or secondary memory) to store your data after the computer has been turned off. The computer will store your work as a file. Its size depends on the amount of data in it, and is measured in bytes. A byte is one data character.

4. Backing storage media includes floppy disks, hard disks, CDs (compact discs), DVDs (Digital Versatile Disks), Zip disks, magnetic tapes, memory cards and memory sticks. A storage device is often needed to make use of the medium.

5. A magnetic tape can store a very large amount of information but there is only serial access to the data – you must start at the beginning, and go through the tape to reach the part you want. For this reason, magnetic tape is mostly used for backing up data.

6. To avoid the loss of data stored on backing storage, a backup copy is made. Backups should be made frequently and automatically. Backups should be kept on hand, in a fireproof safe and in another location. The schedule of backups is adjusted to suit the circumstances in which the computer system is being used.

7. While the computer is running, data and running programs are held in main memory, but the contents will be lost when it is turned off. This type of memory is random-access memory (RAM),

which can be read from, written to and edited while the computer is running. This memory can be accessed in any order (hence 'random').

8. Read-only memory (ROM) is intended for permanent data, necessary for the operation of the computer system. It can also be accessed in any order, but the data stored in it cannot be changed.

9. Erasable programmable read-only memory (EPROM) is a type of ROM where the data stored on it can be changed.

10. Flash memory is type of EPROM. Flash memory is used to store the BIOS (basic input-output system) which makes sure the computer starts up as it should and that all the parts of the computer work together. Portable Flash memory is used as backing storage and is available as, for example, compact flash memory cards for digital cameras and as memory sticks for storing and transferring data between computers.

11. Bit patterns can represent numbers, characters, graphics, sound and colour.

12. Numbers are represented using the binary number system.

13. Characters can be represented as bit patterns using ASCII.

14. Graphics can be bitmapped or vector. Bitmapped files store detailed pictures but can be very large, and picture quality can be degraded if the picture is enlarged. Vector graphics store information about how to set up the graphic rather than the picture itself. File size and quality do not change significantly if the picture is resized.

15. Sound quality depends on the frequency of sampling. Good quality sound files can be very large and audio compression is used to reduce file size.

16. Colours are represented by hexadecimal RGB codes. The component colours of red, green and blue (RGB) can be combined to make a very wide range of colours.

Chapter 3

Software

Software is another name for the programs that run on a computer. A program contains a series of instructions to the computer. When a program is run or **executed**, the computer goes through these instructions one by one, and so accomplishes its tasks.

There are different types of software. **Operating system (OS)** software controls the hardware to give you full use of the computer, and prepares it to run other software. The operating system is **system software**. To actually carry out your tasks on the computer, you need to use **application software** – programs that relate to the things you want to do.

Application software

- **Word processing** is the preparation of typed documents that contain mainly words and some pictures. A **word processor** enables you to manipulate text. You can move whole blocks of text around. You can set the size and shape of your text. You can let the word processor check your spelling and grammar. And you can save and keep a document that you have prepared on the computer. An example of word-processing software is Microsoft Word.

- **Desktop publishing (DTP)** is like word processing but text and pictures are managed in columns as in a newspaper. Many word processors have features similar to DTP software but often do not handle columns as well as DTP software, which is designed to do this. An example of desktop publishing software is Microsoft Publisher.

- A **spreadsheet** is a table of numbers (mostly) arranged in rows and columns with related charts and graphs. Some of the numbers may have been calculated using others in the table, so if you change any of them, a **spreadsheet** will automatically redo the calculation. An example of spreadsheet software is Microsoft Excel.

- **Database** software is used for managing records. Even people who never use a computer are affected by the use of this kind of software, because database software is used to keep records that relate to people. For example, a supplier of domestic electricity will have at least the name, address and meter reading of all its customers. A database stores the records, and also provides many tools for handling and investigating the data it contains. An example of database software is Microsoft Access.

- **Graphics** software is used to manipulate pictures and drawings. Graphics software enables you to produce original art on the computer. You can also open existing pictures and photographs and change them. You can add, distort or erase parts of a picture, and resize it. Examples of graphics software are Microsoft Paint and Adobe Fireworks.

- **Multimedia presentation** software is used to prepare a talk to an audience. The monitor display is projected onto a very large screen during the talk. A presentation will consist of a series of slides with mainly text and graphics, and notes for the speaker. An example of multimedia presentation software is Microsoft PowerPoint.

- In order to access the Web you must have **web browser** software running on your computer. When you are connected to the Internet and you first run your web browser, the home page will be displayed. You can now surf the Internet by using your mouse to click on links or you can enter the web address or **uniform resource locator (URL)** of the website you want to access. A **search engine** enables you to search the Web by entering keywords that describe the information you are looking for. Microsoft Internet Explorer, Google Chrome and Firefox are commonly used web browsers, and Yahoo and Google are popular search engines.

- **Website writer** software is used to create a website. A website is a structured collection of web pages that is accessible via the Internet. Web pages usually include text and graphics, and are written using Hypertext Markup Language (HTML) or software that generates HTML. Most software, including word processors, spreadsheets and databases, will allow you to save your work as a web page, but website writer software gives you more control over this. Website writer software may also include facilities to manage your website. Examples of website writer software are Arachnophilia, Adobe Dreamweaver and Microsoft Expression Web.

- The **e-mail** software that most users are familiar with is an e-mail client running on their computer. Using this you can send and receive e-mails. You can filter the incoming e-mail so that unwanted e-mails (spam) are removed. An example of e-mail client software is Microsoft Outlook.

- There are many **educational software packages**. A particular package might, for instance, teach you how to type. It could look at the keys you press, to measure your speed and accuracy, and could set up personalised typing lessons to help improve your typing.

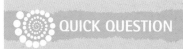

QUICK QUESTION

Which educational software packages have you used?

Other application software

Integrated software packages have many applications bundled into one package (e.g. Microsoft Office or Star Office), or a single program for many general purposes (e.g. Microsoft Works). The software is designed so that data can be transferred easily between different parts of the package. For example in Microsoft Office, a spreadsheet prepared in Excel can be copied and pasted into a Word document.

Specialist application software provides the tools for a specific task, rather than for a broad application area. An example of this would be a program especially for preparing and printing DVD labels. Such software provides limited word processing and drawing facilities but would not be suitable for general purpose typing or drawing. For example, Easy CD & DVD Cover Creator.

General-purpose software, in contrast to **specialised software**, can be used for a variety of tasks but must be set up or customised before use. It is usually **off-the-shelf** software – you can walk into a shop and buy it off the shelf.

Custom-written or bespoke software

Bespoke software is software that has been uniquely created only to meet the needs of a particular business or individual. There are advantages and disadvantages to using custom software.

Advantages:

- You get what you want. Whereas off-the-shelf software may not encompass all your needs, bespoke software is tailored just for your needs or business.

- You have closer control over revisions made to the software. A company that owns the original **source code** for the program can change it as needed.

- A program written for a specific purpose may run faster, because its code is optimised to serve that one purpose only.

Disadvantages:

- Custom software takes time to develop. If the business used an easily available software package instead, it could be off to a quick start in computerising its activities.

- The cost of development for custom software could be higher than the price of off-the-shelf software. This is because you must pay an ICT specialist to design and produce the software.

- A custom package is essentially new, since it has only just been produced. An off-the-shelf package may have been around for some time – other people will have used it, so you can learn from them about its strengths and weaknesses. You cannot fully assess a custom package beforehand.

- General-purpose packages tend to be widely used, so there may be many people who are already familiar with them. People who are looking for a job will even train themselves to use such software. This means that even new employees may already be familiar with the software.

- You may have to spend some time training staff to use custom software as it will not be like other software. In contrast, general-purpose software is usually designed to be easy to use, so you do not need long training periods to prepare staff to use it.

Customised software

An alternative to purchasing specialised software or using off-the-shelf general-purpose software is to **customise** off-the-shelf software. This should let you maintain the familiarity of general-purpose software, while allowing you to add other features that are important to you. It still takes some time to develop, but not as much as developing custom-written software from the very beginning. Many general-purpose software packages are customisable. Customisation may enhance the performance of the software, and enable you to carry out some tasks automatically.

Exercise 3.1

1. Name the type of software that would help you do these tasks. One has been done for you.

Task	Type of software
Write a club newsletter	Desktop Publishing
Write an essay for homework	
Send an e-mail to a friend	
Keep a record of all your music tracks	
Look for information about mobile phones on the Web	

2. Name an example of graphics software and describe what you can do using this software.

3. Name an example of multimedia presentation software and describe what you can do using this software.

4. Name three types of application software and give an example of another task that you could do with each of them.

5. State the name of an integrated software package. Name and describe the different applications that are integrated within the package.

6. Explain what is meant by general-purpose software.

7. Explain what is meant by off-the-shelf software.

8. Discuss the advantages and disadvantages of buying custom-written software compared with off-the-shelf software.

9. One example of specialist application software is a program for preparing and printing DVD labels. Name and describe another example of specialist application software.

10. Integrated software packages rarely give access to a complete range of single-purpose applications. Name an integrated package and describe the different applications that have been integrated within it.

Operating System (OS) software and Graphical User Interfaces (GUIs)

The **operating system (OS)** controls the computer; you could not use the computer without it. The operating system is software that runs between the hardware and application software. It enables application software to use the computer's hardware and other resources. Microsoft Windows 7 is an example of an OS. The OS has many functions, including the following:

- input and output control
- error handling
- resource allocation
- providing a user interface
- allowing users to give commands to the computer
- file handling

Input/output control

The operating system controls all input and output and the transfer of data within the computer. It manages the interfaces with the various devices that make up a computer system, and controls their behaviour so that application software functions smoothly.

Error handling

The operating system manages error handling. For example, when you are printing something, you might get the message in Figure 3.1. The printer has sent a signal to the computer telling it that it is out of paper. The operating system receives this signal, interprets it and displays a message on the screen that you can understand. Errors that arise while a program is running are known as **run time errors**.

Figure 3.1 ▶
An error message displayed when the printer is out of paper

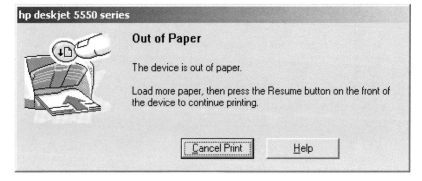

Resource allocation

The operating system ensures that all the software has access to the different resources it needs to run successfully. The programs running on a computer are broken up into processes that need different types of resources in order to run. For example, if you want to print a document you must have the use of the printer. The operating system controls the running and scheduling of all these processes and manages the share of the CPU's processing time that is used by the different processes. If you only have one processor you can only run one process at a time, but you can interleave different processes that need different resources. If you have a dual- or multi-processor computer, you can run more than one process at the same time – this is **parallel processing**.

The operating system manages the use of shared resources on the computer. With more than one process running at the same time, it may well happen that two processes try to use a single resource, for example a printer, at the same time. In this case, the operating system will place the jobs into an orderly queue, and will control the way in which the output gets to the printer. In fact, the operating system has the task of controlling the use of any device that several programs might be trying to use at the same time.

The operating system controls communications between the various devices that make up the computer system. For example, when you move the mouse, you expect the mouse pointer to move on the screen. What actually happens is that a part of the operating system will display a mouse pointer at a particular location on the screen, and will control its movement as the actual mouse moves and sends signals to the computer.

On a PC, the operating system will handle resource allocation during **multitasking**, that is, when one user is using more than one piece of software at a time. For example, when a user is running Word and Excel at the same time.

Commands and User Interfaces

The operating system enables you to give commands to the computer. You could give the computer commands in different ways. You could do any of the following:

- Type in commands on a command line.
- Select an option from a menu-driven system.
- Use a graphical user interface (GUI), and navigate and select using a mouse.

The operating system interprets these commands however they are given to it, and controls the computer so that it carries out the task you have commanded.

Command line user interface

Figure 3.2 shows a command line user interface. The example used here is from Microsoft DOS (disk operating system), that is, MS-DOS.

Command line user interfaces can be difficult to use for various reasons:

- You have to know the exact instruction to type in.
- You have to type in exactly the right instruction otherwise the operating system will reject it.
- To make full use of the operating system, you need to know all the instructions available.
- If you don't know what instruction to use, you have to look it up in the documentation and this could be very time-consuming. However, if you can do this, then command line user interfaces are straightforward and quick to use.

DID YOU KNOW?

If you type **A:** at the C:\ prompt and press the <ENTER> key, the OS will look at the floppy disk in drive A: rather than the hard disk (drive C:). You should see the A:\ prompt appear (see Figure 3.2).

DID YOU KNOW?

If you type **dir** at the A:\ prompt and press the <ENTER> key, the OS will display a list of all the files and directories on the floppy disk. In Figure 3.2, four files are shown (one is *letter.doc*), and there is one directory (or folder) called *administration*.

```
C:\WINDOWS\system32\cmd.exe                                    _ □ ✕

C:\Documents and Settings\Roger Crawford>A:

A:\>dir
 Volume in drive A has no label.
 Volume Serial Number is 0000-0000

 Directory of A:\

19/11/2009  22:27            19,968 summary.doc
19/11/2009  22:28    <DIR>          administration
19/11/2009  22:27            19,968 agenda.doc
19/11/2009  22:33           864,858 report.doc
19/11/2009  22:27            19,968 letter.doc
              4 File(s)        924,762 bytes
              1 Dir(s)           3,584 bytes free

A:\>
```

▲ **Figure 3.2**
A command line user interface

Menu-driven user interface

Figure 3.3 shows a menu-driven user interface that may be displayed when starting up a computer. The user can choose any option from the menu by typing in the number next to the menu option and pressing <ENTER>. Often menus are hierarchical and one menu leads to another menu, which leads to another menu.

A menu-driven user interface can be easier to use than a command line interface because you don't have to remember the commands. However, they can be irritating if there are too many levels of menus to move through. It may not be as easy to move through the levels of menus on a menu-driven user interface as it is using a GUI. If you know the right command, using a command line interface you can run the required option immediately.

Figure 3.3 ▶
A menu-driven user interface

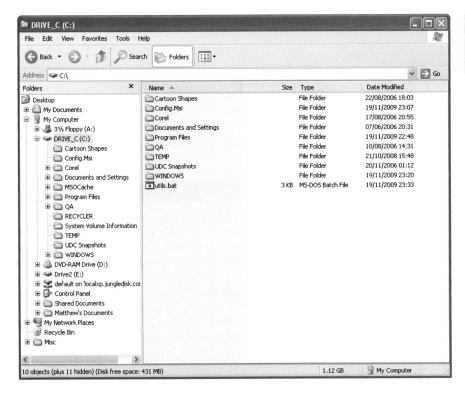

◀ **Figure 3.9**
Windows Explorer has two panes
in a single window

Moving, copying and deleting files

In Windows Explorer, you can move a file within a disk by dragging it to
another folder. You can copy a file from one disk to another by dragging it
from the source disk to the target disk. To delete a file, right-click on the
filename (see Figure 3.10) and select **Delete**. A dialog box will ask you to
confirm that you want to delete the file.

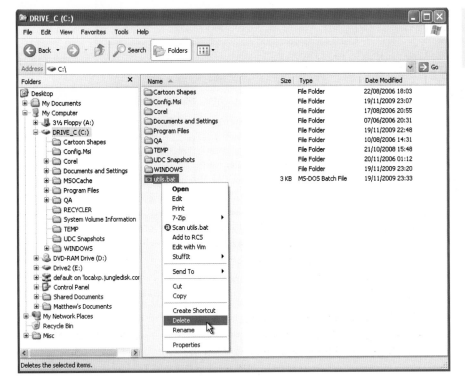

◀ **Figure 3.10**
A right-click menu for the
selected file

File properties

You can set files so that they have important properties, such as being read-only. A read-only file can only be opened; it cannot be saved. This allows others to share a file you have prepared but not to alter it. In Windows, if you right-click on a file, and select the **Properties** item from the menu, it brings up a **Properties** dialog box, which will be similar to the one in Figure 3.11. If the **Read only** attribute is ticked, then no changes can be saved to the file. If the **Hidden** attribute is turned on, the file will be invisible to some operations.

Figure 3.11 ▶
The File Properties dialog box

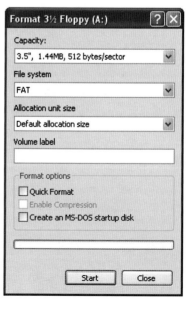

Formatting

The data on a floppy disk or a hard disk is stored in **tracks** that run in rings around the surface. Formatting prepares a disk for use by setting up the tracks and dividing them into **sectors**, and setting up an index that lists the name and location of every file on the disk.

Different operating systems use different file storage arrangements. In Windows, if you right-click on a disk icon in My Computer, one of the options is **Format**. If you select this, a dialog box appears that will guide you through formatting the disk (see Figure 3.12).

Figure 3.12 ▶
A dialog box for formatting a disk

DID YOU KNOW?

If a disk already has information on it, formatting will destroy its contents. For this reason, you should not normally format the hard disk.

Utilities

There are other kinds of system software, some of which are often included as a 'bundle' along with the operating system. **Disk optimising** and **disk error checking** programs are examples of this. **Antivirus** software helps protect your system from dangerous viruses that may seek to destroy the data on your computer; for example, McAfee VirusScan. Such software is often referred to as **utility** software because it does tasks that help you maintain your computer, making the other applications run better.

Help and documentation

Even if software provides a good user interface that is easy to use, you may find it useful to also have access to clear and informative help.

Help can be provided in various ways:

- a printed manual
- help within the software
- online help accessible via the Web
- an e-mail help service
- a telephone help line.

Such help should show you:

- how to use the program
- any hardware requirements
- how to get more information and further help if you need it
- how the software is structured, to make it easier for you to configure it.

Documentation is often categorised as user documentation and technical documentation. **User documentation** is simple instructions to get you started and help you use the software. **Technical documentation** will have more in-depth information about how the software works and will help programmers reconfigure the software.

Software licensing

When buying software, purchasers may acquire some or all of the following:

- A copy of the software on a CD-ROM, or access rights to a website to download the software so that the purchaser can install the software.
- A manual explaining how to use the software. This could be printed or available as help files with the software, or as a documentation file on the CD-ROM.
- A licence to use the software.

A software **licence** gives users rights to use the software under the specific conditions and restrictions stated in the licence. The distribution and use of software is restricted.

If a user does not have a software licence then it is illegal for them to use the software. It is assumed that if software is installed on a hard disk, or there is a copy of it on another backing storage medium, then it is in use. Using software without a licence is known as **software piracy**.

DID YOU KNOW?

Utility software often begins life as an add-on to the operating system, but can be later integrated with the operating system so that it becomes a part of it.

There are three general categories of software with distinctive licensing arrangements:

- Licensed software
- Public domain software
- Shareware.

Licensed software is sold. Purchasers buy the rights to use the software. These rights are typically one or more of the following:

- The right to use the software on one or more standalone computers
- The right to distribute the software over a network for use on a specified number of network stations
- A site licence, giving the right to distribute and use the software on any computer on a particular site.

Public domain software is free software. The owners of the software make it available to anyone who wants to use it, or to specific groups of users, at zero purchase cost. Software producers may place any restriction on the use of the software that they wish. Even so, most public domain software carries no restrictions on its use.

Shareware is licensed software that is initially distributed freely in the manner of public domain software. Users may install the software and try it out. However, if they decide to make regular use of the software, they must pay a licence fee. Users sometimes receive improved versions of the software when a licence fee is paid. Where the licence fee is not paid, continued use of the software is illegal.

A **demonstration disk** is a disk containing a demonstration version of software. Demonstration disks are often sent to intending purchasers so that they can evaluate software for themselves. The software on a demonstration disk may be complete but often there is some essential feature, such as printing, omitted. This is to encourage potential purchasers to buy a licensed copy of the software.

Exercise 3.2

1. Name the type of software you would expect to use these files. One has been done for you.

Filename	Type of software
agenda.doc	
index.htm	Web browser
myfamily.jpg	
format.hlp	
song.mp3	

2. Look at Figure 3.8. Design a file structure for your work and leisure activities.

3. Figure 3.1 shows an error message displayed when the printer is out of paper. Describe another error message.

document and as many times as you like. This process is called **pasting**. You need to make sure that the insertion point is where you want to put the text you have cut.

Copy and Paste

The copy and paste feature allows you to make as many copies of a block of text as you want. The original block of text remains in position in the document. A copy of the block of text is placed on the clipboard. This copy can then be inserted anywhere, as many times as you wish, into any open document. You use the same method as cut and paste but you choose **Copy** instead of **Cut**.

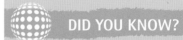

DID YOU KNOW?

In Word, the Cut, Copy and Paste commands are on the **Home** tab.

Moving text from one document to another, or from one application to another

You can use cut and paste, or copy and paste, to move text from one document to another, or from a word processor to another application. Similarly, you can do this from another application into a word processor. This is a very useful feature when you are producing a report or essay and need to include statistics produced in a spreadsheet. You can copy graphs produced in a spreadsheet and paste them into a word processing document.

Extension activity

Produce a word processed report on your weekly spending. Include in it part of a spreadsheet table and a graph that shows how much you spend each week over one year.

Spelling and grammar checks, and proofreading

Errors in spelling and grammar can undermine the professional look of a document. To help create more accurate and professional looking documents, word processors contain tools that check documents for possible spelling and grammatical errors. Words that are spelt incorrectly, grammatical errors or inaccurate spacing between characters can be identified. If a spelling checker does not recognise a word, it identifies the word and displays a list of suggested alternative spellings for you to choose from. A grammar checker will identify possible grammatical errors and suggest how these can be corrected. Spelling and grammar checkers can check your English as you type and will help you correct your spelling and grammar.

Spelling and grammar checkers will detect most but not all errors of this type, and you should carefully proofread your work.

For example, they are unlikely to discover the errors in this sentence:

- The house is over their. They have a big garden with has a large beach tree growing in it.

The correct version is:

- The house is over *there*. *It has* a big garden *which* has a large *beech* tree growing in it.

Proofreading is a careful reading of text. During proofreading you should:

- Look for errors in spelling and grammar that have not been found by spelling and grammar checkers. Make a particular effort to check words that you know you find hard to spell correctly.

- Look for missing words and letters. For example: *a, the, and* and *it* are often omitted.

- Look for transposed words and letters. For example, *friend not freind*.

- Check the correct use of capital letters and punctuation marks (such as question marks, apostrophes, commas and full stops).

- Check homophones are used correctly. These are words that sound the same but are spelt differently and have different meanings. For example: *their and there; weather and whether*.

- Check the spelling of words ending in 'ing'. For example, check that you have used *making* not *makeing and trimming* not *triming*.

- Make sure that sentences are meaningful.

- Make sure that in every sentence the verb and subject agree. For example, 'she was going to the cinema' not 'she were going to the cinema'.

- Make sure that paragraphs are well structured. That is, they start with a sentence which tells you the topic of the paragraph, and this is followed by further explanation, supporting argument, or examples.

Here are some useful proofreading techniques:

- Don't rush. If you do, you could miss obvious mistakes.

- Check the first sentence and the first paragraph very carefully. You may have read this several times and see what you think you have written rather than what you have actually written.

- Check a printout, because it can be harder to find errors when reading text on the screen.

- Have a reliable spelling checker or dictionary on hand to check the spelling of unfamiliar words.

- Read the text to yourself. This will help you spot missing words and meaningless sentences.

- Get someone else to check your writing. They may notice errors you have overlooked.

- Double-check any facts or other information that needs to be accurate, such as web addresses.

Undo and Redo

If you intentionally or unintentionally change a document, you can reverse the changes using the 'Undo' function. You can undo more than one previous action and you can select these from a list of earlier actions. In case you then decide your editing really was better than the original, you can use the 'Redo' function, which allows you to undo an undo!

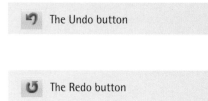

The Undo button

The Redo button

Find and Replace

Find is used to search for a word or phrase in a document. **Replace** is used to replace one word or phrase with another word or phrase.

For example, in Figure 4.5, the **Find and Replace** dialog box has been set up to find the word *change*. When this is found, it is highlighted. You can then choose what to do:

- Do nothing. Click on **Find Next**, and the next occurrence of *change* is highlighted leaving the original unchanged.

- Replace *change* with *alter*. Click on **Replace** and *change* is replaced with *alter*, and the next occurrence of *change* is highlighted.

- Replace all occurrences of *change with alter*. Click on **Replace All** and wherever *change* occurs in the document it is replaced by *alter*.

It is risky to use the **Replace All** option. In the text in Figure 4.5, replacing *change* with *alter* leaves the meaning unchanged. However, the word *change* could have other meanings. For example: 'I paid for the newspaper with a $10 note but when I received my change it was incorrect.' Here *change* refers to money and to replace it with the word *alter* would make the sentence meaningless.

▼ **Figure 4.5**
The Find and Replace dialog box

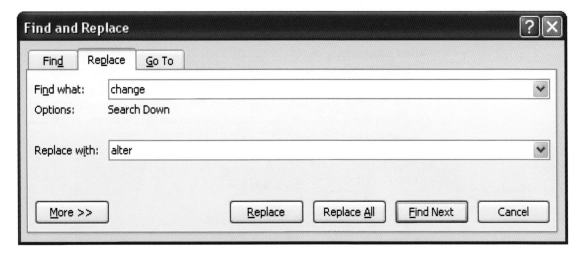

1. Open the document **Tobago** which you saved during Exercise 4.1.

2. Move the lines beginning with *Toobago is a small island* and ending with *The people of Toobago are warm and friendly* so that they come after the paragraph that begins with *Toobago is considered one of the jewels of the Caribbean.*

3. Insert the following piece of text, without the quotes, as a new paragraph at the end of the document:

> The local cuisine in Tobago is truly delightful. A visitor can choose from a wide variety of local and international dishes. Some of the favourite local dishes are curried crabs and dumpling, curried goat and the ever popular bake and fry fish.

4. Find all occurrences of the word *inhabitants* and replace them with the word *population.*

5. Find all occurrences of the word *Toobago* and replace them with *Tobago.*

6. Check your work using the spelling and grammar checker.

7. Type in your name and the date at the bottom of the document.

8. Save the document as 'Tobago *your name*'.

9. Print the document.

10. Proofread your work and, if necessary, save and print it again.

Formatting

The final appearance of a document depends to a large extent on how effectively you can use the many formatting features that are available. We will consider formatting applied to characters, paragraphs and pages. You can change formatting even after text has been typed in.

Character formatting

Many of the features of text that affect its appearance can be changed. A **font** is a complete set of consistently shaped characters; for example, the Times New Roman font. You can change the font type and size; font style (normal, bold, italic, underline – see Figure 4.6); font colour; and font effects (strikethrough, superscript, subscript, shadow, outline, emboss, engrave and caps). In Word, to make these changes you can use the **Home** tab or the **Font** dialog box (see Figure 4.7).

Figure 4.6 ▶
Normal, bold, italic and underlined text

> This is normal text
> **This is bold text**
> *This is italic text*
> <u>This is underlined text</u>
> ***<u>This is normal, bold, italic and underlined text</u>***

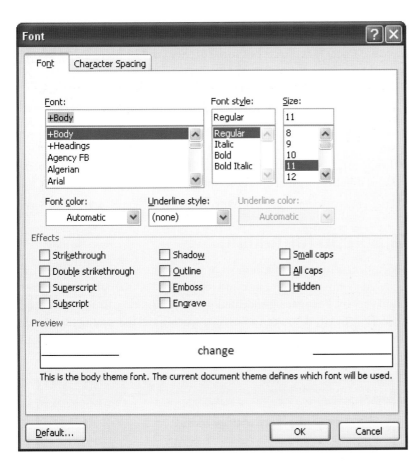

◀ **Figure 4.7**
The Font dialog box

Fonts

A **Font** is a complete set of consistently shaped characters. There are many different fonts, for example: Arial, Comic Sans and Times New Roman.

The Times New Roman font has serifs (see Figure 4.8). Serifs are short extensions of a character. Other examples of fonts with serifs are Courier, Palatino and Century Schoolbook.

Arial and Comic Sans are sans serif fonts, which means they do not have serifs. Other examples of sans serif fonts are Tahoma and Univers.

Font sizes

The size of the text in a font is measured in **point size**. The larger the point size, the larger the character. The font size can be changed after you have typed in your text. This means you can experiment to find the most attractive font for your document. As a general rule, point sizes 11 and 12 are easily readable (see Figure 4.8).

The Arial font in point size 8
The Arial font in point size 10
The Arial font in point size 12
The Arial font in point size 14

The Comic Sans font in point size 8
The Comic Sans font in point size 10
The Comic Sans font in point size 12
The Comic Sans font in point size 14

The Times New Roman font in point size 8
The Times New Roman font in point size 10
The Times New Roman font in point size 12
The Times New Roman font in point size 14

Figure 4.8 ▶
Different fonts in different point sizes

67

▲ Figure 4.9
WordArt

Font effects

There are many font effects but some of these will be more useful to you than others.

- A **superscript** character is one that is raised above the normal line. For example, in the mathematical expression $4x^3 + 5x^2 + x$, the numbers 3 and 2 are superscript characters.

- **Subscript** characters are placed below the normal line. For example, the chemical representation of sulphuric acid is H_2SO_4. The numbers 2 and 4 in the formula are subscript characters.

- There may also be a range of **WordArt** effects (Figure 4.9).

Paragraph formatting

A document is made up of a number of paragraphs. The format of these can be altered to improve appearance and readability. For example, you may be able to vary the line spacing, indentation and justification, or add bullets and numbering. In Word, you can adjust line spacing and indentation using the **Home** tab or the **Paragraph** dialog box (see Figure 4.10). To use this, click the little box in the bottom right of the **Paragraph** area on the **Home** tab.

Figure 4.10 ▶
The Paragraph dialog box

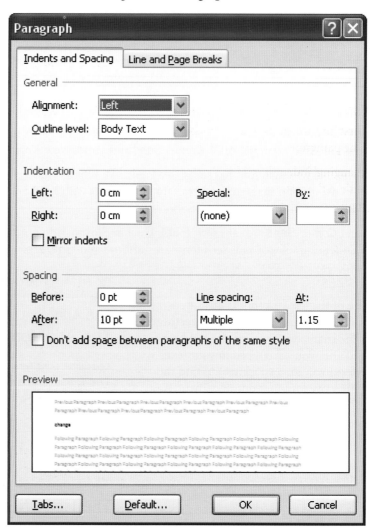

Line spacing

Line spacing is the distance between lines of text. Appropriate line spacing can improve the appearance and readability of a document. Line spacing options include single, 1.5 times and double. Other line spacing may be available; for example, you could alter the spacing between paragraphs, and before and after headings (see Figure 4.11).

This text has been typed in with **single line spacing**. Notice how close together the lines are. With double line spacing the lines are much wider apart and you will get less in the same space although it may be more readable.

This text has been typed in with **1.5 lines line spacing**. Notice how wide apart the lines are. With single line spacing the lines are closer together and with double line spacing they are further apart.

This text has been typed in with **double line spacing**. Notice how wide apart the lines are. With single line spacing the lines are much closer together and you will get more in the same space although it may be less readable.

◀ **Figure 4.11**
Single, 1.5 times and double line spacing

Indents

When you **indent** a paragraph (see Figure 4.12) you move the vertical edge of it inwards from the left or right margin towards the centre of the page. The size of an indent is the distance between the margin and the text.

You can also have special indents:

- A 'first line' indent is one in which the first line is shorter than the rest of the paragraph.

- A 'hanging' indent is exactly the opposite. The first line is indented less than the rest of the lines in the paragraph, so that it appears to be hanging to the left.

The text in italics has been indented from both the left and right margins. The text in italics has been indented from both the left and right margins.

The text in italics has been indented from both the left and right margins. The text in italics has been indented from both the left and right margins.

The text in italics has been indented from both the left and right margins. The text in italics has been indented from both the left and right margins.

This paragraph has a **first line indent** where the first line is shorter than the rest of the paragraph. This paragraph has a 'first line' indent where the first line is shorter than the rest of the paragraph. This paragraph has a 'first line' indent where the first line is shorter than the rest of the paragraph. This paragraph has a 'first line' indent where the first line is shorter than the rest of the paragraph.

This paragraph has a **hanging indent** where the first line is indented less than the rest of the lines in the paragraph, so that it appears to be hanging to the left. This paragraph has a 'hanging' indent where the first line is indented less than the rest of the lines in the paragraph, so that it appears to be hanging to the left.

◀ **Figure 4.12**
Indentation

Figure 4.13 ▶
Justification and centring

This Heading is Centred

This paragraph is **left justified** which means that the text is aligned with the left margin. This paragraph is left justified which means that the text is aligned with the left margin.

This paragraph is **right justified** which means that the text is aligned with the right margin. This paragraph is right justified which means that the text is aligned with the right margin.

This paragraph is both **left and right justified** which means that the text is aligned with both margins. This paragraph is both left and right justified which means that the text is aligned with both margins.

Justification

A paragraph or an entire document can be **left aligned**, which means that the text is lined up with the left margin (see Figure 4.13). Similarly, text can be **right aligned**. Text which is **justified** is both left and right aligned and is stretched across the page, possibly with more than one space between words. This makes paragraphs look neater but the text can be more difficult to read. You can also **centre** text so that it appears in the middle of the line. Headings are sometimes centred. In Word, text can be aligned and centred by highlighting it then clicking the appropriate buttons (see Figure 4.14).

Figure 4.14 ▶
The buttons used to justify and centre text

Bullets and numbering

Bullets and numbering are useful for organising text where you want to emphasise several short points (see Figure 4.15). In Word, to add bullets or numbering, highlight the text and click the appropriate button (see Figure 4.16).

Figure 4.15 ▶
Bullets and numbering

- This is a bulleted list
- This is a bulleted list
- This is a bulleted list
- This is a bulleted list

1. This is a numbered list
2. This is a numbered list
3. This is a numbered list
4. This is a numbered lis

Figure 4.16 ▶
The buttons used to add bullets and numbering

Exercise 4.3

1. Type out the document shown below. The number of words per line may differ, but keep the paragraph structure.

2. Centre the first two lines of the document.

3. Use WordArt effects (or similar) on the heading *The Zenith Oil Company*.

4. Change the font size of the second line of the document to a size larger than the rest of the document.

5. Change the font type of the second line of the document to Comic Sans.

6. Place a blank line between the first two lines of the document and the date.

7. Indent all the text between the first and last paragraphs.

8. Use bold for the words *Cash List Form, Fund Raising Form and Approved Budget 2010/2011* and put a blank line above them and below the words *Fund Raising Form*.

9. Use bullets to emphasise the items approved for the budget.

10. Change the line spacing in the document to 1.5.

11. Check for errors in spelling and grammar.

12. Save the document as 'new procedures'.

13. Print the document.

Here is the document for you to type:

The Zenith Oil Company
Sports and Cultural Club
13th December 2009

The Manager,
Zenith Oil Company Sports Club

As you are aware the present executive has reviewed the accounting and budgeting procedures. In order to promote transparency and proper accounting and record keeping, the following systems will now be implemented.
Cash List Form
This form will be used to record all petty cash transactions.
Fund Raising Form
This form will be used to inform the executive of all fund raising details.
Approved Budget 2010/2011
The items listed below have been approved for the 2010/2011 budget:
Cricket bats
Pair Cricket pads
Table Tennis Rackets
Soccer Balls
Twenty Football Shirts
If there are any questions concerning the new forms please contact the assistant treasurer. We look forward to your continued support.

Treasurer

Page setup

A new, blank word processing document already has a default page setup which is satisfactory for most documents you will produce. It is set to print on a standard A4 sheet of paper (210mm × 297mm). However, you may wish to make modifications:

- change the width of the **margins**, perhaps because you are putting your work in a ring binder and want space for the holes on the left-hand side of the page

- change the **page orientation** from **portrait** to **landscape** (see Figure 4.17); for example, so that you can print a spreadsheet that is wider but shorter than a standard A4 sheet of paper

- change the paper size, perhaps because you want to print addresses on envelopes

- add a header or a footer; for example, so that every page is numbered

- start a new page

Figure 4.17 ▶
The Page Setup dialog box

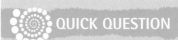

In Word, you can make changes to the margins, page orientation and paper size using the **Page Layout** tab or the **Page Setup** dialog box (see Figure 4.17).

Headers and footers

A **header** is the text or graphics that appears across the top of a page, and a **footer** is the text or graphics that appears across the bottom of a page.

Headers and footers are commonly used to show information such as the filename, chapter title, author's name, page number, date and time. Different headers and footers can be used for odd and even pages. In Word, the header and the footer can be accessed from the **Insert** tab. You can type in text or insert items such as page numbers and the date.

QUICK QUESTION

What is printed in the header on this page? Is it on every page in this chapter? Is it on every page in this book?

What is printed in the footer on this page? Is it on every page in this chapter? Is it on every page in this book?

◀ **Figure 4.18**
A header

Page breaks

Word processors automatically end each page and break up the text from one page to the next. However, you may want to insert a **page break** before the normal end of a page. In Word, you can do this using the **Page Break** button on the **Insert** tab.

Section breaks

It is sometimes useful to divide a document into sections so that there can be different formatting in each section. For example, you may want one or two pages orientated to landscape in a booklet which is mainly in portrait. You would put a section break before the change of orientation from portrait to landscape, and another section break when you change back to portrait.

In Word, to change from Portrait to Landscape, do the following:

- On the **Page Layout** tab, select **Breaks** then **Next Page**.
- Then click on the **Orientation** button and choose **Landscape**.

To change back to Portrait, insert another section break and repeat the same process but select **Portrait**.

Widows and orphans

The final paragraph on a page may not quite fit on it. A **widow** is the final line of a paragraph that is printed at the top of the next page (see Figure 4.19). Similarly, if most of the final paragraph is printed on the next page, the first line printed at the bottom of the previous page is an **orphan**.

Even better than applying widow/
orphan control to selected text
would be to modify your body
text style to turn this setting on.

To avoid widows and orphans in Microsoft Word:

- Select the paragraphs in which you want to control widows and orphans.
- On the **Home** tab, click the little box in the bottom-right corner of the **Paragraph** area.
- In the **Paragraph** dialog box, click the **Line and Page Breaks** tab.
- Tick the **Widow/Orphan control** check box.
- Click on **OK**.

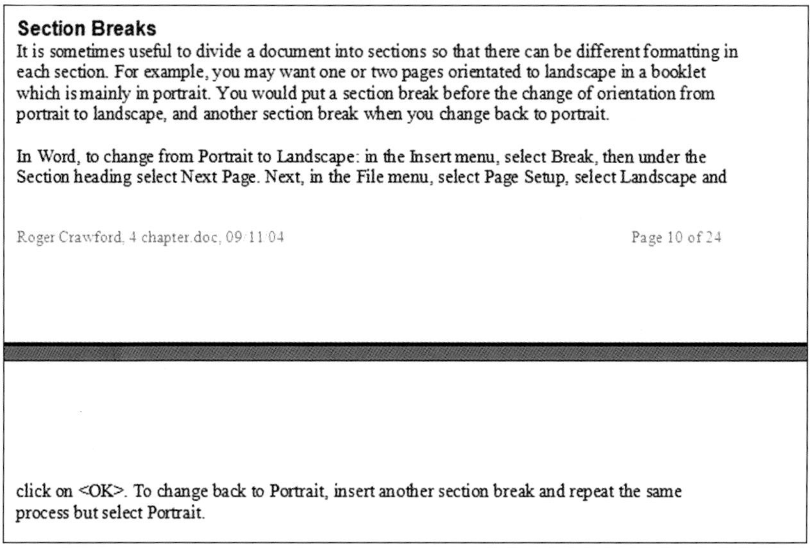

Figure 4.19 ▶
Preventing a widow

Section Breaks
It is sometimes useful to divide a document into sections so that there can be different formatting in each section. For example, you may want one or two pages orientated to landscape in a booklet which is mainly in portrait. You would put a section break before the change of orientation from portrait to landscape, and another section break when you change back to portrait.

In Word, to change from Portrait to Landscape: in the Insert menu, select Break, then under the Section heading select Next Page. Next, in the File menu, select Page Setup, select Landscape and

Roger Crawford, 4 chapter.doc, 09/11/04   Page 10 of 24

click on <OK>. To change back to Portrait, insert another section break and repeat the same process but select Portrait.

Tables

One method of improving the layout of documents is by using tables. Tables are very useful for displaying statistical and numerical data and can also be used for keeping text aligned.

Rows, columns and cells

A **table** is made up of **rows** and **columns**. The intersection of a row and a column is called a **cell** (see Figure 4.20). You can choose the number of columns and rows when you insert a table. In Word, click on the **Insert Table** button (see Figure 4.21) and drag the mouse to set the number of columns and rows.

To add a row to an existing table in Word, do the following:

- highlight a row by left-clicking to the left of it
- right-click to display a menu
- from the menu, select **Insert** then choose from **Insert Rows Above** and **Insert Rows Below**.

Inserting a column is similar but you must click above the column to highlight it.

To delete rows and columns in Word, follow the same process but select **Delete Row** or **Delete Column** from the menu.

You can change column widths and row heights by dragging the frame.

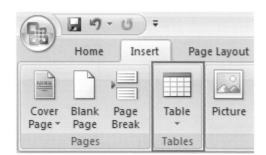

▲ **Figure 4.20**
A table with four columns and five
rows

◀ **Figure 4.21**
The Insert Table button

Cell contents and formatting

You can type in text or insert graphics or other objects in a cell and you
and can apply formatting such as bold; italic; underline; bullets; and
horizontal cell alignment (left, right, centre and justified) to the cell. In
Word, highlight the cell and apply the formatting as you would if the text
or other objects were not in a table.

Borders and shading

The lines that outline the table are visible in Draft view, Print Layout view
and most other views of the document. However, if they are faint, they
will only show on screen not when the document is printed. If you want
borders to show when you print the document, you could use the **Table
Tools Design** tab or the **Borders and Shading** dialog box to set these (see
Figure 4.22). In Word, to display the **Borders and Shading** dialog box,
right-click on the table and select **Borders and Shading**.

To alter the borders, select the **Border** tab, then choose whether you want
none, box, shadow, 3-D or custom borders. Select the line style, colour and
width, and use the buttons around the preview to add or remove the top,
bottom, left or right border. To apply the borders, click on **OK**.

You can also shade in rows, columns and cells in a variety of colours:

- Highlight the rows, columns or cells you want to shade.

- Display the **Borders and Shading** dialog box and click on the **Shading**
  tab.

- Choose the fill colour you want to use.

- Use the **Patterns** drop-down menu to select the intensity of the fill; for
  example, clear, solid, 5%, 10%, etc.

- Click on **OK**.

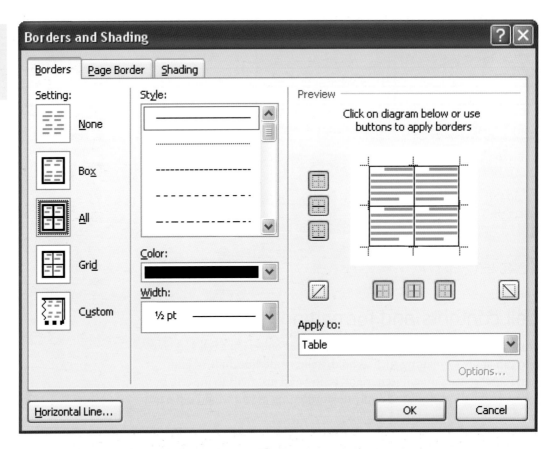

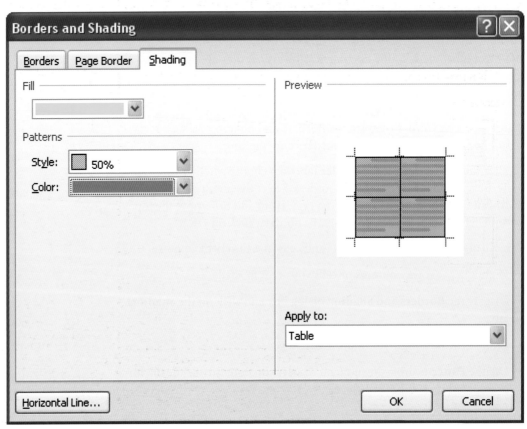

Text orientation in a table cell

You can change the orientation of text in a table cell. To do this in Word, highlight the cell, and in the **Table Tools | Layout** tab select **Text Direction**. This cycles through the available text directions.

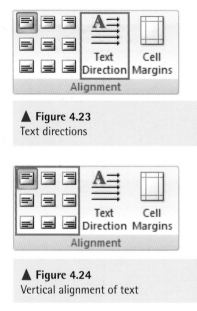

▲ Figure 4.23
Text directions

Vertical alignment within a cell

You can change the vertical alignment of text within a cell (see Figure 4.24).

To do this in Word, highlight the cell, and on the **Table Tools | Layout** tab select the option you require.

▲ Figure 4.24
Vertical alignment of text

Text wrapping around table

You can change how text outside a table aligns with and wraps around a table (see Figure 4.25).

To do this in Word, highlight the table, and on the **Table Tools | Layout** tab click on **Properties**. Click on the **Table** tab, and select left, centre or right alignment (or none or around-text wrapping), then click on **OK**.

◀ Figure 4.25
The Table tab in the Table Properties dialog box

1. Here is a list of some food we eat and the approximate amount of energy we get from it, measured in kilojoules.
   - A portion of fish, 363
   - A portion of potatoes, 129
   - One boiled egg, 380
   - A slice of bread and butter, 180
   - One peanut, 25
   - One carrot, 85

   Using a word processor, do the following:

   a) Create a table with seven rows and two columns.

   b) Put the information above into the table under the column headings, 'Food' and 'Energy'. Make these bold.

   c) Save the document with a suitable filename.

   d) Provide evidence that you have done this.

2. Information about the planets in the solar system is listed below, in the following order: planet, diameter (km), distance from the Sun (millions of km) and length of year.
   - Mercury, 4840, 58, 88 Earth days
   - Venus, 12 200, 108, 225 Earth days
   - Earth, 12 800, 150, 365 Earth days
   - Mars, 6750, 228, 687 Earth days
   - Jupiter, 143 000, 778, 12 Earth years
   - Saturn, 121 000, 1430, 29 Earth years
   - Uranus, 47 200, 2870, 84 Earth years
   - Neptune, 44 600, 4500, 154 Earth years
   - Pluto, 6000, 5900, 248 Earth years

   Do the following:

   a) Create a table with ten rows and four columns.

   b) Put the information above into the table with appropriate headings.

   c) Make sure that numbers are right justified and text is left justified.

   d) Save the document with a suitable filename.

   e) Provide evidence that you have done this.

3. This is a list of five students with their name, student number, weight (kg) and height (cm).
   - Adil Mir, 302001, 40.5,140.5
   - Mike Johnson, 302002, 45.2, 160.3
   - Julie Maynard, 302003, 50.6, 165.0
   - Brian Taylor, 302004, 48.8, 150.2
   - Andrea Campbell, 302005, 65.0, 166.3

Do the following:

a) Put the data in a table with appropriate headings.

b) Edit the table to improve its appearance.

c) Save the document with a suitable filename.

d) Provide evidence that you have done this.

4. The treasurer of the Zenith Oil Company Sports and Cultural Club has prepared a cash listing for the period September 1, 2010 to October 31, 2010. The document is shown below.

Zenith Oil Company
Sports and Cultural Club

CASH LISTING FOR THE PERIOD SEPTEMBER 1st 2010 – OCTOBER 31st 2010

Date	Description	Receipts	Payments	Cash Balance on hand
	Bal b/fwd			0
Sept 02	Raffle (200 sheets @ $10.00 a sheet)	2000		2000
Sept 06	Breakfast Sale	600		2600
Sept 08	Prizes for raffle		500	2100
Sept 09	Cake Sale	550		550
Sept 15	Cost of prizes for cricket presentation		1200	2650
Sept 20	Cost of refreshments for cricket prize giving function		800	1450
Sept 28	Subscription Fees for September	500		650
	Bal c/fwd			1150
Date: November 05 2010				

_____

Treasurer

a) Create the document shown above.

b) Centre the first two lines of the document and change the font size to one that is larger than the rest of the document.

c) Right-align the data in the Receipts and Payments columns, and tidy up the table.

d) Adjust the table so that it takes up the minimum amount of space.

e) Save the document with a suitable filename.

f) Provide evidence that you have done this.

Columns

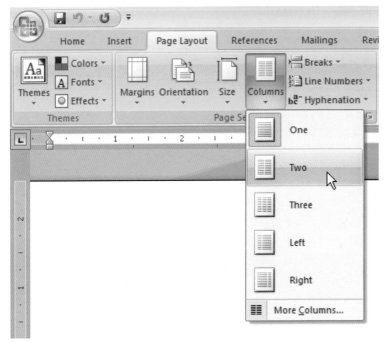

Text **columns** are a very useful layout feature when you want to produce newsletters, newspaper-style documents, indexes or any text that needs to be in continuous columns – so that when the first column is filled at the bottom of the page, the text is started in the next column at the top of the page.

Generally you will use a word processor to produce text that goes across the whole width of the page. This is the default setting but you can lay out a document in one or more **columns**, similar to a newspaper. Even so, if you wish to lay out a document in columns you should consider using desktop publishing (DTP) software – see the section on DTP later in this chapter. In Word you can alter the number of columns in a document or a section of a document using the **Columns** drop-down list on the **Page Layout** tab (see Figure 4.26). The **More Columns** option opens the **Columns** dialog box (see Figure 4.27).

The position at the bottom of a column where the text ends and the next column to the right starts is called a **column break**. If a document has two columns and you reach a particular point before the end of the first column where you would like to start in the next column, you can insert a column break. In Word, you can do this using the **Breaks** drop-down list in the **Page Layout** tab.

▲ Figure 4.26
Columns

Figure 4.27 ▶
The Columns dialog box

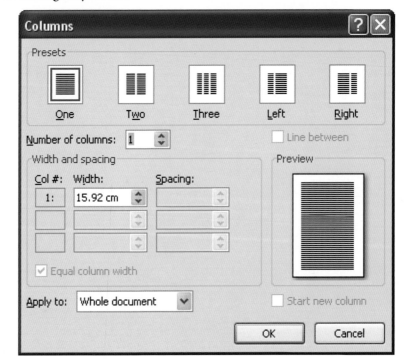

Exercise 4.6

The First Trinidad National Bank has a newsletter called the *Staff Agenda*. The articles shown below are to be placed in the newsletter. You are required to convert the document into an acceptable format by performing the following steps:

1. Type out the document as shown below.

2. At the top insert a heading: *Staff Agenda*.

3. Centre the heading and put it in bold. Ensure that it has a larger font than the rest of the document.

4. Use bold and capitals for the title of each article.

5. Put a blank line between each article and around headings where appropriate.

6. Change the left and right margins to 5 cm and the top and bottom margins to 4 cm.

7. Format the document using two newspaper-style columns. The heading should not be part of any column.

8. Insert the following header into every page of the document:

    Staff Agenda, Volume 1, Number 10

9. Insert the page number into the footer. Centre the page number.

10. Justify the text of each article so it has straight left and right edges.

11. Correct all spelling, grammatical and other errors in the document.

12. Save the document as *Staff Newsletter*.

13. Provide evidence that you have done this.

Here are the articles for the newsletter. When you have done Exercise 4.6, the articles should be much more presentable.

Staff Departures and arrivals

On behalf of the bank, I wish to express our sincere appreciation to and extend best wishes to the following employees:

Mr. John Cardinal, Accounting Supervisor, Fyzabad Branch has resigned with effect from September 25, 2010. Mr. Cardinal served the bank for ten (10) years in the Accounting department.

Mrs. Leanna Achong, Clerk II, Head Office has resigned effective October 10, 2010. Mrs Achong served the bank for eight (8) years in various departments.

New Staff

On behalf of the bank, I would like to welcome the following employees to our institution:

Mr. Larry Phillips has been employed as a Programmer I in the M.I.S. department. Mr. Phillips started on October 6,2010.

Mr. Glenn Singh, has been employed as an Professional Trainee in the Accounting department. Mr. Singh Started on October 6, 2010.

Staff Promotions

On behalf of the bank, I would like to congratulate Ms Teresa Black, Junior Accounting Supervisor, Fyzabad Branch. Ms. Black has been promoted to Accounting Supervisor, effective September 26, 2010.

Sports News

The Bank's annual Sports and Family Fun 2010 day will be held at the Centre of Excellence, Macoya, on January 14, 2011 at 9.00 am. All branches are asked to elect their team captains and to start making preparations for this grand day. There will be events for the entire family. Music will be provided and each employee and their family will receive chits for lunch and refreshments. We look forward to seeing each and every one of you with your family.

Fundraising Events

The Scrabble club will be having a Christmas breakfast on December 14, 2010 to raise funds to purchase hampers for the needy. For further information please contact Ms Gloria Simmons in the Personnel department at Head Office.

Training and Development

Seminar on Money Laundering

The Bank Inspection Department will be conducting a seminar for supervisors on January 17–20, 2010 at the Training centre in Couva. This is the first in a series of seminars and workshops designed to empower our staff with the necessary skills to deal with the problem of money laundering.

Supervisors attending the seminar will conduct knowledge-sharing presentations within their banks upon their return.

Advance Excel Workshop

There will be a three-day Advance Excel workshop to be held on January 21–23, 2011 at the Training Centre in Couva. The workshop is designed for members of staff who have completed the Introductory Excel course. Notification will be sent to managers of respective branches, who would then make arrangements for individual employees to attend.

Examinations

The Bank would like to congratulate the following employees on obtaining their Institute of Bankers Diploma:

Mr. Kevin Khan

Mr. Daniel Ramjohn

Ms Roanna Gill

A Note on Customer Service

With the increasing competition from our competitors we must seek to differentiate ourselves, by standing out from the others. We believe this could be achieved by customer service. Customer service is the perception the public has of our institution. It is about delivering to our customers what we advertise, the personal touch that makes a customer feel special. Remember that poor customer service is an unpleasant experience and could lead to loss of business. Good customer service is a pleasant experience and leads to further business.

At this point in our bank's development, we would like all our employees to remember that good customer service is one of the main contributors to the growth of our organization.

Staff Christmas Diner

This years' annual Christmas diner will be held at the Main Ball Room of the Mohogany Hotel. All employees are invited along with a guest. Cocktails will be from 7.30 to 8.30 and Diner will be from 8.30 pm. Music will be provided by a DJ and a live band. Look forward to seeing all employees.

Templates

If you want to use the formatting and page setup of a document over and over again you could set up the document as a **template**. A business might want to do this so it can have a consistent house style for all the letters and other documents that its staff send to other companies. To use a template, you have to select it when you are setting up a new document. This opens a new document with the formatting and page setup of the template.

To use a template in Word, click on the Office Button and select **New**. The **New Document** dialog box appears (see Figure 4.28). You can then select a template document. Your new document will have the formatting and page setup of the template.

To set up a template in Word, you produce a document with the formatting and page setup you want, and then save the document as a template not as a word processing document.

It is often quicker to start with an existing template and edit this to your requirements. To do this in Word, follow these steps:

- In the **New Document** dialog box, click on **My Templates** and highlight the template you wish to edit.
- Under the heading **Create New**, select **Template** and click on **OK**.
- A new document will open which will have your chosen template. Edit this, then save it with a new filename – the file type (*Document Template*) and location should be set automatically.

When you want to use this template, you select it in the **New Document** dialog box as before.

▼ Figure 4.28
The New Document dialog box

Mail merge

Using the **mail merge** feature, you can produce personalised letters, mailing labels, memos and many other communications to send to a large number of people without having to type each one individually. For example, many companies send standard letters to customers in which the body of the letter is the same but the name, address and a few pieces of additional information may be different. This type of correspondence can be done easily using mail merge.

Mail merge uses two files: **a main document** (containing a **standard letter** or similar), and a **data source** containing the personal information. Data from the data source is inserted into the main document to produce personalised documents. Figure 4.29 shows the merging process. Figure 4.30 shows a standard letter in Word before merging with the data source shown in Figure 4.31. Figure 4.32 is one of the mail merge letters produced.

Figure 4.29 ▶
How mail merge works

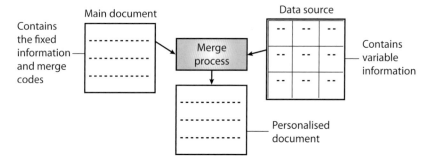

Figure 4.30 ▶
A standard letter before a mail merge

Happy Valley School
12 Valley Line Road
Ocho Rios

04-01-2010

Dear «Title» «Last Name»

You are requested to attend the school's annual parents' day with your «child» «student's name» of «formclass» on January 22nd 2010.

We look forward to seeing you.

Yours truly,

C. Johnson
Headteacher

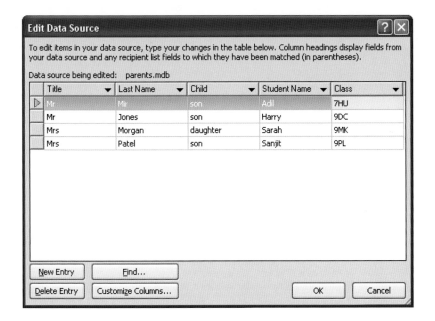

◀ **Figure 4.31**
The mail merge recipients list

Happy Valley School
12 Valley Line Road
Ocho Rios

04-01-2010

Dear Mrs Morgan

You are requested to attend the school's annual parents' day with your daughter Sarah of 9MK on January 22nd 2010.

We look forward to seeing you.

Yours truly,

C. Johnson
Headteacher

◀ **Figure 4.32**
One of the personalised letters after the mail merge

In Word, one way to do a mail merge is to use the **Mail Merge Wizard**. Open a new document and in the **Mailings** tab, click on **Start Mail Merge** and select **Step by Step Mail Merge Wizard**. Follow the instructions:

- Select document type: *letters*. Click **Next**.
- Select starting document: *start from existing document*. Click **Next**.
- Select recipients: *type a new list*. Click **Create**.
- In the **New Address List** dialog box you will need to customise the field names. Change them to those needed in the standard letter (see Figure 4.30). Type in the new entries for your mail merge. When you have finished, close the dialog box and you will have the opportunity to save your data. Click **Next** to write your letter.
- As you write your letter you can insert the **merge fields**. To do this, select **More items** and the **Insert Merge Field** dialog box appears. Select the required field and click on **Insert**. Click **Next**.
- Before completing the mail merge, save your standard letter.
- Click **Next** again and your mail merge is complete.

1. The Happy Valley High School is having its annual parents' day and wishes to invite parents. The principal wants each parent to receive a personal invitation. The school secretary has been asked to send personalised invitations to parents and is going to do this using mail merge.

> Happy Valley High School
>
> 12 Valley Line Road
>
> Ocho Rios
>
> 04-01-2011
>
> Dear <<Title>> <<LastName>>
>
> You are requested to attend the school's annual parents' day with your <<child>>, <<student_name>> of <<formclass>> on January 22nd, 2011.
>
> We look forward to seeing you.
>
> Yours truly,
>
> C.Johnson
>
> Headteacher

- When you type in this letter, centre the name and address of the school, and insert blank lines where these are necessary; for example, between the line beginning with 'Dear' and the following line.
- When you save this document, give it the filename 'Open Day'.

The data source is to contain this information:

Title	Mr
Last Name	Jaffar
child	son
student_name	Ronald
formclass	8MX

Title	Mrs
Last Name	Morgan
child	daughter
student_name	Sarah
Form class	9MK

- When you enter this data, add at least eight records of your own.
- When you save this data, give it the filename 'Parents'.
- Mail merge the standard letter with the data source and print all the letters.

2. Customers who do not pay their monthly instalment by the fifteenth day of the following month are sent the following reminder letter by Makhan Furniture Shop:

Makhan Furniture Shop
Broad Street Bridgetown
Barbados

<<Title>><<First Name>><<Surname>>

<<First line of address>>

<<Second line of address>>

Dear <<Title>><<Surname>>

Please be informed that our accounts are showing that you have not paid your monthly instalment of <<amount>> towards your purchase on <<date>>. Kindly pay this amount to your account, number <<account number>>, to avoid any inconvenience.

Yours truly,

_____

Lenore Brown

Manager

These defaulters were found in the current month:

Title:	Mr
First Name:	Kelvin
Surname:	Harry
First line of address:	3 Hisbiscus Lane
Second line of address:	Christ Church
Amount:	$450
Date:	08 08 2010
Account Number:	Aug134

Title:	Mr
First Name:	Conrad
Surname:	Lewis
First line of address:	10 Wilson Avenue
Second line of address:	St Lawerence Gap
Amount:	$650
Date:	12 10 2010
Account Number:	Oct256

Title:	Ms
First Name:	Sherry
Surname:	Roach
First line of address:	8 Railroad Street
Second line of address:	Blackrock
Amount:	$875
Date:	15 08 2010
Account Number:	Aug150

a) Add seven records of your own.

b) Using mail merge, print personalised letters to the customers who have defaulted on their payments.

c) Add a new field called *Item* and fill in possible names for the items for each customer.

d) Change the amount owing for Mr Lewis to $785.

e) Save all changes, produce personalised letters to the customers who have defaulted on their payments using mail merge, and provide evidence you have done this.

Macros

Macros are useful if you wish to automate tasks that you do repeatedly. A macro is a series of instructions and commands to the software that you can group together so that they become a single command.

For example, if you want your name, the date and the filename of a document to appear in the footer of the documents you produce, you could create a macro to do this (see Figure 4.33). So instead of going through the lengthy process needed to do this each time you create a document, you could do it using a single command which could be accessed in a toolbar or a menu.

In Word, you could create this macro by following three steps: turning on the macro recorder, editing the footer and turning the macro recorder off again.

To turn on the macro recorder:

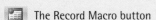
The Record Macro button

- Click on **Record Macro** in the **Macros** drop down menu in the **View** tab.

- Give the macro a name, e.g. 'footer', and click on **OK**.

Everything you do between turning on the macro recorder and turning it off is recorded and becomes a part of the macro:

- In the **Insert** tab, select **Footer** then **Edit Footer**.

- In the footer, type in your name.

- Insert the filename (select **Quick Parts**, **Field**, **FileName** and click on **OK**).

- Insert the date (select **Date and Time**, choose a format and click on **OK**).

Turn off the macro recorder:

The Stop Recording button

- Click on **Stop Recording** in the **Macros** drop down menu in the **View** tab.

In Word, to use the macro you have created, do the following:

- On the **View** tab, select **Macro**, select the macro **footer** and click on **Run**.

Macros can also be written in Visual Basic. In Word, you can see the Visual Basic code generated by the macro **footer**: in the **View** tab, select **Macros**, select the macro **footer** and click on **Edit**. The Visual Basic code is displayed. You can edit this code if you wish.

Footer

Roger Crawford, Chapter 4.doc, 01/11/2009

▲ **Figure 4.33**
The 'footer' macro puts your name, the filename of the document and the date in the footer

Graphics
Including graphics in a word processed document

Depending on the nature of your document, you may be able to enhance its appearance by including graphics. There are many ways to do this:

- Insert clip art from a clip art library

- Input a photograph from a digital camera

- Insert a scanned image of a drawing or picture

- Download graphics from the Web

- Cut or copy a graphic from another application

- Copy the whole or part of the screen and paste it into the document.

Inserting a graphic

In Word, insert a graphic in a document as follows:

- Place the insertion point where you want the graphic displayed.

- On the **Insert** tab, select **Clip Art** (or **Picture** if the graphic is stored in a file).

- Next, select a picture and click on **Insert**.

Including the whole or a part of the screen in a document

On an IBM compatible personal computer, pressing the **Print Screen** key on the keyboard will copy an image of the screen display into the clipboard. Pressing the **Alt** key and the **Print Screen** key at the same time will copy the active window (or dialog box) into the clipboard. In Word, the contents of the clipboard can be included in a document by selecting **Paste**. Figure 4.31 is an example of a dialog box which has been pasted into a word processed document.

When you have inserted a graphic, you may find that you want to change its size, move it to a new position, allow text to flow round it or put a border on it. These tasks can be done in a word processor.

Extension activity
Create a macro to put your name, the filename, the file size, the date and a page number in the footer.

DID YOU KNOW?
As an alternative, you can cut or copy a graphic from another application or document and paste it into a word processing document.

Changing the size of a graphic

When a graphic has been inserted, you may wish to change its size. This can be done by resizing and cropping. When a graphic is **resized**, the whole graphic is enlarged or reduced, but when a graphic is **cropped**, part of the graphic is removed.

Resizing a graphic

A graphic is resized when it is enlarged or reduced but the whole graphic is retained. In Word, click once on the graphic and it is displayed with eight selection handles around it (see Figure 4.34).

- You can change the height of the graphic using the selection handles at the top or bottom to stretch the graphic vertically.

- You can change the width of the graphic using the handles at the sides to stretch the graphic horizontally.

- To reduce or enlarge the graphic proportionately, drag the corner handles away from the centre of the graphic to enlarge its size or towards the centre of the graphic to reduce its size. This preserves the **aspect ratio**, which means that any changes to the graphic keep the same shape.

Figure 4.34 ▶
Selection handles surrounding a graphic

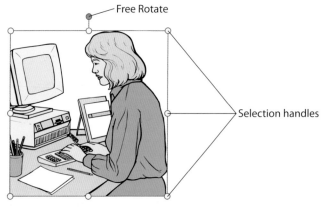

Cropping a graphic

When a graphic is cropped, it is reframed and the part of it outside the new rectangular frame is deleted. In Word, in the **Picture Tools | Format** tab, click on the **Crop** button and reframe the graphic. When you are satisfied this is as you want it, click on the crop button again and the part of the graphic outside the new frame is deleted. If you wish, you can now resize the cropped graphic.

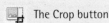 The Crop button

Changing the position of the graphic

When a graphic has been inserted, you may wish to move it to another position in the document. You could highlight the graphic then drag it to the desired position. Alternatively, you could cut or copy and paste the graphic.

Rotating or reflecting a graphic

Graphics can be rotated and reflected (flipped). In Word, select the graphic and select **Rotate**. You can use the **Free Rotate** selection handle at the middle top to achieve any degree of rotation.

Wrapping text around a graphic

When a graphic is placed in a document, the text around the graphic is placed at the top and bottom of the graphic but not at the sides. However, for newsletters, newspapers and magazines, you may want the text to flow or wrap around the graphic. This can save space and enhance presentation. Figure 4.35 shows a graphic within a border with text wrapped around it.

In Word, you can wrap text around a graphic by selecting it and using the **Text Wrapping** options on the **Picture Tools | Format** tab.

Text wrapped around graphic ——

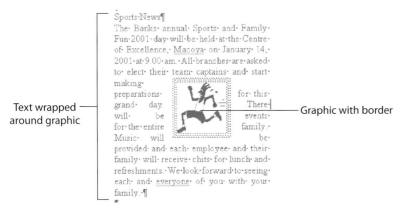

—— Graphic with border

◀ **Figure 4.35**
Text wrapped around a graphic

Inserting a border around a graphic

You can put a border on a graphic to emphasise it rather like a picture frame. In Word, select the graphic and in use the **Picture Border** options on the **Picture Tools | Format** tab to select the border you want.

Inserting symbols and special characters

Some documents may need symbols that do not appear as keys on the keyboard. For example, α, Π and Σ are all symbols that might be part of a document. In Word, these symbols can be found listed in the **Symbol** drop-down list on the **Home** tab.

Drawing tools

Many word processors now have a range of drawing tools so that you can add commentary to illustrations and graphics.

Drawing tools that can be found in word processors include the following:

- Autoshapes – a variety of lines, arrows, connectors, flowchart symbols, callouts and other shapes. These will be available in different styles and shapes.
- Preformatted diagrams; for example, organisational charts.
- Text boxes.
- Colour which can be used to fill shapes.
- Shadow and 3-D effects.

To access these tools in Word, click the **Shapes** button on the **Insert** tab.

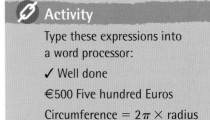

Activity

Type these expressions into a word processor:

✓ Well done

€500 Five hundred Euros

Circumference $= 2\pi \times$ radius

$m \propto A$

Desktop publishing (DTP)

⌀ Activity

Write a story about your holidays. Put pictures of your holidays in the story, and wrap the text round the pictures. Use callouts to point out particular features in the pictures.

DTP software is used to produce leaflets, brochures, newspapers, magazines, etc. Popular examples are PageMaker and Microsoft Publisher. DTP software has many features in common with word processors – for example, you can open, save and print documents, enter and edit text, change the font type and size, and insert new pages in a very similar way to when you use a word processor. However, DTP has much better controls for handling page layout. For example, Microsoft Publisher has templates for business cards, letterheads, flyers and brochures.

Very early word processors did not allow you to format text using columns and tables and you could not import graphics. The DTP software available at the time provided these facilities but would not allow you to enter and edit text. Text had to be entered using a word processor then imported to the DTP software. This is sometimes still the case. However, as word processor software and DTP software have been improved over the years, a considerable overlap has developed and these now have many features in common. Even so, professional typographers would tend to use DTP software rather than word processing software to produce published materials such as magazines.

▼ **Figure 4.36**
The Microsoft Publisher opening screen

At present, the main difference between DTP and word processing software is that DTP software emphasises page layout. When you are setting up a new DTP document you have to decide on the page layout before you can enter text, import clip art and other graphics.

To illustrate the emphasis placed on page layout in DTP software, consider the options presented to the user when Microsoft Publisher is opened. First, you are presented with a screen that asks you to select from a variety of page layouts (see Figure 4.36). Having selected a page layout you are guided through a range of layout and design options before entering text or inserting your own graphics.

If you immediately exit the opening screen, the software still persists in encouraging you to select a page layout. It does this using the **Format Publication** task pane (see Figure 4.37). Working through the various options you would take the following steps:

- Add suggested objects.
- Choose a colour scheme for your background.
- Choose a font scheme.
- Choose a template.
- Change the page size.

If you avoid both the opening screen and the **Format Publication** task pane and click on the page and start typing, a text frame is created for you. A text frame is a layout feature, as explained below.

Frames

Frames are a layout feature, and all text and graphics or any other object inserted into Publisher must be entered into a frame. In Publisher, you can insert frames using the toolbar shown in Figure 4.38. To do this, you click on the appropriate button and insert the required object.

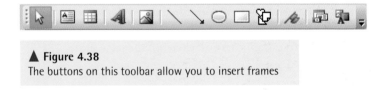

▲ **Figure 4.38**
The buttons on this toolbar allow you to insert frames

Inserting a text frame

To insert a text frame you click on the **Text Box**. Dragging the mouse pointer across the page creates a text frame. When you type, the text appears in the text box.

Inserting a picture frame

To insert a picture frame you click on **Picture Frame Tool**. Dragging the mouse pointer across the page creates a picture frame. Double-click on the picture frame and a dialog box appears. Using this dialog box you can choose a picture file and this will be imported into the picture frame.

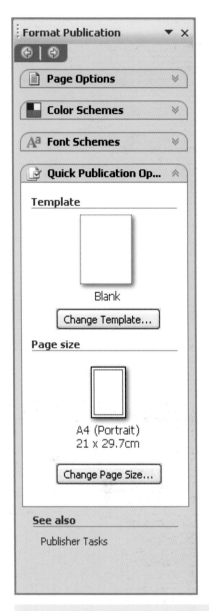

▲ **Figure 4.37**
The Format Publication task pane

Importing from other applications

You will also need to use an appropriate frame if you import an object from another application. For example, in Publisher, when importing part of a spreadsheet by copying it from Excel and pasting into Publisher, the software will create a table frame for you.

Manipulating frames

Page layout is controlled by resizing and moving frames. Having inserted a frame you can resize it using the selection handles in a way similar to that described for resizing a graphic earlier in this chapter.

Manipulating graphics

The crop feature works in much the same way as it does in Word. You can also move a graphic, rotate or reflect it, wrap text around it and put a border on the frame in much the same way as you would in Word.

Text flow

An important feature of DTP is the ability to make text flow between different text frames that are separate and in different positions on the page or on different pages. You will want text flow to work when you resize frames so that they can contain more or less text, and when you delete or insert text.

Let us suppose you want to type a story in two or more frames. In Publisher, you would create a text box and begin to type in the text. When the text box is full, the **Text in Overflow indicator** (see Figure 4.39) appears on the lower right-hand corner of the text frame. Create another text frame then click on the original text frame. Next, click on the **Create Text Box Link** button (see Figure 4.40) then click on the second text frame. The two frames are now linked and the story pours into the second text frame. These frames can now be manipulated so that the second text frame appears elsewhere on the page or on another page.

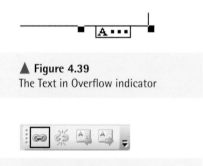

▲ **Figure 4.39**
The Text in Overflow indicator

▲ **Figure 4.40**
The Create Text Box Link button

Business cards, letterheads, flyers and brochures

Microsoft Publisher has **templates** that allow you to create business cards, letterheads, flyers, brochures and many other common forms of printed communication.

For example, here is how to create business cards in Publisher:

- From the opening screen, click on the **Business Cards** publication type.
- The templates for business cards with different layouts are displayed. Select one of these then press **Create**.

- To customise your design, you choose from a range of colour schemes and fonts.

- To personalise the business card, you enter your details, such as your name and business name, address, telephone number, fax number and e-mail address.

- You can also decide whether to include a logo, the orientation and the number of copies to be printed on each sheet of paper.

- To print or save your business card, in the **File** menu, select the appropriate option.

 Activity

Write a booklet about the place where you live. This could have several different articles describing how different people live, work and enjoy themselves. This should include photographs of local people, houses and industrial buildings. The booklet should be up to four pages long.

Summary

1. A word processor allows you to prepare letters, reports, memos, books and other correspondence. These can be saved to be worked on later or printed.

2. When entering text, the word wrap feature moves you to a new line automatically. You press the Enter key only if the line is a short line or to move to a new paragraph. You can also insert graphics and symbols into documents.

3. A word processor contains many editing and proofing features that enable users to make changes to a document quickly and easily. Some of the editing features include the following:
   - **Delete** (characters, words and blocks of text can easily be deleted).
   - **Insert** (characters, words and blocks of text can easily be inserted).
   - **Drag and Drop** is the easiest way to move text within a document.
   - **Cut, Copy and Paste** (characters, words and blocks of text can be removed or copied from one part of a document and placed in another part of the same document, in another document or in another application).

4. You can check a document for accuracy using tools such as spelling and grammar checkers. You should also proofread your work carefully.

5. If you make a mistake in a document and immediately want to reverse the change, you use the **Undo** function. If you then decide you preferred the changed document you can use **Redo** to reapply the change.

6. **Find** is used to search for a word or phrase in a document. **Replace** is used to replace a specific word or phrase with another word or phrase.

7. **Formatting** determines the final appearance of a document. Formatting can be carried out at three levels: character, paragraph and page.
   - Characters can be formatted using font type (Arial, Times New Roman, etc.), font size (height of a character), font style (regular, bold, underline, italic), font colour and special effects (superscript, subscript, strikethrough, shadow, outline, emboss, engrave, caps).
   - Paragraph formatting includes line spacing, alignment (centre, left, right and justified) and indenting, bullets and numbering.
   - Page layout can be adjusted by changing the margins, changing the page orientation to landscape or portrait, altering the paper size, and by including headers and footers.

8. **Headers** can be used to display text or graphics across the top of the page (for example, the title of a document). **Footers** can be used to display text or graphics across the bottom of the page (for example, the page number).

9. **Page and section breaks** are used to control the start of new pages and sections of a document.

10. A **widow** is the final line of a paragraph that is printed at the top of the next page, and an **orphan** is the first line of a paragraph printed at the bottom of a page. It is desirable to avoid these.

11. **Tables** can be inserted into a document to display statistical and numerical data. Rows, columns and cells can have borders and can be shaded for emphasis. The text in a cell can be left and right aligned or centred, and it can have different vertical orientation and alignment. Text outside a table can be wrapped round the table in different ways.

12. **Columns** are a useful feature for producing newsletters and newspaper-style documents.

13. Templates can be used to create new documents with the same format. This is useful for businesses wanting a consistent house style.

14. The **mail merge** feature allows you to produce personalised letters, mailing labels and memos without having to type each one individually. Mail merging requires two files: the main document or *standard letter*, and the *data source*. The standard letter contains the letter and the merge fields, which are positioned where the personalised information from the data source will be placed. The data source contains the personalised information needed to complete the standard letter.

15. **Macros** are use to automate tasks which are done repeatedly. A macro is a series of instructions to the software which are grouped together and can be run using a single command.

16. **Graphics** can be included from many sources. For example, images from a clip art library, photographs from a digital camera, scanned images and graphics downloaded from the Web. **Symbols** and special characters can be inserted.

17. Word processors have many tools for manipulating graphics. Graphics can be resized preserving the aspect ratio or stretched. They can be cropped, moved, rotated and reflected. Borders can be put on them and text can be wrapped round them.

18. **Drawing tools** are used to create graphics in a word processor. These might include auto shapes including callouts, preformatted diagrams, colour, shadow and 3-D effects.

19. **Desktop publishing (DTP)** software is used to produce leaflets, newspapers and magazines.

20. DTP software has many features in common with word processing; for example, open, save, print, enter and edit text, change font type and size.

21. DTP software emphasises the importance of **page layout**. You cannot enter any information into DTP software until you have used some page layout features.

22. Information is inserted into DTP software in **frames**. There are different types of frame for text, pictures and other objects.

23. An important feature of DTP is the flow of text between different frames. These may be on the same page or on different pages.

Chapter 5

Spreadsheets and modelling

Spreadsheets enable you to store numerical data and **formulae**, which can be used to carry out operations on the numerical data. These formulae are applied to the data whenever you make a change to it. If you change any data values, the entire spreadsheet is **automatically recalculated**. This is one of the most important features of a spreadsheet. The ability to represent the numerical data quickly and easily as a graph is another important advantage.

A spreadsheet can also be used to set up numerical and financial models that can be used to help novices learn how these work and to forecast future events.

Here are some examples of the uses of spreadsheets:

- Loan calculations

- Financial plans — e.g. budgeting

- Keeping accounts in a club or for a business

- Statistics — e.g. finding averages or calculating the standard deviation

Spreadsheets are made up of several worksheets. It is the active worksheet that you see on the screen. Multiple worksheets can be used to hide complex data and calculations so that the user is presented with a simplified summary. This feature is very useful in modelling.

Various spreadsheet software is available, such as the *Calc* spreadsheet (part of OpenOffice), *Lotus 1-2-3* (part of Lotus SmartSuite) and *Excel* (part of Microsoft Office). The examples in this chapter are illustrated using Microsoft Office Excel 2007 running on the Windows XP operating system.

Basic concepts

Spreadsheet software initially displays on the screen a large grid divided into rows and columns. This is the **active worksheet**. A typical screen display has horizontal rows from left to right which are numbered, and columns up and down the screen which are named using letters. What is displayed on the screen is only a small part of the available worksheet. For example, the initial screen displayed by Excel is shown in Figure 5.1.

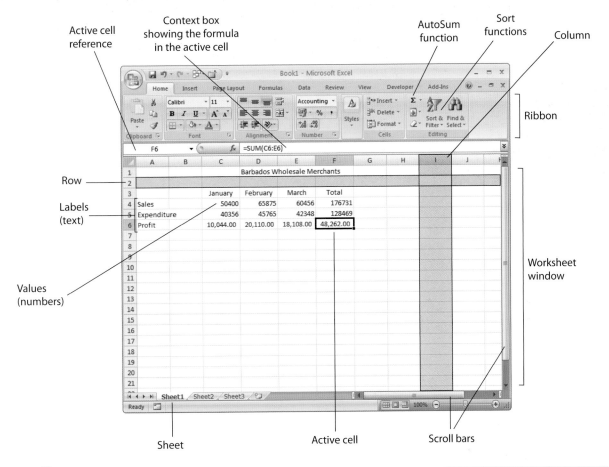

Cell contents

The intersection of a row and a column is called a **cell**. A cell can contain different types of information, for example: **label** (text), **value** (number) or **formula**.

- A **label** can be used as a title or heading. It can contain any string of characters (letters or numbers) but must start with a character that does not indicate a formula or number. A label cannot be used in a calculation.

- A **value** is numerical data that can be used in a calculation.

- A **formula** is an instruction to perform operations on values. A formula must start with a special symbol (e.g. **+, −, @, =**) to identify it as a formula. For example, in Excel formulae start with **=**, and in Lotus 1-2-3 formulae begin with **@**.

Cell references

Each cell in the active worksheet can be identified by its **cell reference**, which is the column position and the row position combined. For example, the address **F6** means that the cell is in column **F** and row **6**.

The **active cell** is the cell which is currently selected. For example, in Figure 5.1, the cell **F6** is the active cell. The cell reference F6 only refers to a single cell, but you can use **a cell range reference** to refer to a range of cells. For example, in Figure 5.1, the data for January is contained in cells **C4:C6** in column C, and the sales figures are in cells **C4:F4** on row 4.

▲ **Figure 5.1**
A typical spreadsheet

HINT!

If you are using a spreadsheet other than Excel, you must remember that formula may not start with =.
You should change any = you find used in this chapter to your special symbol that indicates a formula.

To refer to a rectangular block of cells, you would give the cell reference of the top left-hand corner and the bottom right-hand corner; for example, in Figure 5.2, the rectangular block that has been selected has the cell range reference **B2:D4**.

Figure 5.2 ▶
Sample spreadsheet with the range B2:D4 selected

	A	B	C	D	E
1		Trinidad Wholesalers Ltd.			
2		January	February	March	
3	Sales	50400	65875	60456	
4	Expenditure	40356	45765	42348	
5					

Moving around a worksheet and entering data

You can move around a worksheet using the mouse and the cursor control keys (or arrow keys). Before data can be placed in a cell, the cell must be selected. You can do this by moving the cursor to it and clicking the left mouse button or by using the cursor control keys. Notice that when you type data, it is displayed in the selected cell and in the content box at the top of the window. The data enters the cell only when the **Enter** key or an arrow key is pressed.

Exercise 5.1

1. Write down the name of the spreadsheet package you are using.

2. Describe what is meant by the following and give examples to illustrate your answer:
   a) Cell   b) Cell reference
   c) Range reference d) Value
   e) Formula   f) Worksheet

3. Look at the spreadsheet in Figure 5.3.

Figure 5.3 ▶
Sample spreadsheet for Exercise 5.1

D4	▼		f_x	42348

	A	B	C	D
1		Trinidad Wholesalers Ltd.		
2		January	February	March
3	Sales	50400	65875	60456
4	Expenditure	40356	45765	42348
5				

   a) Write down the number of rows and the number of columns that are shown.
   b) Write down the content of cell **C4**. State whether it is a label, a number or a formula.
   c) Write down the cell reference of the active cell.

4. Give two situations where a spreadsheet may be used. Give reasons for your answers.

5. Create the worksheet shown in Figure 5.3. Save the spreadsheet giving it the file name **Sales**.

The advantage of using the SUM function

Suppose that the Premium Furniture Store has reorganised and introduced an additional sales area called Home. This is to be inserted in the spreadsheet of Figure 5.5 above the sales data for the East area. The sales data for the Home area will become row 8, and current rows 8 and 9 will become new rows 9 and 10. If the formula in cell B10 was =**B6+B7+B8+B9** instead of =**SUM(B6:B9)**, this formula would become incorrect and need editing. The spreadsheet will adjust the formula =**SUM(B6:B9)** to =**SUM(B6:B10)** as the new row is inserted. This is also true for the formula in cells C10 and D10. This is a major advantage of using the SUM function.

Relative cell addressing

Notice that in the spreadsheet shown in Figure 5.5, the formulae that would be entered in cells E6, E7, E8 and E9 are very similar except that the row numbers are different. You could enter the different formula into each of the four cells separately but there is a faster way of doing this. Instead of entering the four different formulae, a spreadsheet will let us enter one formula and copy this to the other cells and it will adjust the copied formula. The structure of the formula remains the same, but the addresses of the cells used in the formula will change relative to the position of the formula. This feature is called **relative cell addressing**. For example, if the formula **B3*C3** was in cell D3 and you copied this to cell D4 then the formula in D4 would be **B4*C4**.

Exercise 5.4

1. Create the worksheet 'Premium Quarterly Sales' as shown in Figure 5.5.

2. In column E, calculate the total sales for the four branches using the SUM function.

3. In row 10, use the SUM function to calculate the total sales for all the branches for the months January to March.

4. In cell E10 calculate the grand total.

5. You are going to change the value in cell B6. Write down the cell references of the cells you think will change automatically. Print the worksheet.

6. Change the value in cell B6 to 20050. Write down the cell references of all the cells that are automatically recalculated.

7. Adjust column widths and row heights so that the data in all the cells can be seen.

8. Right-align the headings in row 5.

9. Save the spreadsheet with the name **Premium**.

10. Print the worksheet.

Absolute cell references

You can copy a formula to other cells in a row or column and a spreadsheet will change the formula relative to the position of the cells (this is *relative cell referencing*). However, there are situations where you do not want the spreadsheet to adjust the cell references when a formula is copied from one location to another. To prevent this adjustment we use **absolute cell references**. In Excel, these are constructed by placing two dollar ($) signs in the cell reference. For example, in Figure 5.7, we would want formulae that refer to the percentage mark-up and the percentage VAT always to refer to cells B1 and B2 where their values are stored. To achieve this when we write formulae that refer to cells B1 and B2 we would enter B1 and B2 instead. These absolute cell references remain unchanged no matter where they are copied or moved to in the spreadsheet.

Copying a formula

You can cut or copy and paste a formula in the same way that you cut or copy and paste other cells. However, in Excel there is a particular method of copying cells that is useful when you copy formulae. You can copy a formula in the active cell to the cells in the same column immediately above or below it by dragging the fill handle. You can also copy to the left and right on the same row using this method, which is called *replication*.

Figure 5.6 ▶
The fill handle on the active cell

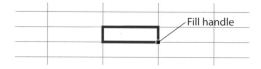
Fill handle

Figure 5.7 ▶
Data for calculating a final selling price

Exercise 5.5

A store owner would like to build a spreadsheet to calculate the final selling price of each item in his store. The store owner first adds a mark-up of 20% to the cost price, to produce the marked-up price, and then adds 15% VAT to the marked-up price to get the final selling price.

	A	B	C	D	E
1	MARK-UP	20%			
2	VAT	15%			
3					
4	Item	Cost price	Marked-up price	Vat	Final selling price
5	Hat	$20.00			
6	Shirt	$75.00			
7	Pants	$235.00			
8	Jersey	$145.00			
9	Shoes	$225.00			

1. Enter the data as shown in Figure 5.7.
2. Move to cell C5. Type the formula =B5+ (B5* B1).
3. Copy the formula to cells C6, C7, C8 and C9.
4. Move to cell D5. Type the formula =C5 * B2.

106

Exercise 5.7

The spreadsheet in Figure 5.11 shows a list of books from a supplier to the Small Book Store. Do the following:

1. Create the worksheet.

2. Make the title and the labels in row 3 bold.

3. Sort the data into ascending order by author and then by title. Save the spreadsheet as 'Small Books'.

4. Add a column to calculate the total cost for each title.
    (Total cost = No. of copies * Unit cost)

5. Adjust column widths and row heights so that the data in all the cells can be seen.

6. Save the spreadsheet.

7. Print the spreadsheet.

▼ **Figure 5.11** Book list

	A	B	C	D	E
1		The Small Book Store			
2					
3	Author	Title	Classification	No. of Copies	Unit Cost
4	Mars Richard	Star Chase	Science Fiction	6	$ 39.00
5	Lucas Gary	Dracula	Horror	4	$ 40.00
6	Brown James	Faith Healers	Religious	10	$ 45.00
7	Brown James	Back to God Head	Religious	5	$ 50.00
8	Lucas Gary	Bad Omens	Horror	6	$ 54.00
9	Richards Jenifer	Outer Planet Experience	Science Fiction	5	$ 65.00
10	Jaira Kadine	Eagle and the Falcon	Thriller	3	$ 75.00
11	Lucas Gary	The Dark Side	Horror	6	$ 76.00
12	Jaira Kadine	Apocalypse	Thriller	3	$ 78.00
13	Mohammed Afzal	In Touch with God	Religious	3	$ 80.00
14					

Creating graphs and charts

Graphs and charts are important because they can simplify numerical data and make it easier to interpret. They get your attention almost instantly and allow information to be interpreted quickly. Therefore charts can be important tools for data analysis and the presentation of data.

The first step in creating a chart is to select the data values you want to place in it. A spreadsheet package enables you to plot any row or column of data against any other row or column of data. For example, if we want to represent the first quarter sales for the months of January to March for the four branches of the Premium Furniture Store for the values shown in Figure 5.9, we need to select the range A5:D9.

After selecting the data values, you need to select an appropriate type of chart. The type of chart you choose depends on the type of data you have and how you want to represent it. Some charts are best for representing certain types of data. For example, the sales data may best be displayed using a column graph. Data that represents portions of a whole might best be represented using a pie chart.

If any values in the data selected are changed after the chart has been created, they are immediately reflected in the chart. Also, more data can be inserted between the first and last rows or columns. These changes will also be automatically included in the chart. Before creating a chart, make yourself familiar with the elements of a chart. Figure 5.12 shows a completed chart for the first quarter sales of the Premium Furniture Store.

Figure 5.12 ▶
A sales chart with its elements named

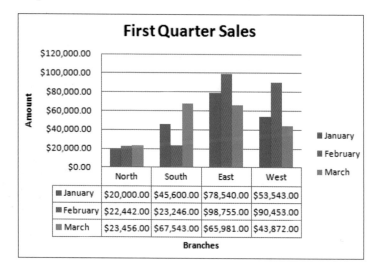

Chart elements

A graph or chart has several elements:

- **Axes** – The vertical and horizontal lines against which data is plotted. The horizontal X-axis is referred to as the **category axis** and the vertical Y-axis is known as the **value axis**.
- **Titles** – There are three titles: for the chart, the category axis and the value axis.
- **Data range** – The range of cells selected to create the chart.
- **Data labels** – The actual value, percentage or name of a bar or segment of a chart.
- **Data table** – The range of values, included at the bottom of the chart, that is used to draw the graph.
- **Series** – The data in a row or column that makes up the range of values that is used to create the graph.
- **Legend** – A cross-reference showing how each series is represented in the chart.
- **Gridlines** – Lines parallel to each axis that help you read values from the graph more easily.

Creating a chart

In Excel, you can use the **Insert** tab to create graphs and charts, as follows:

- Select the data to be displayed and click the **Insert** tab.
- Choose a type of graph from the **Charts** area.
- You can fine-tune the chart using the options in the **Chart Tools** tabs.

Enhancing a chart

Charts can be customised or enhanced for variety and emphasis.

A slice of a pie chart can be offset from the main body of the pie, perhaps for emphasis. In Figure 5.13, the slice representing the number of Ford vehicles in a car park has been offset slightly from the main body of the pie chart so it stands out.

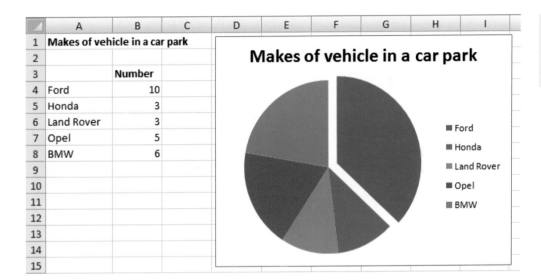

To offset a slice of a pie, create a pie chart, select the pie, then click on the slice to be offset. Drag the slice out of the pie.

Several features of the slice of a pie can be changed, including its colour. Select the slice you wish to change, right-click it and select **Format Data Point**. The **Format Data Point** dialog box appears (see Figure 5.14). Click on the **Fill** tab then click on **Solid fill** and select a colour.

You can use the **Chart Tools** tabs in the Ribbon to enhance the whole chart or a single data point.

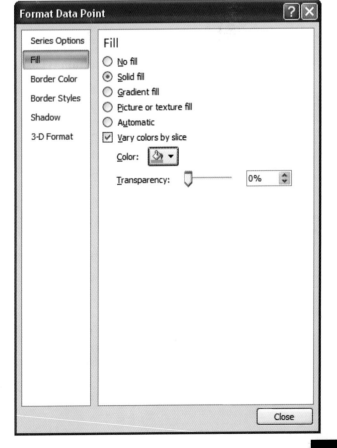

Figure 5.14 ▶
The Format Data Point dialog box

The IF function

The **IF** function tests a condition to see if it is true or false.

The general form of the **IF** function is as follows:

=**IF**(**condition, what to do if the condition is true, what to do if the condition is false**)

When the function is executed, the first instruction *(what to do if the condition is true)* is executed if the condition is true, and the second instruction *(what to do if the condition is false)* is executed if the condition is false. Either instruction can be text, a number, a formula, a function or a cell address. If an instruction is text or a number then this is displayed. If the instruction is a formula, function or cell address, the result, and not the instruction itself, will be displayed. For example, consider the function =**IF**(**F5 > 50000, 10, 8**). If the value in cell F5 is greater than 50 000, the number 10 will be displayed in F5. If the value in F5 is less than 50 000, the number 8 will be displayed.

The logical operators which can be used in the **IF** function are as follows:

Operator	Meaning
>	Greater than
=	Equal to
>=	Greater than or equal to
<	Less than
<=	Less than or equal to
<>	Not equal to

 **EXTENSION QUESTIONS**

Cell E4 contains this formula: **IF(D4<50, "reorder", "stock levels adequate")**.

- Write down what will be displayed in cell E4 if the value in cell D4 is 55.
- Write down what will be displayed in cell E4 if the value in cell D4 is 23.

Exercise 5.12

1. Set up the price forecast model on a spreadsheet and use it to forecast:
   - the price of a car worth $9,500 in 10 years if inflation is 2.5%
   - the price of a house worth $80,000 in 5 years if the price of housing is increasing by 15% each year
   - the value of $500 in ten years time if it is invested in a savings account with an interest rate of 2.75%.

2. a) Set up a supermarket queue model.
   A supermarket has five checkouts and the checkout operators take an average of 3 minutes to get a customer through the checkout.
      - If there are 20 customers and 5 checkouts open, calculate how long the last customer will have to wait.
      - If there are 15 customers and an acceptable waiting time is 10 minutes, calculate how many checkouts need to be open.
   b) A retail company is building a new supermarket. Describe how the supermarket queue model could be used to help with the design of the supermarket.

Testing a model

A model is based on rules which attempt to describe the real-world situation that the model represents. These rules should be tested in the way that any ICT system is tested (see Chapter 11) and the examples of spreadsheet models given in this chapter should be tested in this way.

In addition, because a model is intended to mimic a real-world situation, it should be tested against this situation to see if it does make accurate predictions. For example, in the supermarket queue model, the average waiting time for customers should be manually measured using stopwatches and the results compared to the predictions of the model. This comparison is likely to show whether the rules built into the model are reasonable. A likely finding is that the measured average waiting time is longer than that predicted by the model. This is because the model assumes that customers distribute themselves evenly between the checkouts that are open; in the real world, customers do not do this.

The supermarket manager could respond to this information in various ways:

- accepting the model, as the difference in average waiting time results from customers' choices and could be minimal

- introducing ways of managing the queues of customers so that they distribute themselves evenly between checkouts

- changing the rules built into the model to make it more accurate.

Other types of modelling

More complex models can be built based on specific application software. They include games, simulations, science experiments, economic models and weather forecasting. These can be virtual reality models. These types of models are far more complex than those based on spreadsheets and are described in a later chapter.

Exercise 5.13

1. A student receives an allowance of $50.00 a week. This is how the student spends the money each day.

	Monday	Tuesday	Wednesday	Thursday	Friday
Travelling	4	4	4	4	4
Lunch	2	3	2	4	6
Snacks	3	2	1	2	2
Games World	10	9	5	6	10

Using a spreadsheet, complete the following tasks:
a) Calculate the total money spent each day of the week.
b) Calculate the total money spent on each item for the week.
c) Calculate the total expenses for the week.
d) Calculate the amount left from the student's allowance.
e) Add currency symbols.
f) Centre all headings.
g) Save the spreadsheet as 'Allowance' and print it.
h) The student is spending more than the weekly allowance. Propose ways to reduce spending to an acceptable level.

2. Figure 5.24 shows the names of students and their marks in five subjects. Enter the data into a spreadsheet as shown.

▼ Figure 5.24
Students' marks in five subjects

	A	B	C	D	E	F	G	H
1				RB College Barbados				
2								
3			Form 3.1	Mark	Sheet			
4	Names	Maths	Biology	Chemistry	Physics	English	Total	Average
5	Victoria Bishop	67	76	45	55	23		
6	Renee Eastman	76	42	45	57	45		
7	Ravi Omar	58	67	42	61	65		
8	Melissa Cardinal	79	56	67	84	56		
9	Donny Seepersad	87	43	64	83	76		
10	Gary Fredricks	65	67	38	76	62		
11	Shimona Vaughn	61	65	56	65	45		
12								
13	Subject	Highest mark	Lowest mark					
14	Maths							
15	Biology							
16	Chemistry							
17	Physics							
18	English							
19								
20	Class Average							
21								

Using the **Blank Database** area, select a location to store the database, give your database a filename and click on **Create**. A window having the name of the database is displayed along with the database objects, as shown in Figure 6.3.

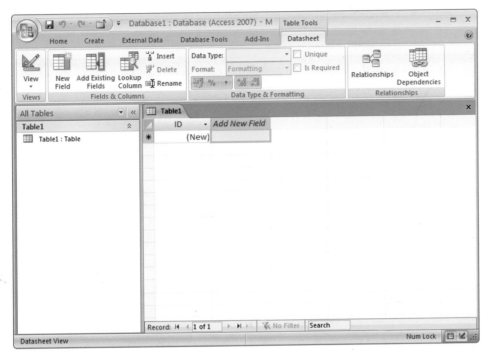

◄ **Figure 6.3**
The Database window showing a named database with objects

The database objects available are listed at the left-hand side of the Database window. Those used in this chapter are listed below with their meanings.

Object	Description
Table	A collection of related data about a subject (person, place or thing). One or more tables make up a database **file**. A **flat file database** will have only one table in the database file, whereas a **relational database** will have more than one table in the database file.
Query	You would use a query to **search** a database.
Report	A customised printout of the information in a table or from a query.
Macro	A series of instructions that can be saved and used over and over again.

Designing a database

Designing a database is the first and most important step towards providing easy and fast access to information. If you plan your database carefully you will save time and inconvenience when you are creating queries and reports. The steps involved in designing a database are as follows:

- **Determine the purposes of the database.** By determining your purposes, you will be able to define what data should be stored on your database. For example, one purpose might be to keep track of the stock in a supermarket.

Here are some example purposes:
- I need to know which items are selling well.
- I want a list of the best-selling items and their selling prices.
- I need to know who supplies a particular item and at what cost.

- **Analyse each purpose.** Break down what you need to know into a series of well-defined needs and wants.
- **Determine the data you need.** Write down all the data items that you will need in order to meet these purposes.
- **Design your tables.** Separate the data items into groups, depending on how each is related to the others. This will allow you to decide what data will be in each table.
- **State the field names and define each field.** Give each data item a unique field name and describe its properties. For example, a person's first name could be given the field name 'firstname'; its data type would be alphabetic; and it would probably be sufficient to give it a length of 10 characters.
- **Determine how the tables will be related.** Two tables are related if the records in both share some common fields. Creating relationships between tables allows the tables to be linked so that information can be cross-referenced. You may need to add further fields to tables to create the necessary relationships.

Tables

A **table** is an organised collection of related records about a specific subject (for example, customers). A table is divided into rows and columns. Each row holds a record and each column represents a unique field.

A **record** is a group of related fields (for example, about one customer).

A **field** is a data item within a record (for example, the customer's name).

Figure 6.4 shows part of a table about students. All the information about one student is contained in a single row or record. The first row of the table consists of the field names.

▼ **Figure 6.4**
Part of a table about students

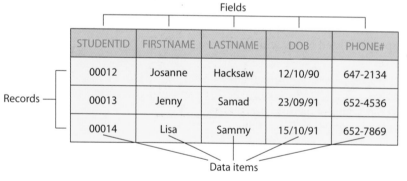

Creating tables

In Access, you can create a table using any one of the following methods:

- **Design View** — This method enables you to create a table by naming the fields and selecting their data types and properties. You can precisely determine all the characteristics of the table.
- **Table Wizard** — This is the easiest and fastest method of creating a table. The table wizard guides you through a process that is very easy to follow, although the resulting table may not meet your exact requirements.
- **Datasheet View** — You enter data into the datasheet grid, which consists of rows and columns labelled *Field 1, Field 2, Field 3* and so on. The database software determines the data type based on the data you enter.

This chapter describes how to create a table in Design View, because this will show you more about how data is organised in a database.

Creating a table in Design View

Click on the **Create** tab then on **Table Design**. The **Table Design View** window appears, as shown in Figure 6.5.

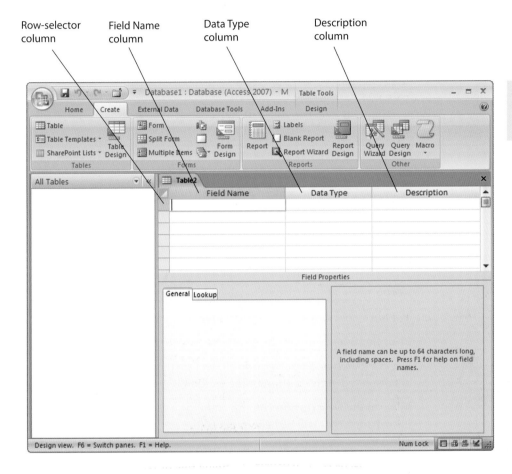

Row-selector column

Field Name column

Data Type column

Description column

Defining and adding fields

The **Table Design View** window (Figure 6.5) shows four columns:

- The **row selector** enables you to select the field in which you wish to enter, change or delete information, by using the mouse or the up and down arrow keys. The selected row has an arrow in the row selector column.

- The **Field Name** column is where you type in a field name.

- The **Data Type** column enables you to select an appropriate data type from a drop-down list. Various data types and their descriptions are listed in the table below. Some of these data types are used in Access but others are included which are used elsewhere. In Access, when you have selected a data type, the **Field Properties** pane appears at the bottom of the window. Access provides default field properties that are suitable for many applications, but you can change these.

- The **Description** column is for your use in typing out a short description of the field as a form of documentation.

Data type	Description
Number	Contains a number. Use this type for data to be used in calculations, except calculations involving money.
Real number	Stores any number expressed as a decimal number, e.g. *54.371*.
Integer	Stores a whole number, which can be positive, negative or zero, e.g. *+5*.
Text or Alphanumeric	Can store any alphanumeric character (alphabetic or numeric) and special characters, such as punctuation marks, e.g. '*27 Parkland Avenue, Bolton BL7 4RT*'.
Memo	Used to hold notes about a record.
Date/Time	Stores the date and time in one of several different formats.
Currency	Holds a monetary value and is used in calculations involving money.
Logical or Boolean	Holds one of two values, e.g. 1 or 0; yes or no; true or false.
OLE Object	Contains an object created by another application. If the object is edited or updated in the other application, the change will also be made in the database.
AutoNumber	Used to generate unique numbers in a specific field each time a record is added.
Hyperlink	Stores a web address (a URL).

Adding fields to a table in Design View

The process for adding fields to a table in Design View is as follows:

1. Type in a field name in the **Field Name** column.

2. Press the **Tab** key or use the mouse to move to the **Data Type** column.

3. Select a data type from the drop-down list (the default field properties are displayed at the bottom of the window).

4. Move to the **Description** column and type a short description of the information that will be held in the field.

5. Once you have done this for all the fields, click on the **Office** button.

6. Select **Save** or **Save As** to save the table within the current database. (The **Save As Table** dialog box appears, as shown in Figure 6.6.)

7. Type in a name for the table and click **OK**.

Figure 6.6 ▶
The Save As Table dialog box

Adding a field between two rows

Open the table in Design View. Place the record selector in the row below where you want the new field to be inserted. Right-click and select **Insert Rows**. A blank row appears. Type in the new field name, data type and description.

132

Deleting a field

Open the table in Design View and select the row to be deleted. Right-click and select **Delete**.

Primary keys

A **primary key** (often referred to as a **key field**) is a field such that the contents of the field uniquely identify each record. When a primary key is set, an index is created for the field. Using a primary key field has the following benefits:

- It can speed up data retrieval and the running of queries.

- It enables you to establish relationships between tables.

To define a primary key in Access, display the table in Design View, then select the field, right-click in the row containing it and select **Primary Key**.

If you do not select a primary key while building the structure of a table, the message box shown in Figure 6.7 will appear when you try to close the table. If you click on **Yes**, Access adds an **AutoNumber** field to the table and defines it as the primary key. If you click on **No**, the table is saved without a primary key being defined.

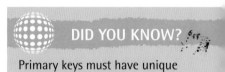

DID YOU KNOW?

Primary keys must have unique values. This is why **AutoNumber** is a good choice of data type.

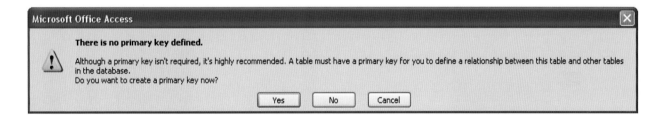

▲ **Figure 6.7**
'There is no primary key defined' message

Deselecting a primary key

In Access, display the table in Design View and select the **Primary Key** field. On the **Table Tools | Design** tab, the primary key should show as being selected. Select the **Primary Key** option to deselect the primary key.

Foreign keys

A record can have only one primary key, but there is no restriction on the number of foreign keys it can have. A **foreign key** is a primary key from another table. It shows the relationship between the current table and the other table.

For example, an autoparts database, where each record stores details about a part used in manufacturing a car, might have a foreign key which identifies the warehouse where the part is kept. If the part is available from several different warehouses, there could be several different foreign key fields in the record.

1. Explain what is meant by a database.

2. Explain what is meant by the following, giving examples of each.
   a) Table
   b) File
   c) Record
   d) Field
   e) Key Field

3. Explain why every record should have a primary key.

4. The manager of Betterprices Hardware wants to move away from the manual method of stock keeping to a computerised method. He decides to place the information about his stock into a database. Complete the following tasks:
   a) Create a database called **Betterprices Hardware Stock List**.
   b) Create a table called **Stock** within the database, with the structure shown below.

Field Name	Data Type	Description
Itemno	Text	The number used to identify each item
Itemdesc	Text	Name of each item
Quantity	Number	Amount in stock
Sectstored	Text	The hardware section in which the item is stored
Price	Currency	The selling price of the item

   c) Define **Itemno** as the primary key field.

Help with this question

To create a table called **Stock**:

- Create a new database named **Betterprices Hardware Stock List**.
- A default table is created. Click on **View**, **Design View** and save the table as **Stock** when prompted. The **Table Design View** window appears, as shown in Figure 6.5.
- Place the cursor in the **Field Name** column in the first row.
- Type **Itemno** into the column.
- Move to the **Data Type** column. The default data type, **Text**, will be displayed.
- Move to the **Description** column. Type *The number used to identify each product*.
- Move to the second row and enter the field name, data type and description for the second field.
- Do likewise for all the remaining fields.

To define **Itemno** as the primary key field (if this doesn't happen automatically):

- Click anywhere in the **Itemno** row.
- Right-click and select **Primary Key**.

To save the table structure:

- Pull down the **Office Button** menu.
- Select **Save**.
- Type the table name, **Stock**, into the **Save As** dialog box.

The complete structure for the **Stock** table is displayed in Figure 6.8.

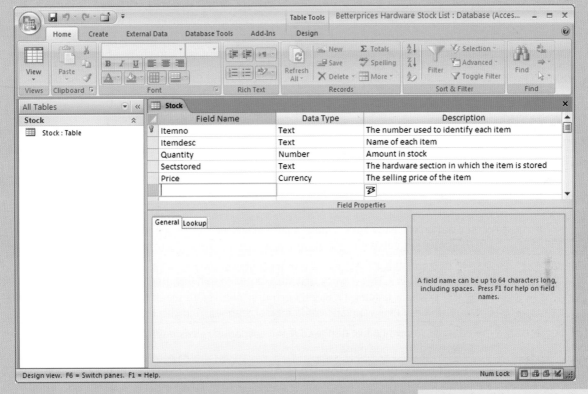

5. Create a database named **Employees**. Create a table in the database with the following structure (include field names, data types and descriptions). Make **EmpID** the primary key and give the table the filename **Salary**.

▲ Figure 6.8
Structure of the Stock table

Field name	Data type	Description
EmpID	Number	Number assigned to each employee when hired
Surname	Text	
Firstname	Text	
Age	Number	Age of employee
Phone	Text	Employee home phone number or contact number
Department	Text	Department in which employee is currently working
Salary	Currency	Gross salary

 SOFTWARE NOTE

If the database package you are using is **not** Microsoft Access, investigate and write down how you would perform the following operations.
a) Creating a database
b) Creating a table
c) Defining, adding, editing and deleting fields
d) Creating a primary key field

Field properties

A field's properties determine how it is stored, what can be done with it and how it is displayed. Default field properties will be assigned to each field, depending on the data type. The default field properties are appropriate for many databases but you can change them if you wish.

Validation checks help ensure that the data stored in each field is reasonable and accurate. Some of the different field properties that can be used to validate data in Access are listed below.

Field property	Description of field property and validation check
Field size	The field size specifies the maximum number of characters that can be stored in a field, so that a **field length** check can be carried out. For instance, the field size for a student's first name could be 10. If a name longer than 10 characters were to be entered, the computer would reject it.
Input mask	Enables you to define a character string to act as a template so that a **format** check can be carried out on the data. For example, a date may have to be entered in dd/mm/yyyy form for the UK. Dates not entered in this form would be rejected.
Validation rule	Despite its name, this field property is a generally considered to be a type of validation check called a **range** check. This ensures that the values entered into the field are within a specific range. For example, a domestic gas bill might be checked to see if it lies between $0 and $500. Bills outside this range would be considered exceptional and checked for errors.
Validation text	The message you would like displayed if the validation rule is not satisfied. In our example, the message could be 'Value must not exceed $500'.
Required	This is a **presence** check. If a record is selected but no value is inserted in this field, the record will be rejected and an error message displayed, such as 'Employee name is required for an Employee table'.
Default value	A value that is automatically entered in a field in each record of the table.
Allow zero length	Allows a text or memo field to be filled with blanks or with a string of zero length.
Indexed	Builds an index on a field. Tables are searched or sorted faster when a field is indexed. A primary key field is always indexed.
Format	Determines the way a field is displayed or printed. For instance, a date could be displayed as short (15/01/10) or medium (15 Jan 2010).
Caption	A label other than the field name that you can use for forms and reports.

Field sizes

If you select **Number** as the data type in Access, you can choose different field sizes. Some of these are listed below.

Numeric field size	Description
Byte	A number in the range 0 to 255
Decimal	A decimal number with up to 28 digits of accuracy
Double	A double-precision floating-point value with about 15 digits of accuracy
Integer	A number in the range -32 768 to 32 767
Long Integer	A number in the range -2 147 483 648 to 2 147 483 647
Single	A single-precision floating-point value with about seven digits of accuracy

Exercise 6.2

1. In the Betterprices Hardware Stock List database (created in Exercise 6.1) open the table named **Stock** and perform the following tasks:

   a) Change the field sizes of the following fields to their new field size:

Field name	New field size
Itemno	6
Itemdesc	30

   b) Delete the **Sectstored** field.

   c) Insert the following new field:

Field name:	SupplierID
Data type:	Text
Description:	The number used to identify each supplier
Field size:	5

   d) The **Quantity** field must not hold a value greater than 1000. Include a validation rule that would ensure the condition is met, and validation text to display an appropriate message if the entered value falls outside the limit.

   e) Save the table.

Help with Question 1

To change the field sizes for **Itemno** and **Itemdesc**:

- Display the **Stock** table in Design View.
- Click anywhere in the **Itemno** row (the **Field Properties** pane will be displayed).
- Click on the **Field Size** box; delete **50** and type in **6**.
- Do similarly for the **Itemdesc** field.

To delete the **Sectstored** field

- Click the row selector column for the **Sectstored** field (the row becomes highlighted).
- Right-click and select **Delete Rows**.

To insert the **SupplierID** field:

- Click in the next empty row in the **Betterprices Hardware Stock List** table in Design View.
- Type **SupplierID** in the **Field Name** column (*Text* will be displayed in the **Data Type** column).
- Move to the **Description** column and type *The number used to identify each supplier*.

To add a validation rule and validation text for the **Quantity** field:

- Click on the **Quantity** field row.
- Move to the **Field Properties** pane and click on the **Validation Rule** box.
- Type in **= 1000 or <1000**.
- Click on the **Validation Text** box and type *Quantity is greater than 1000. Please re-enter.*

Figure 6.9 shows the new field properties for the **Quantity** field.

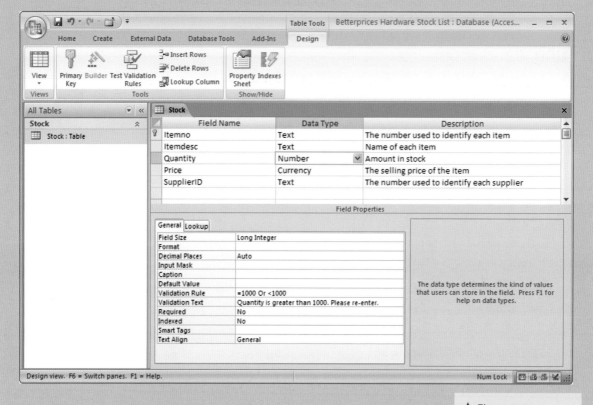

▲ **Figure 6.9**
Field properties for the Quantity field

2. Using the **Salary** table from the **Employees** database created in Exercise 6.1:
   a) Change the field sizes of the **Surname** and **Firstname** fields to 25.
   b) Include the following validation rule and validation text for the Salary field:
      • Validation rule: "<10000"
      • Validation text: "Salary cannot be more than $10 000"
   c) Explain why it is better to store the date of birth of an employee than their age.
   d) Delete the **Age** field, and insert the **DOB** (Date of Birth) field between the **Firstname** and **Phone** fields.

Entering records into a table

Save the table, and you can then insert data into each field of each record. To do this from the database window shown in Figure 6.3, select the **Tables** tab to list all the tables in the database and double-click on the table you wish to use.

You can now enter the data for each record on one row making sure that the appropriate values are entered in each column. Continue until you have entered data for all the records.

Deleting a record

Open the table in Datasheet View. Select the record to be deleted, right-click and select **Delete Record**.

2. Using the **Salary** table created within the **Employees** database in Exercises 6.1 and 6.2:

a) Make any changes needed to the fields.

b) Change the validation rule to allow a salary of $12,000.

c) Enter the records shown below:

EMPID	SURNAME	FIRST NAME	DOB	PHONE	JOB	SALARY ($)
10	Viera	Edison	19/03/79	648-5432	Manager	12,000.00
25	Moore	Ian	04/11/78	677-5865	Janitor	2,500.00
46	St. Louis	Allan	17/07/80	634-7806	Engineer	8,000.00
56	Moore	Sean	15/10/62	648-2343	Accountant	8,000.00
63	Neptune	Kent	23/09/68	658-4533	Programmer	6,000.00
75	Achong	Lisa	26/06/80	656-7687	Secretary	4,000.00
81	Sakawat	Amit	14/03/75	678-9651	Systems Analyst	9,000.00
125	Baptiste	Lisa	11/08/76	634-5478	Clerk	3,500.00
131	Griffith	Viola	25/10/73	697-2532	Engineer	9,500.00
143	Alexander	Anthony	02/03/83	622-5667	Janitor	3,000.00
187	Rattiram	Nalini	21/04/72	687-3213	Secretary	3,800.00
245	Moore	Gillian	15/10/65	615-1234	Clerk	4,000.00

d) Delete the record for employee 75.

e) Change the name of employee 187 from **Nalini Rattiram** to **Nalini Ramrattan**.

f) Sort the table on surname and then on first name, in ascending order.

g) Index the table on job.

Queries

Queries are used to **search** a database and extract information. A **query** enables you to find and view data stored in one or more tables. You can also do calculations and other operations on the data and view the results. Queries can be saved and used again.

After you run a query, the answer is displayed in a **dynaset** − a group of records that answers a query. It looks and behaves like a table but is really a dynamic subset of data from one or more tables that has been selected and sorted as specified in the query. Information in a dynaset can be modified like information in a table, and the changes are automatically reflected in the relevant tables.

Types of query

There are several types of query but we will consider only the following:

- **Select query**: This is the most common type. It is used to search tables to retrieve data that satisfies the query, and to display the data as a dynaset.

- **Update query**: This is a type of action query. It makes specified changes to a group of records, or to all records, in one or more tables.

- **Append query**: This adds a group of records from one or more tables to the end of one or more other tables.

- **Delete query**: This deletes a group of records from one or more tables.

Creating a new query from scratch

Open the database and the **Database** window appears (see Figure 6.3).

On the **Create** tab click on the **Query Design** button.

The **Show Table** dialog box shown in Figure 6.15 appears with the **Select Query** design grid behind it. The **Show Table** dialog box enables you to select (add) the tables that contain the data you wish to be included in the new query.

Click the **Tables** tab and select the required tables from the list (see Figure 6.15). Click **Add** to add them to the upper part of the query design window (see Figure 6.16), and then click **Close**.

▲ **Figure 6.15**
The Show Table dialog box

Removing a table from a query

Select the table in the **Select Query** design window and right click the mouse. Select **Remove Table**.

Creating joins or relationships with tables

A query can operate on a single table but if you want to extract data from more than one table, you have to create a join or relationship between the tables.

The relationship between tables can be of these types:

- A **one-to-one** relationship exists when each record in a table corresponds to exactly one record in the other table.

- A **one-to-many** relationship exists when each record in one table corresponds to many records in the other table.

- A **many-to-many** relationship exists when multiple records in one table correspond to multiple records in the other table.

You can create a join or relationship as follows (you will try this in Exercise 6.4):

1. Open the database. The **Database** window appears (see Figure 6.3).

2. In the **Database** tab, select **Relationships** (the **Relationships** and **Show Table** dialog boxes appear). If the **Show Table** dialog box does not appear, in the **Relationships Tools | Design** tab select **Show Table**.

3. In the **Show Table** dialog box, select the tables between which you want to create joins or relationships, then click **Close**.

4. In the **Relationships** dialog box, click the field name you would like to join in one table and drag this onto the field name in the other table. The **Edit Relationships** dialog box appears, showing the names of the two tables and the fields you would like to join.

5. Click on **OK**. A line connecting the two fields is displayed in the **Relationships** dialog box, as shown in the upper part of Figure 6.16.

6. Save the relationships.

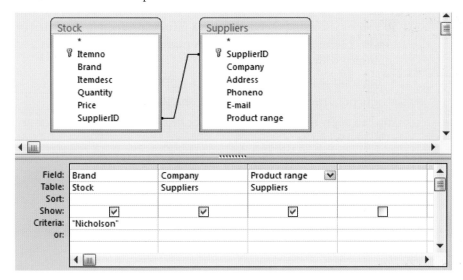

◀ **Figure 6.16**
A Select Query design window, showing a relationship between tables

When you have created relationships between the tables, you can proceed to create queries.

Working with a Select query

Figure 6.16 shows a **Select Query** design window. The top part of the pane holds the tables and shows the relationship between them. The bottom part of the pane is the **query by example grid** or **design grid**, consisting of rows and columns. The row labels and a description of what they are used for is shown below:

Row label	Explanation
Field	Select the field to be searched.
Table	Select the table that the selected field is taken from.
Sort	Select any fields you would like sorted in ascending or descending order in the query.
Show	Specify whether you want the field to be displayed.
Criteria	Specify the criteria used to select a record during the search.
Or	Specify any additional criteria.

Setting up a Select query

In a Select query, you define what data values you want to find in what fields, and what fields you want to display. You can use a Select query to view specific data, reorganise data and calculate data.

1. Click in the leftmost column, which is blank. Click on the row labelled **Table** and select the table from which the field is to be chosen.

2. Click in the same column on the row labelled **Field** and select a field.

3. Click in the same column on the row labelled **Sort** and select **Ascending** or **Descending**.

4. The **Show** row contains a check box in each column. If you would like the value in a field to be displayed, tick the box. You do not have to show all the fields used to select the data, and the fields shown do not have to be part of the selection criteria.

5. To specify selection criteria, enter a value or expression in the **Criteria** row. A criterion can contain values or expressions, which can be combined with the following:

   - the relational operators $>$, $<$, $>=$, $<=$, $=$ and $<>$
   - functions such as **ADD, OR**, **NOT** and **BETWEEN**.

   You can apply these to date or number fields to return records within a designated range.

6. Repeat steps 1 to 5 for each field involved in the selection.

7. Select **Save** to save the query.

Running a query

To carry out or run a query, click the **Run** button.

! The Run button

Using logical AND and OR and NOT in a query

Logical AND and OR are used to connect the criteria used in setting up a query.

AND tests two or more criteria, and if they are **all** individually true, then AND is true.

OR tests two or more criteria, and if **at least one of them** is individually true, then the OR is true.

In Access, when setting up a query in the **Select Query** design window (see Figure 6.16):

- if the criteria are on the same row then **AND** is implied
- if the criteria are in the same column then **OR** is implied.

NOT is true if the criteria is not true.

AND example

Looking at the **Salary** table in Exercise 6.2, suppose we wanted to find out which employees were engineers and earned more than $8,500.00 salary. We would need an **AND** condition which can be paraphrased as follows:

JOB is Engineer AND SALARY is more than $8,500.00.

To set up this condition in Access, in the **Select Query** design window, for the fields **JOB** and **SALARY**, the criteria $=$*"Engineer" and >8,500.00* would be set up **on the same row**.

OR example

Looking at the **Salary** table in Exercise 6.2, suppose we wanted to find out which employees were engineers or programmers. We would need an **OR** condition which can be paraphrased as follows:

JOB is Engineer OR JOB is Programmer.

To set up this condition in Access, in the **Select Query** design window, for the field **JOB** the criterion =*"Engineer"* is set up, and **in the same column** on the row underneath, the criterion =*"Programmer"* would be set up.

NOT example

Looking at the **Salary** table in Exercise 6.2, suppose we wanted to find out which employees were not engineers. We would need a **NOT** condition which can be paraphrased as follows:

JOB is NOT Engineer.

To set up this condition in Access, in the **Select Query** design window, for the field **JOB** the criteria =*not "Engineer"* is set up.

Working with an Update query (extension material)

An update query makes changes to a group of records, or to all of the records, in one or more tables.

Creating an update query

1. Create a new query as you did for a Select query, just completing the **Field**, **Table**, and **Criteria** rows as appropriate.

2. In the **Query Tools | Design** tab, click on **Update**.

Notice that the **Sort** and **Show** rows have been replaced by an **Update To** row. This is where you will be able to enter a formula, value or expression to make changes to records in the tables.

Building a formula and running an update query

1. Click on the **Update To** cell where the formula will be placed.

2. Right-click the mouse and select **Build**. The **Expression Builder** dialog box appears, as shown in Figure 6.17. The top pane of the window is a clear area used to display the formula. Buttons for the relational and arithmetic operators are displayed under the typing area. The bottom pane is divided into three columns. The first column is a list that includes folders called **Tables**, **Queries**, **Forms**, **Reports** and **Functions**.

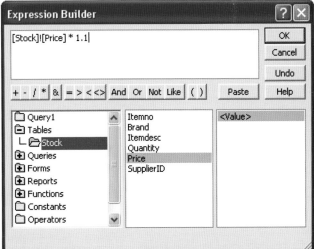

3. Double-click on the **Tables** folder (a list of all the tables in the database is displayed).

4. To select fields from a particular table, click once on its name (its fields are displayed in the second column).

▲ **Figure 6.17**
The Expression Builder dialog box

5. Double-click on a field that will be part of your formula (the field together with the table it comes from is displayed in the top pane).

6. Click on any of the operators (for example, ***** or +) to begin to build a formula, which is displayed in the top pane.

7. Click on other fields and operators, or type values directly into the top pane, to complete the formula.

8. Click on **OK** (the formula will be displayed in the **Update To** cell of your query grid).

9. Click on the **Run** button (a message box appears to ask you to confirm that you want to update the database).

10. Click **Yes** to make the changes to the database.

Working with a Delete query (extension material)

A Delete query deletes a group of records from one or more tables.

1. Create a new query as you did for a Select query.

2. In the **Query Tools | Design** tab, select **Delete**.

3. The bottom pane of the query design window changes and should now include rows for **Field**, **Table**, **Delete** and **Criteria**. Complete these rows.

4. Click in each **Delete** cell that has criteria below it, and select **Where** from the drop-down list.

5. Run the delete query.

Creating a calculated field

A **calculated field** contains an expression that calculates a value by referencing one or more fields from one or more tables. The value derived is placed in a new field, which is displayed in the query. Calculations can only be performed on numeric, date and text fields.

1. Display the query in Design View.

2. Select an empty field in the design grid.

3. Type in the new field name, followed by a colon (:), followed by the field names that form part of the expression, each in square brackets and with the relevant operator in between each pair. For example:

> *Totalrentalcost: [Daysrented] * [Dailycost].*

Including totals in a query

You can adapt your query to produce a list of statistical information from the numeric fields you retrieve. Some of the functions that you can use are shown below:

Function	Description
Sum	Calculates the total of all the values in a field
Avg	Calculates the average of all the values in a field
Min	Returns the lowest value in a field
Max	Returns the highest value in a field
Count	Returns the number of values in a field, ignoring null values
StDev	Calculates the standard deviation of all the values in a field
Var	Calculates the variance of all the values in a field
First	Returns the first value in a field
Last	Returns the last value in a field

1. With the query design grid displayed, in the **Query Tools | Design** tab, select **Totals** (a *Total* row is added to the query design grid).

2. To find the total for a particular field across all the records:
   a) Click on the arrow in the **Total** cell of the appropriate field (a drop-down menu appears, listing the functions shown above).
   b) Select **Sum**.
   c) Run the query.

Displaying the highest values

Access enables you to sort the data in a table and select as many of the top values as you want displayed. For example, a teacher may want a listing of the names and percentages of the top ten students in a class, or a bookstore owner may want to know which book has sold the most copies for a particular month.

1. With the query design grid displayed, select the fields you want displayed.

2. Click in the **Sort** row under the name of the field from which you would like to select the data.

3. Click on the arrow in the cell and select **Descending**.

4. Click on the arrow in the **All** box in the Ribbon.

| All | ▼ | The All box |

5. Select from the options provided or type a value into the box.

6. Run the query.

Exercise 6.4

1. Within the database called the Betterprices Hardware Stock List create a table called **Orders** with the structure shown below:

Field name	Data type	Description	Field size	Format
Date	Date/Time	Date order was placed		Short Date
Orderno	Text	Order number	5	
Itemno	Text	Item number of product	6	
Quantity	Number	Quantity ordered		
SupplierID	Text	Supplier identification number	5	

2. Enter these records into the **Orders** table (note that the dates are listed here in mm/dd/yy format so you may have to swap the months and days).

Date	Orderno	Itemno	Quantity	SupplierID
06/04/00	A0100	H0005	8	SP010
06/06/00	D0800	TR0090	10	SP010
05/12/00	B0079	FK0035	45	SP015
06/08/00	E0450	H0006	5	SP015
05/07/00	B0067	H0007	25	SP020
05/10/00	D0432	SH0011	15	SP020
06/12/00	E0500	SP0015	15	SP020
06/15/00	F0120	SP0040	20	SP020
05/04/00	A0051	FK0025	20	SP030
05/06/00	A0051	SH0010	12	SP030
05/15/00	C0056	SH0110	14	SP050
05/20/00	D0567	TR0078	10	SP060
05/25/00	B0089	PD2000	5	SP075

3. Create another table called **Suppliers** within the **Betterprices Hardware Stock List** database with the structure shown below:

Field name	Data type	Description	Field size
SupplierID	Text	Supplier identification number	5
Company	Text	Name of company	30
Address	Text	Address of supplier	50
Phoneno	Text	Phone number of supplier	8
E-mail	Text	Supplier's e-mail address	20
Product Range	Memo	Name of products sold by supplier	

4. Enter these records into the **Suppliers** table.

SupplierID	Company	Address	Phoneno	Email	ProductRange
SP010	S and S Distributors	18 West Cost Drive, Arima	632-6778	sdist@hotmail.com	Superior Brand Tools: Hammers, Shovels, Spades, Forks, Trowels, Hatchets, Spirit levels
SP015	Tools Specialist	25 Royal Road, Pt. Lisas	654-4435	tools@tstools.net.tt	Nicholson Tools: Files, Hammers, Shovels, Forks, Spades, Pigfoot, Hacksaw blades, Saws
SP020	Star Wholesalers	12 Hammond Drive, Pt. Fortin	648-2356	star@hotmail.com	Star Tools and merchandise
SP030	BD Suppliers	3 Main Road, Cova	636-7894	bdog@hotmail.com	Bulldog Tools

6. Add 10 records of your own to each table.

7. Change the DOB of Fyzool Ali from 5/10/91 to 15/10/91.

8. List the name and date of birth of each female student in the class.

9. List the name and date of birth of each student born before 1991.

10. Sort the **Students** table by surname and then by first name.

11. List the students who scored more than 70 in their Maths test.

12. List the students, their marks in each subject and their total mark.

13. List the students and their total mark, and their father's name and occupation. Display the list in alphabetic order on the surname.

Representing data graphically

It is sometimes easier to see patterns in data if we show it in a graph. For example, consider the **Parents** table from Exercise 6.5, Question 2. The school may wish to analyse the occupations of students' fathers. A convenient way to do this might be to produce a report showing all the records with a column chart summarising the fathers' occupations (see Figure 6.34).

The column chart in Figure 6.34 was generated in Microsoft Access in a report but you can also do this in a form. There are a variety of chart types to choose from and data from different tables can be included.

In Access, to generate a column chart in a report:

- Select **Create** in the Ribbon.

- Click on **Report Wizard**, and use the wizard to create a report which has in it the field **Fatheroccup**.

- View the report in Design View.

- Click the **Insert Chart** button on the **Report Design Tools | Design** tab. The mouse pointer changes shape.

- Drag the mouse pointer to position the chart. For example, you could put this in the **Detail** section or the **Page Footer**. The **Chart Wizard** dialog box will open.

- Select the table to be used to create the chart (i.e. **Parents**) and click **Next**.

- The field containing the data to be used in the chart is **Fatheroccup**. Transfer this to the right-hand column and click **Next**.

- Select the chart type you want and click **Next**.

- Preview the chart and, if it is what you want, click **Next**.

- You do not want the chart to change from record to record because you want to summarise data from all the records. Make sure no fields are showing, and click **Next**.

- Ensure the title of the chart is *Fathers' Occupations* and click **Finish**.

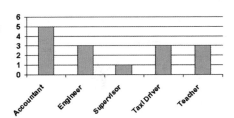

Fathers' Occupations

▲ Figure 6.34
Column chart summarising the occupations of students' fathers

- View the report using **Print Preview** and print this. You may need to adjust the layout and the size of the chart. To do this you may have to toggle between Print Preview and Design View.

Loading data from an existing file

Data in an existing file can be loaded into a table in a database. Imported files often have these file types: **.csv** (comma-separated variables), **.txt** (text) and **.rtf** (rich text format).

For example, consider the file **events.txt** with data in this format in it:

> "105","Judo","Experienced","Fitness","Gymnasium","Saturday",10.00
>
> "109","Tennis","Novice","Racquets","Tennis Courts","Sunday",13.30

In Access, to create a table with this data in it:

- Click the Office Button and select **Open**.
- In the **Open** dialog box, browse to the file **events.txt** and open it.
- The **Link Text Wizard** dialog box appears.
- Choose the delimiter used. The delimiter separates one item of data from the next. In **events.txt**, this is a comma. Click on the **Next** button.
- Name each field. Click on **Next**.
- Click on the **Finish** button.
- The data in the file **events.txt** is imported into a table.

Macros

A macro is a set of actions that you can create to help you to automate common tasks.

Creating a macro

When creating a macro in Access, you cannot simply turn on the macro recorder as you can in Word and Excel, then perform the actions you want in the macro and turn off the macro recorder. You have to select the actions you want the macro to perform.

You are going to set up a simple macro that will open all the tables in your database and beep when this has been done. Suppose you are working on a library database with three tables: **books**, **loans** and **members**. Each time you start work you want to open these three tables. As the tables get bigger, this can take some time so you want the computer to beep to let you know when all three tables are open.

1. In the **Create** tab, select **Macro**. A new macro is created and displayed (see Figure 6.35).

2. Click in the **Action** column in the top blank cell; the down arrow appears. Click on this to reveal an extensive list of possible actions. Select **OpenTable**.

3. In the **Action Arguments** section at the bottom of the dialog box, click in the **Table Name** and click on the down arrow to choose a table.

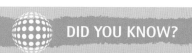

- **Coaxial cable**. Coaxial cable is more expensive than twisted pair and is used to transmit voice, video and data. It is ideal for a medium-sized network. Coaxial cable has an inner core and an outer sheath of copper wire that are insulated from each other.

- **Fibre optic**. Fibre optic cables enable large volumes of digital data to be transmitted extremely fast and virtually error free. A single strand of a fibre optic cable is a hair-thin piece of flexible glass tubing. The inside acts as a mirror, allowing a light beam to travel along it. A cable consists of thousands of these hair-thin strands.

Connection to a cabled LAN

A computer must be connected to a cabled LAN using a **network interface card** (**NIC**). The network cable is plugged into the NIC.

LAN topologies

The **topology** of a LAN describes the structure of the connections between the computers attached to it. The most common topologies for a LAN are line or bus, and star.

Line or bus topology

This is a single line or cable with nodes at different points. Servers, computers and other devices can be connected to any of the nodes on the line, as shown in Figure 7.1.

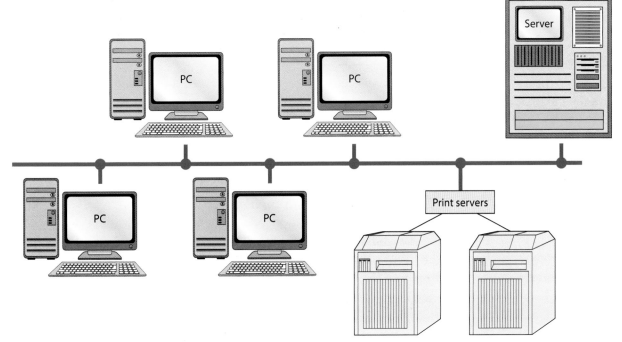

Advantages of a line or bus topology

- Extending the network is very easy. New equipment can be connected to it simply by attaching it to the end of the network or by adding a short spur.

- Only a single network cable needs to be installed.

▲ **Figure 7.1:**
A line or bus network

Disadvantages of a line or bus topology

- Any problems with the main cable may cause the whole network to malfunction.
- Data travels in both directions along the network cable. Packets of data may collide, which may slow down transmission speed and data may be lost.

Star topology

All the computers on the network are connected to one another through a central server incorporating a hub (see below) as shown in Figure 7.2.

Figure 7.2 ▶
A star network

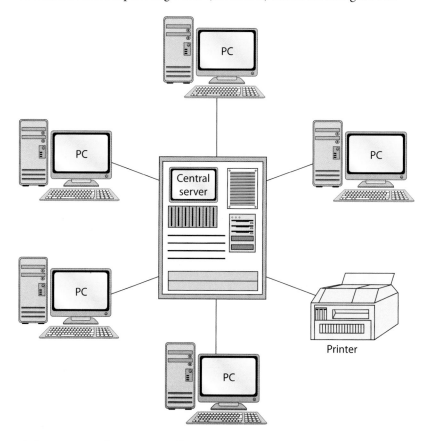

Advantages of a star topology

- Extending the network is very straightforward. New equipment can be connected to the network simply by connecting it to the server.
- If one computer stops working, the network is not affected.
- If a cable stops working, only one computer is affected.

Disadvantages of a star topology

- It requires more cabling because each computer has its own cable to the hub.
- It may be more difficult to connect a new computer to the network because a separate cable is needed from the computer to the server and this may be difficult to install because of the physical layout of the building.
- A star network topology requires more cable than a line network.

Wireless LAN (WLAN)

Wireless LANs have been around for a while but their high installation costs and slow speeds were prohibiting factors. Today, with the reduction in cost of many wireless devices and an increase in speed, more businesses and homeowners are opting for a WLAN.

A WLAN differs from a cabled LAN in that computers can use a wireless link to connect to the network instead of being attached using a cable. The wireless connection is made possible by three sets of components: **wireless access points**; wireless **network interface cards (NICs)** and **routers**.

A wireless access point is a device attached to a LAN. It contains a radio receiver, encryption and communications software so that it can broadcast and receive wireless communications. It translates computer signals into wireless signals (and back), so that it can broadcast to and receive signals from wireless NICs on the network. NICs equipped for wireless communications have a fixed or detachable radio antenna instead of the usual coaxial cable. Routers enable several computers to communicate through a wireless access point at the same time.

A WLAN can be used where it may be difficult or impractical to use a cabled LAN (for example, in homes, large offices, warehouses and lecture halls). A device can be as far as 100 metres from an access point and it may still be able to access the Internet. In a building with many rooms or large halls, several access points may be needed. A user may take a laptop and walk from one room to the next or from one end of a building to the other and still have access. This is because the laptop will lock on to the strongest signal from an access point and will transfer its link to another access point if the signal there is stronger.

A WLAN has the same features that are available in a wired LAN. In addition, access to it can be more flexible. Users can be in any location in a building or outside, and still have access to Internet services. Wireless access points are now installed in public places, so that, for example, someone waiting for a train can connect to the Internet using a laptop. However, WLANs have relatively slow transmission speed, and other users or devices could interfere with the operation of the network. Illegal access is also a major concern, since anyone with a compatible NIC can access the network.

WiFi (Wireless Fidelity)

The wireless access point and the NIC communicate with each other using WiFi. WiFi uses the 802.11 standard for wireless access. More recent wireless access products use the 54 Mbps 802.11g standard. Current products are based on the 802.11n standard, which has a faster data transfer rate of 74 Mbps and has an indoor range of 70 metres.

Bluetooth

Bluetooth is a form of wireless communication designed to enable PDAs, mobile phones, computers and similar devices to share information and to synchronise data. Bluetooth requires a transceiver chip in each device. The data transfer rate is 720 Kbps with a 10 metre range.

DID YOU KNOW?

Mbps is short for *megabits per second*. A megabit is just over a million bits.

Bluetooth has a much slower data transfer rate than WiFi and a much shorter range, and is designed for communication between devices that are next to each other. For example, a mobile phone could communicate with a separate GPS antenna using Bluetooth, enabling it to run satellite navigation software for guiding cars and other vehicles to their destination.

Wide area networks (WANs)

A WAN can connect networks across a large geographical area, such as a city or a country or even internationally. Information can be transmitted in many ways; for example, using high-speed telephone lines, fibre optic cables, microwave links and satellite links, or a combination of these. WANs are used mainly by universities, large companies and banks with branches in different countries, to share information and processing loads. Figure 7.3 shows LANs in different countries connected together to form a WAN, using telecommunications links.

Figure 7.3 ▶
A wide area network (WAN)

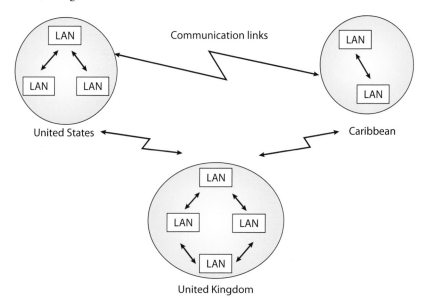

Data transmission

Data communication can be broadly described as the transmission of data from one location to another for direct use or for further processing. A data communication system is made up of hardware, software and communications facilities. It may consist of computer terminals and other input/output devices linked together locally or it can consist of computers linked on a global scale. No matter what type of data communication system it is, data transmission channels are needed to carry the data from one location to another.

Data transmission channels carry the data from one location to another and can be classified according to bandwidth. The **bandwidth** determines the volume of data that can be transmitted in a given time. The wider (higher) the bandwidth, the more data it can transmit. The terms narrowband and broadband are used to describe the capacity of transmission channels, but these terms are not exact.

to another. The packets are sent along by **routers**. A router is a specialised computer or a piece of electronic hardware designed specifically for routing and it chooses the best route to send data to its destination. Data arriving at the destination computer is reassembled. If a packet does not arrive or is corrupted, the entire file does not have to be resent; only the packet that was lost or corrupted.

World Wide Web

The World Wide Web (or the Web) is a multimedia service that runs on the Internet. It was originally developed to help physicists at CERN in Geneva, Switzerland to exchange data and research materials quickly with other scientists. Many people believe the Internet and the Web to be one and the same, but this is not so.

The Web consists of **hypertext** and **hypermedia** documents. A **hypertext** document is a document that contains a **hyperlink** to another document located on the same computer or on another computer in any part of the world. Hypertext allows you to move easily from one document to the next. For example, if you have used the help files in any of Microsoft Office's application programs, you have already encountered hypertext. You may have asked for help with a certain topic and been shown an explanation, in which you saw certain words highlighted in blue. If you clicked on such a word, you would get an additional help screen. The word is associated with a hyperlink to somewhere else either in the same file or in a different file on the computer or on a web server.

Hypermedia is a general name for documents that contain links to text, graphics, sound or video files. A computer that stores and makes available hypertext and hypermedia documents is called a **web server**, and a computer that requests such a document is called a **client**. All the information that can be accessed using the Internet is often referred to as **Cyberspace**, which is made up of all the websites and all the files accessible over the Internet.

Browsers

A web browser (see Figure 7.5) is software that lets you access the information available on the Web. Popular browsers include Microsoft Internet Explorer and Mozilla Firefox. All web browsers operate in a very similar manner and have similar features.

Internet addresses

Each computer on the Internet has a unique address that identifies it. This unique address is a number called the **IP address (Internet Protocol address),** which is a 32-bit address consisting of four sets of up to three digits each, separated by full stops, e.g. 196.161.232.4. The IP address could be **static** (it remains the same every time you connect to the Internet) or it could be **dynamic** (it is a temporary address that changes each time you connect to the Internet). To connect to a computer on the Internet, your computer needs to know its IP address.

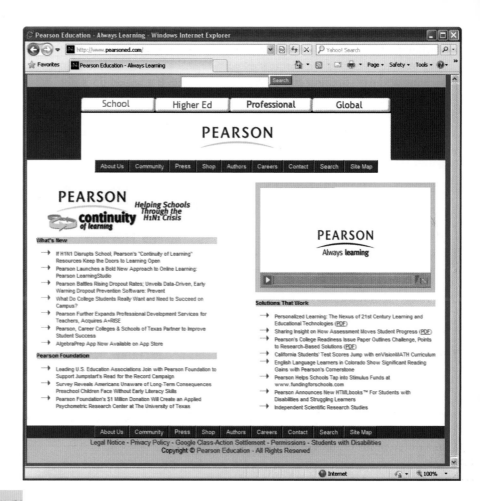

 **DID YOU KNOW?**

**HyperText Transfer Protocol
(HTTP)** is a set of rules that
controls how data travels between
web servers and clients.

Web addresses or URLs

The IP addresses used by software are difficult for humans to remember
so URLs (Uniform Resource Locators) or web addresses are used instead.
Every web address is unique and is constructed like this:

TypeOfResource://HostComputer.Domain/Directory/SubDirectory/Filename.Extension

The different components are as follows:

- *TypeOfResource* identifies the type of resource. There are several
  different types; for example, **http://** identifies a web page and **mailto://**
  identifies an e-mail address.

- *HostComputer* is the name of the host computer or web server. This
  must be unique within the domain.

- *Domain* identifies the type of organisation that owns the website. There
  are several different types of domain, for example:
  .com identifies an international commercial organisation
  .co.uk identifies a UK-based commercial organisation
  .ac.uk identifies a UK-based university or other academic institution
  .org.uk identifies a UK-based non-commercial organisation

You can also go to search engines directly using their web addresses; for example:

- www.google.co.uk
- www.yahoo.co.uk
- www.bing.com
- www.altavista.com
- www.lycos.com
- www.excite.co.uk

Each search engine has its own database of web documents. Items are continually added to the database by a program called a **spider**, which searches the Web looking for new pages. Most search engines will allow you to submit the web address of your own website to make sure the spider visits it. Some search engines charge for this, while others provide this service free. In addition to giving access to information in its database, a search engine site may also provide services such as free e-mail, chat rooms, news and facilities for online shopping.

Searching the Web using keywords

You can also find information by typing into a search engine one or more **keywords** or key phrases that indicate the topic you would like to search for. For example:

- Type one or more keywords or a phrase into the search box (e.g. 'West Indies cricket').

- Click on the 'Search' or 'Go' button.

- A list of sites that are related to the **search terms** will be displayed. Figure 7.10 shows one of the websites found by Excite when the words 'West Indies cricket' were typed in and the 'Search' button was clicked.

◄ **Figure 7.10**
A web page found by searching for 'West Indies cricket'

Advanced search syntax

All search engines give you the option of an advanced syntax to narrow down searches, so that you can find specific information more quickly. The syntax used may differ between search engines, but here is some of the advanced search syntax used by Yahoo!

Required and specific search words

- Placing a plus sign ('+') in front of a word tells Yahoo! that the word *must* be included in all search results.

- Conversely, placing a minus sign ('-') in front of a word specifies that the word *must not* be included in any of the search results.

Phrase matching

- Placing double quotes ("...") around a string of words tells Yahoo! that all search results must contain the string in that exact sequence.

Finding information using a web bot

Bot is short for *robot*, and a **web bot** is software that can run automatically on the Web once it has been set up. Web bots can be useful for searching the Web and alerting you if there is news you are interested in, books you may want to buy, or if information you gathered earlier has been updated. Some examples of web bots are:

- Copernic is a search bot that will search many search engines from a single search condition. The results are ranked in order of relevance to the search condition.

- Various sniping tools can automatically place bids on auction sites in the last few seconds of the auction, so that you don't forget to bid for an item you want, and avoid price increases due to bidding against other buyers. For example, PowerSnipe.

- WebWhacker and other similar tools will download a copy of an entire website and save it on a server or local hard disk so that it can be used when there is no web connection available or instead of connecting to the Web. When you do connect to the Web, your copy will be automatically updated. These tools can increase the speed at which you can view web pages and reduce the frequency of web access. Schools can significantly increase the speed at which web pages can be viewed using this software.

Intranets

An **intranet** is like a local version of the Internet within a company or organisation. It offers many of the same features as the global Internet, but in a localised environment such as a factory site or an office. Many companies make large volumes of information — such as training manuals, company reports, job adverts, and newsletters — available to their employees on an intranet.

Authorised users within a company can use the company's intranet to find information easily and quickly. An intranet uses the same browsers, TCP/IP and other software as used for the Internet. If a company has an intranet and allows limited access to it by people outside the company, the intranet is referred to as an **extranet**.

TASK

Auction sniping
What are the advantages and disadvantages of auction sniping tools?

Electronic mail (e-mail)

E-mail is one of the most popular and widely used services on the Internet today. It enables users to send electronic messages to an individual or group, and to receive messages from others. Messages can include text, pictures and hyperlinks. An e-mail can have other files of any type attached to it and sent with it.

E-mail is usually much faster than mail delivered by the traditional postal system. An e-mail can be sent to an e-mail subscriber in any part of the world in a matter of seconds (although this can sometimes take much longer). Apart from the cost of equipment and the fixed fee that a subscriber has to pay to an ISP for Internet access, sending e-mail is free. You can send as many e-mails as you like at no additional charge and at your own convenience, any time of the day or night. This does not cause any problems for the person receiving it, who does not have to be present to receive the e-mail.

In order to send or receive e-mail, each user must have an **e-mail address**, which is unique to the user and consists of two parts separated by the '@' ('at') symbol. The first part is the user name, which can be a real name, a shortened form of a real name or some made-up name. The second part is the location of the account on the Internet. For users living in Trinidad and Tobago who have the Telecommunications Services of Trinidad and Tobago (TSTT) as their ISP, their e-mail addresses could look like the following:

- vern30@tstt.net.tt
- bobonline@tstt.net.tt

Internet users can also use the **free e-mail services** offered by websites such as Yahoo! and Hotmail. You simply fill out an online form to open an account and get an e-mail address. Examples of these addresses are:

- nick@yahoo.com
- kamo@hotmail.com

For an e-mail message to be sent and received, the following must be in place:

- **e-mail server** − This is a computer on the Internet that receives incoming messages and delivers outgoing messages. It allocates a certain amount of storage to hold mail for registered users. The area of storage allocated to you is your **mailbox.** You can retrieve your mail by supplying your username and password. This is necessary to protect your e-mail from unauthorised access.

- **e-mail client** − This is a program that enables you to read and compose e-mail messages and to send and access e-mail from the server, e.g. Microsoft Outlook.

Sending an e-mail message

In Microsoft Outlook, with the Inbox open on screen, click on the **New** button in the toolbar to open a new e-mail message. Figure 7.11 shows the e-mail screen for creating a new message. The format for other e-mail software is similar.

To send an e-mail:

- In the **To:** field, fill in the e-mail address of the person you are sending it to.

- If you send a copy of the e-mail to other people, enter their e-mail addresses in the **Cc:** field.

- If you want to send a copy of the e-mail to someone and want to hide this from others, enter their e-mail address in the **Bcc:** field. This field may be hidden. To locate it, click on the **To:** field and it will be visible in the **Select Names** dialog box.

- In the **Subject:** field, enter a phrase that describes what your e-mail is about.

- Type your message.

- You can also send **attachments** along with the original e-mail. An attachment can be, for example: a word processed document, a spreadsheet file, a database file, a picture file, a sound file or a video file. When a file is attached, a new field showing the name and size of the file is displayed below the **Subject:** field. In Microsoft Outlook, to attach a file to an e-mail, with the new e-mail open, in the **Insert** tab, select **Attach File**. The **Insert File** dialog box appears. Locate the file and click on **Insert**.

- To send the e-mail, click on the **Send** button in the toolbar and the e-mail will be stored in the **outbox** ready to be sent. To send all your e-mail, click on the **Send/Receive** button in the toolbar.

▶ **Figure 7.11**
An e-mail message

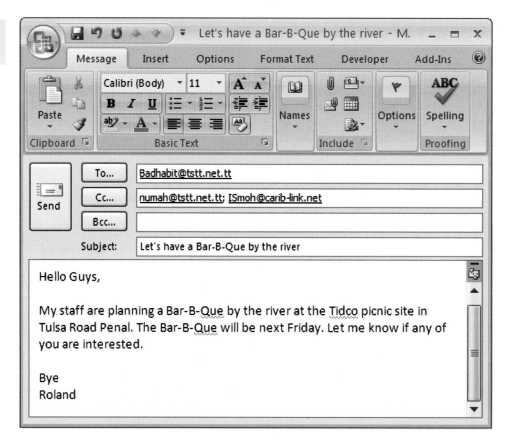

Receiving and replying to an e-mail message

Open the e-mail client and, if you are using Outlook, click on the **Send/ Receive** button in the toolbar. The e-mail software connects to the e-mail server and downloads your e-mail into the **inbox**. To read the e-mail in your inbox, you can either read them in the preview section of the screen, or double-click on each e-mail to open it.

Having read the e-mail you could do any of these things:

- **Delete.** Click on the **Delete** button in the toolbar to delete the e-mail.
- **Reply.** If you click on the **Reply** button, a new message opens. This is addressed to the person who sent you the original e-mail.
- **Reply to All.** If you click on the **Reply to All** button, a new message opens. This is addressed to the person who sent you the original e-mail and all e-mail addresses in the **Cc:** field.
- **Forward.** If you click on the **Forward** button, a new message opens. You will have to fill in all the e-mail addresses you want the message sent to.
- If you reply to or forward an e-mail, when you have finished writing your message, to send it, click on the **Send** button in the toolbar to store the e-mail in the outbox ready to be sent. To send all your e-mail, click on the **Send/Receive** button in the toolbar.

Storing e-mail messages

Outlook sets up folders to store e-mail messages. You can see these folders in the **Navigation** pane. If this is not visible, in Outlook, in the **View** menu, select **Navigation Pane** and then **Normal**.

Here are some common folders:

- **Deleted Items.** When you delete an e-mail, it is saved in the **Deleted Items** folder. If necessary, you can retrieve a deleted e-mail from this folder. If you right-click on the folder and select **Empty 'Deleted Items' Folder**, all the e-mails in the folder are deleted.
- **Drafts.** If you Save an e-mail you are working on, it will be saved in this folder.
- **Inbox.** As e-mails are received, they are put in the inbox.
- **Junk E-mail.** E-mail can be filtered to remove spam and this is put in the **Junk E-mail** folder. You should check this occasionally to make sure that only junk e-mail has been filtered out.
- **Outbox.** E-mail that is ready to send may be stored in the outbox. This e-mail can be opened and re-edited if necessary – click on the **Outbox** folder and double-click on the e-mail. To send e-mail stored in the outbox, click on the **Send/Receive** button in the toolbar.
- **Personal.** It is likely that most of the e-mail you receive will be deleted as soon as you have read it. If you need to save e-mail, you can do this in the **Personal** folder. If you save a lot of e-mail, you can organise this in sub-folders you can create. For example, you might have a sub-folder called *Shopping* where you put e-mails from online shops; or a sub-folder called *Finance* where you put e-mails from your bank or credit card issuer or other e-mails related to managing your personal finances; or a sub-folder called *Family* where you put e-mails from your family.

- **Quarantine.** A virus scanner may put in this folder e-mails that are found to have viruses.
- **Sent Items.** When e-mail is sent, a copy could be placed in this folder.

E-mail messages are files and can also be saved on backing storage. You might find it convenient to store e-mail messages received at school or work on a memory stick so that you can take them home. In Microsoft Outlook, select **File**, **Save As**, chose an appropriate location in the **Save As** dialog box and click on **OK**.

Contacts

Contacts are entries in an address book. In Microsoft Outlook, you can access your contacts by clicking on **To:**, **Cc:** or **Bcc:** in an open e-mail message, or by clicking on the **Address Book** button in the toolbar. In the dialog box that appears, type the name of the contact you wish to access in the **Type Name** or **Select from List** field and the contact will appear automatically. Double-click on the contact to display the **Contact** dialog box (see Figure 7.12)

To set up a new contact for someone who sent you an e-mail:

- Click on their e-mail address in the **From:** field in the message, and select **Add to Outlook Contacts**. Alternatively, you could click on the **New** button in the Outlook toolbar and select **Contact**.

- Fill in the details you wish to record in the **Contact** dialog box (see Figure 7.12). The fields, such as **Full Name**, **Job title** and **Company** are pre-set. You can add notes and a photograph. The picture of Victoria Cave shown in Figure 7.12 would more usually be a picture of the contact. To change the picture, right-click on the picture and select **Change Picture**. A dialog box appears. Locate the new picture and click on **OK**.

To save the contact, click on the **Save and Close** button in the toolbar.

To delete a contact, open the contact and, in the **File** menu, select **Delete**.

Address Book button in Microsoft Outlook

▶ **Figure 7.12**
The Contact tab

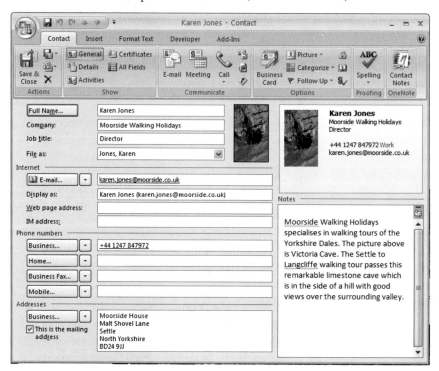

a topic. Everyone currently in the room is notified that a new person has entered the discussion. You are identified by a name, but many users prefer to use a **handle** (a name that they want to characterise their personality). You can see the comments made by other participants and can type out a reply on any of the comments to everyone who is connected at the time, or only to selected people in the group. You may wish to start a topic of your own. Users can enter and leave a chat room as they wish.

Internet Relay Chat (IRC) — This is a real-time conference system that lets you talk with as many people as you like, grouped together on **channels** by topics, using text messages. Once you have accessed IRC, you can find out what topics are being discussed and how many users are involved. You can then search for a channel that suits your interest. IRC can be considered as a type of text-based chat where each chat room (channel) is dedicated to a specific topic, and where users are not allowed to discuss topics unrelated to the channel's purpose.

Instant messaging — This enables you to chat privately with another person. Messages are sent instantly. Messages are usually in text and can be sent using a mix of e-mail type systems and mobile phones.

Multimedia chat — With multimedia software, you can use the microphone in a computer to talk to another user anywhere in the world over the Internet. If you each have a webcam connected to your computer, you will also be able to see each other.

Video conferencing

Video conferencing is essentially the same as multimedia chat but is likely to involve more people communicating at the same time. Video camera systems are often more sophisticated than a simple webcam and may have the facility to zoom out to see the whole group or to zoom in on an individual who is speaking. The video image is more likely to be displayed on a large screen or several monitors, so everyone involved can see it, rather than being displayed on a single monitor. Video conferencing technology tries to avoid problems with the speed of communication channels and bandwidth on the Internet by using private communication systems. These were originally analogue video and satellite links but increasingly they use compressed digital images transmitted over wide area networks or the Internet.

Web rings

A **web ring** is a way of interlinking a group of websites that have information on related topics or themes. The websites are linked so that you can visit each site one after the other, eventually (if you keep going) returning to the first website. Users can also elect to go backwards through the web ring or see a list of all the websites on the ring. A web ring is managed from one website which is able to omit websites that have dropped out or are no longer reachable. The advantage of a web ring is that if you are interested in the topic on one website you can quickly connect to another website on the same topic.

Web broadcasting

You can listen to radio programmes (see Figure 7.16) and watch television programmes and movies. These could be broadcast live or could be a recording. You can see and hear information as the programme is transmitted. You do not have to wait until all the information is downloaded before you can see and hear it. These new services are currently restricted by copyright problems, and bandwidth and transmission speed, and as these increase, there will be a wider choice of programmes.

Setting up your own website

You can advertise your business by setting up your own website. To do this you would create your own web pages and put them on the Web.

You can write web pages in HTML (Hypertext Markup Language), or use software that generates HTML. HTML is a programming language that you can use to create web pages. It contains standard codes that are used to specify how a web page is structured and formatted. These codes determine the appearance of the web page when it is displayed by your browser. HTML also contains tags that are used to create hyperlinks to access related information on the Web.

Software is available that will help you write HTML by generating the structure of the code which you then fill in. You could use software that is specifically designed to help you write web pages in both HTML code and in a manner similar to using DTP software. Such software will also help you manage the structure of your website. Examples are Adobe Dreamweaver and Microsoft Expression Web (the replacement for Microsoft FrontPage).

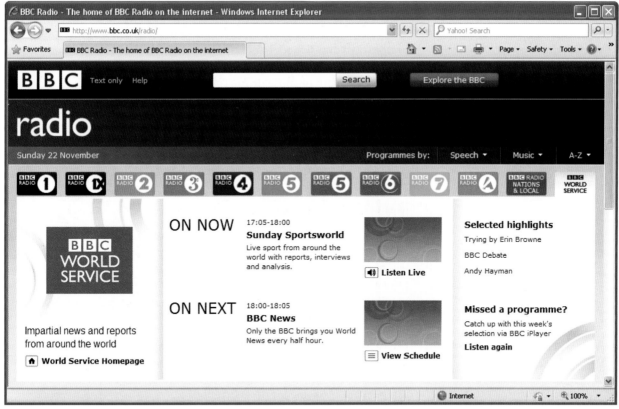

Image of the BBC Radio homepage reproduced with the written permission of the British Broadcasting Corporation. © BBC 2009

▲ Figure 7.16
Broadcast radio from the BBC

Many applications can produce output as a web page; for example, you can save Word files as web pages. Having written your website, you must upload it to a web server before it is generally accessible over the Web. More information on how to set up a website is given in a later chapter.

Web 2.0

Web 2.0 describes a trend in web design and development towards a second generation of web-based communities and services. These include, blogs, wikis and social networking websites which aim to facilitate creativity, collaboration, and sharing between web users. They often have features in common but combine these in different ways.

For example, **Facebook** (**www.facebook.com**) states that it 'gives people the power to share and makes the world more open and connected'. It goes on to say: 'Millions of people use Facebook everyday[sic] to keep up with friends… and learn more about the people they meet.' Facebook allows members to set up a personal profile. Other members can be accepted as friends and will then have access to a member's personal profile. Members can upload text, images and videos to their personal profile and share links to other web pages from it. Similarly, **YouTube** (**www.youtube.com**) provides an online video streaming and sharing service that enables members to upload videos and allows anyone to view them. It also allows members to set up their own page with a personal profile, and there are community forums.

Upload and download digital media

Many sites allow digital media in the form of images or video or music to be uploaded and shared. For example, Facebook allows images and videos to be uploaded and shared as a part of a personal profile and sharing video is the main purpose of YouTube.

Some sites specialise in uploading and sharing images. For example, on **Worldisround** (**www.worldisround.com**) you can upload images and share them. Travellers could use Worldisround to make a record of their experiences around the world by uploading digital photographs so that friends and family back home could keep up with what they were doing. You could use Worldisround for other purposes, such as showing the world around the place where you live.

Downloading music is very popular and may replace the sale of music on CDs and other physical media. Websites such as **iTunes** (**www.itunes.com**) and **Napster** (**www.napster.co.uk**) sell digital music downloads, and these can be downloaded to portable devices so that music can be enjoyed on the move. iTunes also has features that allow users to organise and browse their entire collection of music.

Bit Torrent (**www.bittorrent.com**) is a peer-to-peer file-sharing service that allows users to share any digital content. This could be images, video or music. Files can be downloaded to any registered computer and any file can be made available for downloading.

Blogs

Blogs are online personal diaries with narrative, pictures and hyperlinks. Anyone can set up a blog and these could be on almost any topic.

Here are some examples:

- The Adam Smith Institute promotes free-market economic and social policies in its blog on **http://www.adamsmith.org/blog/**

- Warwick University has blogs by its staff and students on **http://blogs.warwick.ac.uk/directory/people/**

- There are many blogs about music on **http://www.blogtoplist.com/music/**

- There is a directory of blogs on **http://www.blogcatalog.com/directory/**

- You can create your own blog using a hosted service, for example on **http://www.blogger.com**.

Wikis

Wikis enable you to describe and comment on topics in collaboration with other web users. A wiki is a database of web pages which you can edit. You can also search the wiki's content, and view updates since your last visit. In a moderated wiki, the owner of the wiki can review edits before they become a permanent part of the wiki.

Chapter 8

Graphics, presentation and website writer software

In this chapter, you will look at software that will enable you to do the following:

- create and edit simple graphics
- prepare a presentation
- set up a website.

Graphics software

Software that enables you to create and edit graphics can be very useful, especially when preparing a presentation or setting up a website. There is a wide range of such software; for example, Adobe Photoshop. A more straightforward example that is free on computers with Windows is Microsoft Paint. We will have a brief look at how to use this. In Windows, Paint can usually be found in the **Accessories** group in the Programs menu. Select this and the software will display the opening window shown in Figure 8.1.

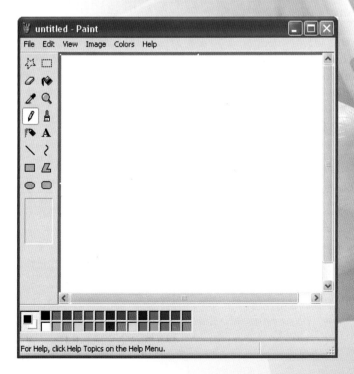

◀ **Figure 8.1**
The opening window of Microsoft Paint

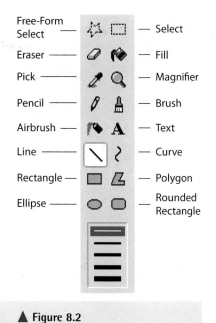

Free-Form Select — Select

Eraser — Fill

Pick — Magnifier

Pencil — Brush

Airbrush — Text

Line — Curve

Rectangle — Polygon

Ellipse — Rounded Rectangle

▲ **Figure 8.2**
The toolbox

Figure 8.3 ▶
The colour box

Tools

On the left-hand side of the window (see Figure 8.1) you can see the toolbox (see also Figure 8.2). The tools available allow you to create and edit graphics. These are the functions of some of the tools:

- **Pencil** and **Brush** both allow you to draw on the work area. Different nib and brush shapes can be chosen.

- **Airbrush** allows you to spray paint onto the work area.

- **Text** allows you to type in text. You drag the mouse to create a rectangular text box, and then type in the text.

- The **Eraser** is used to rub out parts of the graphic.

- **Fill** allows you to fill an enclosed space with colour. You create an enclosed space; select a colour (see Figure 8.3) by clicking on it, and click inside the enclosed space.

- **Pick** allows you to choose an existing colour already present on the graphic you are editing. This can then be used with other tools.

- **Magnifier** allows you to magnify your view of the graphic. This helps you to do more detailed editing.

- There are also tools for drawing a variety of shapes, such as lines, curved lines, ellipses (hold down the **Shift** key to draw a circle), rectangles (hold down the **Shift** key to draw a square), polygons and rounded rectangles.

- **Select** allows you to select a rectangular part of a graphic by dragging the mouse and then releasing the mouse button. **Freeform select** is similar but the shape of the selection does not have to be a rectangle.

Foreground ——
Background ——

The menus in Paint

File menu

In the **File** menu, you will find familiar options such as **Save**, **Save As** and **Print**. You can save graphics in several common file formats, such as **.bmp, .jpg** and **.gif**. There is also a useful option entitled **From scanner or camera**. This will input an image directly from a scanner or digital camera connected to the computer without need to cut or copy and paste the image.

Edit menu

The **Edit** menu options include **Copy, Cut** and **Paste**, and other options which are likely to be familiar.

To copy a part of a graphic, select the part to be copied and in the **Edit** menu select **Copy**. Next, again in the **Edit** menu, select **Paste**. The block copied appears on the work area and it is selected. Drag this across to the location you wish to place it in.

View menu

The **View** menu allows you to turn on or off the display of the toolbox, colour box and status bar. It also allows you to choose to zoom in on the graphic so that you can edit it in detail.

Image menu

In the **Image** menu (see Figure 8.5) you can choose to flip, rotate, stretch or skew an image. For example to reflect in a vertical axis (or mirror line): select the part of the graphic to be reflected; in the **Image** menu select **Flip/Rotate**; in the **Flip and Rotate** dialog box (see Figure 8.6) select **Flip vertical** and click on **OK**.

▲ **Figure 8.4**
A repeating pattern produced using graphics software

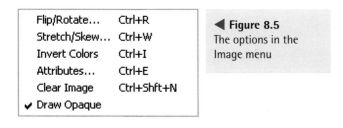

◀ **Figure 8.5**
The options in the Image menu

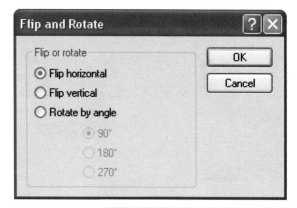

▲ **Figure 8.6**
The Flip and Rotate dialog box

Colors menu

In the **Colors** menu you can define custom colours. Select **Edit Colors** and the **Edit Colors** dialog box appears (see Figure 8.7). Click on **Define Custom Colors** and the colour spectrum appears. Click on the colour that you want in the spectrum and click on **OK**. This colour will now be available in the colour palette, and you can use it with the other tools.

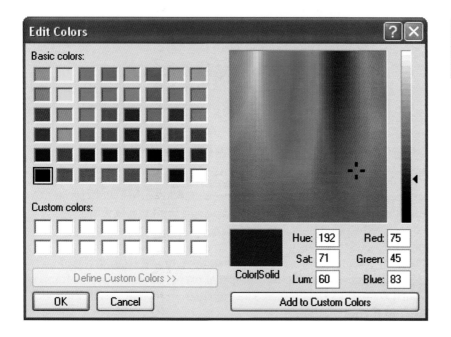

◀ **Figure 8.7**
The Edit Colors dialog box after Define Custom Colors has been selected

Screen images

Paint has only a very restricted range of tools and options but it is readily available. It is very useful when you want to write help documentation and user guides because it is very easy to capture parts of the screen and edit them in Paint.

- To capture the whole screen, follow these steps. On the keyboard, press the **Print Screen** key. This copies an image of the screen into the paste buffer. In Paint, in the **Edit** menu select **Paste**. This places the screen image into the work area where it can be edited. If you only wanted an image of the whole screen, you could paste this directly into Word or other software.

- To capture part of the screen, the process is similar. Capture the whole screen, and then in Paint select the part of the screen you want. Copy this and paste it into Word or other software. You can use this method to capture images of icons and menus.

- To capture a dialog box, you can hold down the **Alt** key when you press **Print Screen**. The dialog box is copied to the paste buffer. This can now be pasted into Paint, Word or other software.

Exercise 8.1

1. Using drawing software, draw a logo for a construction company and colour it in.

2. Using drawing software, create a repeating textile or wallpaper pattern using copy and paste (see Figure 8.4).

3. Write a help sheet that shows someone how to create, save, print and close a document for the first time in a word processor. This should include images of the following items:
   - The **File** menu
   - The **Save As** dialog box
   - The **Save** button
   - The **Print** and **Close** buttons

4. Write a help sheet that shows someone how to open an existing spreadsheet, edit it, save and print it. You should illustrate this with the menus, icons and buttons used.

Presentation software

Presentation software can be helpful when you are preparing to give a presentation to an audience. Such presentations are usually a series of slides projected onto a large screen using a multimedia projector connected to a computer. What appears on the computer's monitor is projected onto the screen. The slides may have links to, for example, pictures, documents or websites, so that these can be easily accessed during the presentation. One example of presentation software is Impress which is a part of OpenOffice. The presentation software used below is Microsoft PowerPoint.

Preparing slides

When you open Microsoft PowerPoint, the default opening screen has a template for an introductory slide, and you enter the title of the presentation. Next you add the slides that make up your presentation.

Adding a new slide

To add a new slide to your presentation, on the **Home** tab of the Ribbon select **New Slide**. The new slide is added after the current slide. The default layout and design of the slides following the introductory slide is shown in Figure 8.8.

If you click in the appropriate box, you can add a title and some text. Text is automatically bulleted.

Inserting images

Images, such as clip art and pictures can be inserted. To insert clip art, on the **Insert** tab, select **Clip Art**. A selection of clip art appears in the task pane on the right-hand side of the screen. Click on the clip art you want to insert and it appears on the slide. Newly inserted clip art looks like that in Figure 8.9.

You can drag the rotation handle to turn the clip art. Dragging a resizing handle changes the size of the clip art. Dragging a handle on a corner changes the size but keeps the proportions (the **aspect ratio**) the same. Dragging a handle on a side stretches the clip art in the direction of movement.

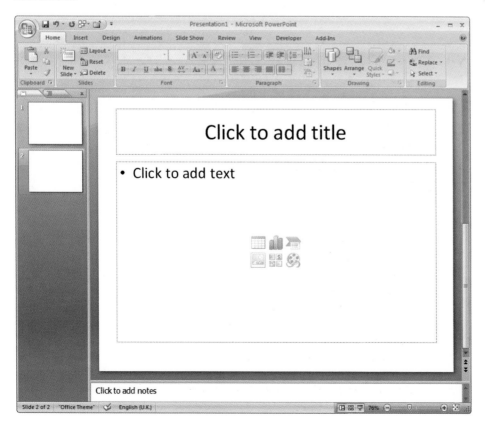

◀ **Figure 8.8**
The default for slides following the introductory slide in Microsoft PowerPoint

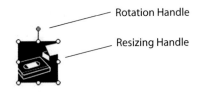

— Rotation Handle

— Resizing Handle

Inserting a picture is a similar process. You are asked to use a dialog box to identify the picture file you want to insert. When you have done this, click on **OK**.

You can add animation to an image, which will play when it is first displayed. To do this, switch to the **Animations** tab and select **Custom Animation**. The **Custom Animation** task pane is displayed. Select **Add Effect**, then **Entrance** and you can choose from several animations, such as *Diamond*, *Fly In* and *Wheel*. Select each in turn and play them to see their effect. You can add several animations to one image which will be played in turn when the image is displayed.

Inserting charts

Powerpoint allows you to insert and modify charts. For example, in PowerPoint, on the **Insert** tab, select **Chart**. The **Insert Chart** dialog box appears, which you can use to change the type and settings of the graph to be generated.

To alter the data which is displayed in the chart you edit the data in Excel.

You can also insert charts by cutting and pasting from a spreadsheet.

Slide layout

PowerPoint has a range of **slide layouts** that you can use. These are available from the **Layout** drop-down menu in the **Home** tab. Select a slide layout by clicking on it. You can do this repeatedly until you find a suitable layout. Notice that some layouts already have bullets built into them so that when you type in text, bullets appear.

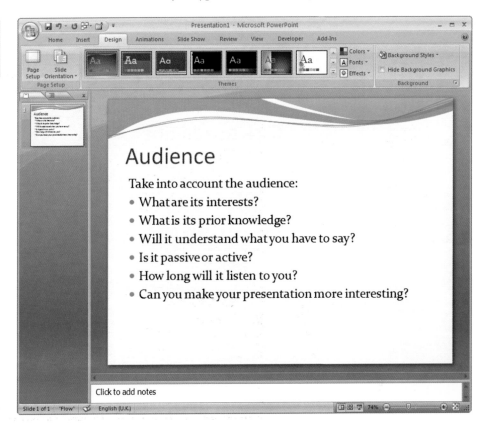

Themes

PowerPoint also has a range of slide **themes** that you can use. In the **Design** tab, hover over a theme to preview its effect and then click on the one you wish to choose.

You can change the **colours** used in the theme you have chosen by selecting **Colors** from the **Design** tab and choosing a colour scheme.

DID YOU KNOW?

You can use animation schemes to control how the title and lines of text are added when a slide is displayed. You have already seen how to do this for images.

Master slides

You can create **your own layout and design**, and use other features, such as a footer that includes the **date**, **footer text** and **automatic page numbering**, by editing the master slide. Whatever is shown on the master slide is visible on every slide in the presentation and cannot be changed when editing them.

The master slide is not normally visible. To display the master slide, on the **View** tab, select **Slide Master**. This can then be edited as you would edit any other slide. You can do the following:

* Set up the styles to be applied to the title and text.

* Insert an image that will appear on every slide. For example, the logo of your company.

* Insert the date, automatic slide numbering and a footer on every slide.

To insert the date, automatic slide numbering and a footer on every slide:

* On the **Insert** tab, select **Header and Footer**.

* In the **Header and Footer** dialog box (see Figure 8.11), select **Date and time, Update automatically** or **Fixed** and select from the available formats in the drop-down menu.

* Select **Slide number** to activate automatic slide numbering.

* Select **Footer** and type in whatever text you want in the footer.

* Click on **Apply to All**.

The date, the footer text and the slide number will appear on every slide.

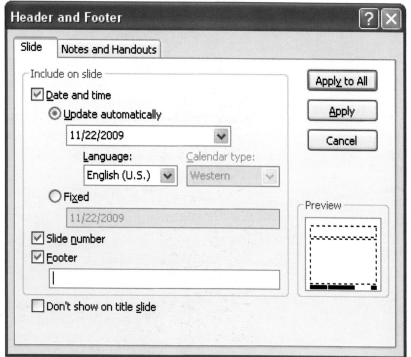

Figure 8.11 ▶
The Header and Footer dialog box

209

Saving

The Save button in PowerPoint

Your presentation can be saved in the usual manner: click on the **Save** button. You should save your work on disk before showing the whole presentation or printing it.

Showing a presentation

The Slide Show button – click this to show your presentation

To **show the whole presentation**, click on the **View** tab and select **Slide Show**. When you do this the slide show is shown on the whole monitor screen as it will appear when projected. Left-click on the mouse to move through the presentation; to **end the show**, right-click and select **End Show**.

Slide transitions

A slide transition takes place as you move from one slide to another as you show a presentation. The default transition is to quickly move from one slide to the next; however, there are many transitions available. In the **Animations** tab the range of transitions available is displayed. For example, you can choose from *blinds horizontal, box out, checkerboard down, comb horizontal* and many more. You can vary the speed of the transition and add a sound (for example, a drum roll) which plays during the transition.

To use the same transition between all the slides in the presentation, click on **Apply To All**. If you want a different transition for different slides, highlight a slide or group of slides in the slide pane on the left-hand side of the screen and select a transition. This will be applied only to the slide or group of slides.

Printing slides

The Office Button

To print your presentation, click the **Office Button** and select **Print** from the **Print** menu. The **Print** dialog box appears, and if you click on **OK** the default settings will print all your slides one to a page. If you want to give your audience copies of your slides, you can print several on one page. You can print six slides on a page by selecting the following:

- Print what: handouts
- Slides per page: 6

Exercise 8.2

1. Prepare a presentation about yourself:
   a) Choose a slide layout, design template, colour scheme and animation scheme.

b) The first slide should introduce you to your audience.

c) Next, include one slide on each of the following:
- Your likes and dislikes
- Your family
- Your home
- Your school
- Your ambitions

d) Save your work.

e) Print your work showing six slides on one page.

f) Show your presentation.

2. You need a loan from your bank manager to buy a local business. Prepare a presentation to be given to the bank manager about the business.

a) Choose a slide layout, theme, colour scheme and animation scheme.

b) The first slide should describe the business.

c) Next, include slides on each of the following:
- The opening hours
- How to find the business
- The products sold
- The staff
- The monthly sales figures for the previous year displayed as a column graph.

d) Put the date, your name and the slide number on every slide.

e) Use slide transitions to stimulate your audience.

f) Save your work.

g) Print your work showing six slides on one page.

h) Show your presentation.

Notes pages

When your presentation is shown to an audience by projecting it onto a large screen, if the font size is too small your audience will not be able to read it. As a result, when you enter text on a slide this is usually in a much larger font size than you would use in a word processor. Consequently, you cannot get much detail on one slide. However, you may want to write detailed notes that underpin the bullet points made on a slide. This can be done using the **notes page** attached to each slide.

To use the notes pages, in the **View** tab select **Notes Page** (see Figure 8.12). Click to add text, and you can type in notes for the slide as you would type text into a word processor.

To return to the normal view showing only one slide, in the **View** tab select **Normal**.

Figure 8.12 ▶
A notes page

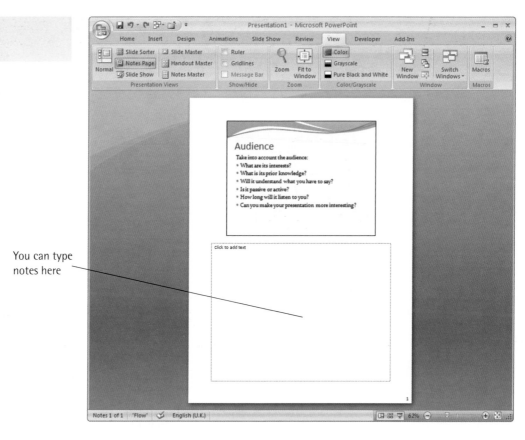

You can type notes here

Printing notes pages

To print your presentation and notes, click on the **Office Button** and select **Print** from the **Print** menu. The **Print** dialog box appears. If you want to print a copy of each slide with its associated notes on the same page, set **Print what** to **Notes Pages**, and click on **OK**.

Links

During a presentation you may want to refer to materials that are not a part of your presentation. For example, you might want to refer to a website or a document you have prepared in a word processor or spreadsheet.

The Hyperlink button in PowerPoint

To insert a **link to a website**, in the **Insert** tab select **Hyperlink**, and the **Insert Hyperlink** dialog box appears (see Figure 8.13). In the dialog box, do the following:

- Set **Link to** to **Existing File or Web Page**
- Set **Text to display** to **Huddersfield University**
- Set **Address** to **http://www.hud.ac.uk**
- Click on **OK**

A hyperlink is inserted into your PowerPoint slide. If you show your presentation on a computer that is connected to the Internet, you can click on this link and the display will change to the Huddersfield University web page. To return to your presentation, close the web browser.

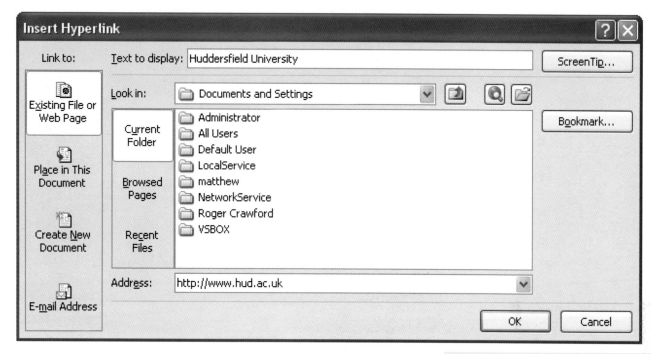

To insert a **link to a word processed document**, the technique is the same but you select a file instead of typing in a URL.

If you show your presentation, you can click on this link and the display will change to the word processed document. To return to your presentation, close the word processor. Using this method you can also link to spreadsheets and other files during a presentation.

Exercise 8.3

1. Prepare a presentation about search engines:
   a) Choose a slide layout, theme, colour scheme and animation scheme.
   b) The first slide should introduce the topic to your audience.
   c) Next, slides should prompt you to explain:
      • Why you would want to use a search engine
      • What search engines do
      • How you use a search engine
   d) In order that you can demonstrate the why, what and how of search engines, include one slide that links to each of the following search engines:
      • Google
      • Yahoo!
      • Bing
   e) The final slide should have a summary and conclusion.
   f) Put the date, your name and the slide number on every slide.
   g) Save your work.
   h) Print your work showing six slides on one page.
   i) Show your presentation.

2. Prepare a presentation about tourism in the Yorkshire Dales, UK.
   a) Choose a slide layout, theme, colour scheme and animation scheme.
   b) The first slide should describe the topic.
   c) Next, include slides on each of the following:
      - Where the Yorkshire Dales region is located.
      - Why tourists go on holiday to the Yorkshire Dales.
      - Where you could stay if you went on holiday to the Yorkshire Dales, including the accommodation available in self-catering cottages, hotels and campsites.
      - The cost of accommodation and how you could book.
   d) Put the date, your name and the slide number on every slide.
   e) The final slide should have a summary and conclusion.
   f) Save your work.
   g) Print your work showing six slides on one page.
   h) Show your presentation.

Publishing a website

If you want to publish a website you must follow these steps:

- Create the web pages that will be part of the website

- Link them together

- Upload these pages to a web server

Creating web pages

We will briefly look at how to create web pages using these methods:

- Using applications software, such as Word, Excel and Access

- Writing the HTML directly using a text editor such as Notepad

- Using an HTML generator, such as Arachnophilia

- Using website writer software, such as Adobe Dreamweaver, that allows you to write web pages as they appear on screen and in HTML, and that provides you with tools to manage a website.

All web pages are saved as HTML (Hypertext Markup Language) files; however, you do not have to create them by writing HTML as there are many ways that web pages can be created.

All web pages will have filenames ending in **.htm** or **.html**. However, it is good practice for HTML files to have filenames that:

- Are in lower case

- Have no spaces in them

- End in .html

A **website** is a group of web pages linked together. It is best if this is done in a structured way, because this makes navigation easier. The structure of many websites is broadly hierarchical but there are nearly always links from each page to a range of other pages.

Website writer software

HTML generators can make writing code much easier and more manageable but, even so, this can quickly become very complicated. Unless you prefer this approach, using **website writer** software that allows you to write web pages both as they appear on screen and in HTML may be easier. In addition, such website writers often provide tools for managing your website. An example of such software is Adobe Dreamweaver (see Figure 8.15), formerly developed by Macromedia.

Notice that the work area is divided into Code View and Design View. The balance of this division can be changed by dragging up or down the horizontal line that divides them. In **Code View** you can write HTML, and in **Design View** you can work on the appearance of the web page as you would in a word processor. Because each view is of the same web page, as you work in Code View or Design View they are each kept up to date with the alterations you make.

Creating a new website

Before you can write a web page in Dreamweaver, you need to start a new website. In Dreamweaver, in the **Site** menu select **New Site**, and the **Site Definition** dialog box appears (see Figure 8.16). You should fill in this information:

- **Site Name:** Give the site a name, for example, *myfirstsite*.

- **Local Root Folder:** This is the folder on the local hard disk where you will store all the files used in your website.

▼ Figure 8.15
Dreamweaver

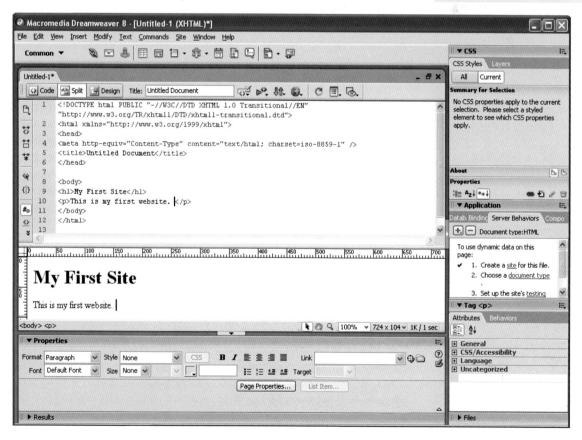

Figure 8.16 ▶
The Site Definition dialog
box

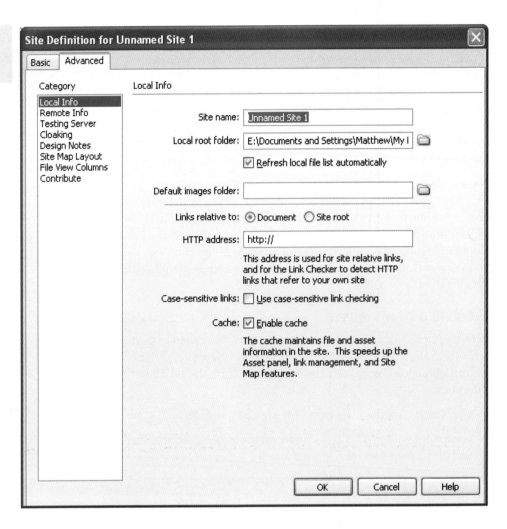

Site Definition for Unnamed Site 1 ☒

Basic | **Advanced**

Category | Local Info

Local Info
Remote Info
Testing Server
Cloaking
Design Notes
Site Map Layout
File View Columns
Contribute

Site name: Unnamed Site 1

Local root folder: E:\Documents and Settings\Matthew\My I 📁

☑ Refresh local file list automatically

Default images folder: 📁

Links relative to: ◉ Document ○ Site root

HTTP address: http://

This address is used for site relative links, and for the Link Checker to detect HTTP links that refer to your own site

Case-sensitive links: ☐ Use case-sensitive link checking

Cache: ☑ Enable cache

The cache maintains file and asset information in the site. This speeds up the Asset panel, link management, and Site Map features.

OK | Cancel | Help

- **Default Images Folder:** It is good practice to keep all your pictures and graphics in a separate folder. It is usual to call the folder *images*.

- **HTTP Address:** This is where you will enter the web address of your site on the web so that it can be easily updated; however, it is not required when you are initially setting up the website.

Click on **OK** and a new blank web page appears.

Creating a new web page

In the **File** menu select **New**, and the **New Document** dialog box appears (see Figure 8.17). Click the **General** tab and you can choose from a wide variety of templates by selecting different categories and page designs. Your choice is shown in the **Preview** pane.

When you have made your choice, click on **Create** and the new page is shown. This will have dummy text and you replace this with your own. Generally, it is easier to use Design View to do this.

Save your new page, and this will appear in the Site Panel. The **Site Panel** (titled **Files** and shown in the bottom right of Figure 8.15) shows the

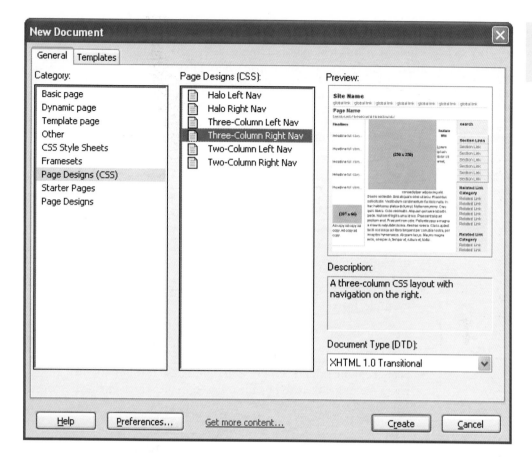

◀ **Figure 8.17**
The New Document
dialog box

location of all the pages and other resources used in your website. As you add more web pages, the **Site Panel** becomes a useful way of accessing your web pages. You can open an existing web page by finding it in the **Site Panel**, and double-clicking on it. When you have more than one website, you can switch between these using the drop-down menu in the **Site Panel**.

Images

To **insert an image** or picture in a web page in Dreamweaver:

- If necessary, create a folder called *images* in your website folder.

- Using Windows Explorer, save the picture file in the images folder in your website folder.

- Using Dreamweaver, find this file in the **Site Panel**, and in Design View drag it across on to the web page.

ALT text

Alternate (or **ALT**) text associates a text description with an image. The text is downloaded and displayed on the web page before the image. When you point at the image, the text is displayed but otherwise it is not shown.

To associate ALT text with a picture in a web page in Dreamweaver:

In Design View, select the image and in the **Properties** panel, type in the text in the **ALT** box.

> **HINT!**
>
> Alternatively, you can insert this HTML code in Code View:
> `<img src="images/`
> `yourpicturename.jpg"`
> `width="285" height="405"`
> `align="center">`
> The size of the image on the web page is given by the width and height, and its position is given by align.

Alternatively, you can insert HTML code in Code View, for example:

<img src="images/myhouse.jpg" width="285" height="405" align=" center" alt=" The house where I live">

The advantages of using ALT are as follows:

- Disabled people may find text on your web page easier to see than images, or they may use software that can read out the descriptions to them.

- If the image is not displayed, the text will be displayed. This can be very helpful; for example, some e-mail software will block images to speed up the downloading of e-mail. The ALT text downloads quickly and tells the user what the image is. If the user wants to look at the image, they can choose to download it. This avoids wasting time downloading unwanted images.

- A few browsers are text-based and these do not download images, for example, Lynx.

- You can use ALT text to point users to other interesting features of your web page.

- Search engine spiders recognise the content of text but not images. Web pages are more likely to be fully indexed in the search engine if images have ALT text.

Background

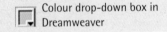
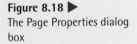
Colour drop-down box in Dreamweaver

To set a **background colour**, in Dreamweaver in the **Modify** menu select **Page Properties**. The **Page Properties** dialog box appears (see Figure 8.18). Click the drop-down box next to **Background** and select a colour. Click on **OK**.

Figure 8.18 ▶
The Page Properties dialog box

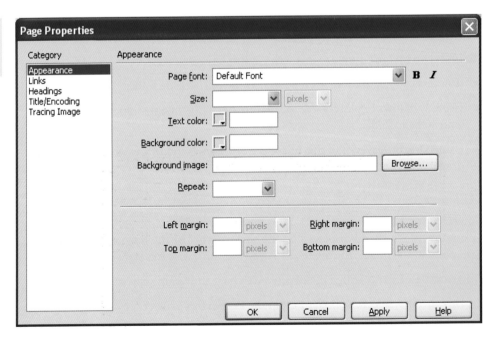

To set a **background image**, in Dreamweaver in the **Modify** menu select **Page Properties**. The **Page Properties** dialog box appears (see Figure 8.18). Browse to find a background image (in the *images* folder) and click on **OK**. The image is tiled over the background.

Text

To change the **size** of text, in Dreamweaver in Design View, highlight the text. In the **Text** menu select **Size**, and select the size of text you want. Click on **OK**. The text changes to the size you chose.

To change the **colour** of text, in Dreamweaver in Design View, highlight the text. In the **Text** menu select **Color**. The **Color** dialog box appears. Select the colour you want and click on **OK**. The text changes to the colour you chose.

To change the **font** of text, in Dreamweaver in Design View, highlight the text. In the **Text** menu select **Font**, and select the font you want. Click on **OK**. The text changes to the font you chose.

Links to other web pages

To insert a link to another web page in Dreamweaver, in Design View in the **Insert** menu select **Hyperlink**. The **Hyperlink** dialog box appears (see Figure 8.19). Fill in the **Text** box with the text to be displayed, and the **Link** box with the full web address of the web page to go to, and click **OK**. The example shown in Figure 8.19 would create a link shown as <u>Google</u> on your web page. If the page was running in a browser, this would link to the Google search engine.

In HTML code, this has the same effect: **<a href="http://www.google. co.uk">Google</a>**

To insert a **graphic link** to another web page, in Dreamweaver, in Design View, insert the graphic, highlight it and enter the full web address of the web page to go to in the **Properties** panel in the **Link** box.

In HTML code, the following creates a link to the web address **http://www.pearsoned.com** from the image **myhouse.jpg** which has been inserted on the web page.

<a href="http://www.pearsoned.com"><img src="myhouse.jpg "></a>

 DID YOU KNOW?

The HTML tag for a link is **<a>...</a>**, which stands for **anchor**. You can think of the page you are linking to as being anchored to the underlined text in the page.

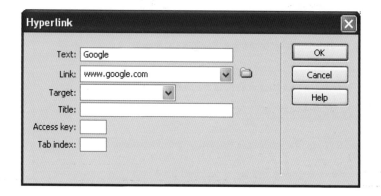

◀ **Figure 8.19**
The Hyperlink dialog box

Links within a page

Links within a page are useful for navigating within large pages. A typical page where links within a page could be used is shown in Figure 8.20. The letters of the alphabet are shown across the top of the page and each of these is a hyperlink to a jump point lower down the page. Lower down the page, there are hyperlinks back to the top of the page.

For example, suppose the page has been saved as **glossary.html**.

The letter **B** is a hyperlink to a jump point called **Bwords** lower down the web page where the words beginning with B start.

<a href="glossary.html#Bwords"> B</a>

Clicking on B navigates to the start of the words beginning with B at the jump point called Bwords, which is marked by the code:

<a name="Bwords"></a>

At the end of the words beginning with B, there will be a hyperlink back to the top of the page:

<a href="glossary.html#Top">Top of Page</a>

At the top of the page is the jump point Top:

<a name="Top" ></a>

▼ **Figure 8.20**
A web page that uses links within a page for navigation

This coding is done for each letter of the alphabet and provides an easy way to navigate within a page.

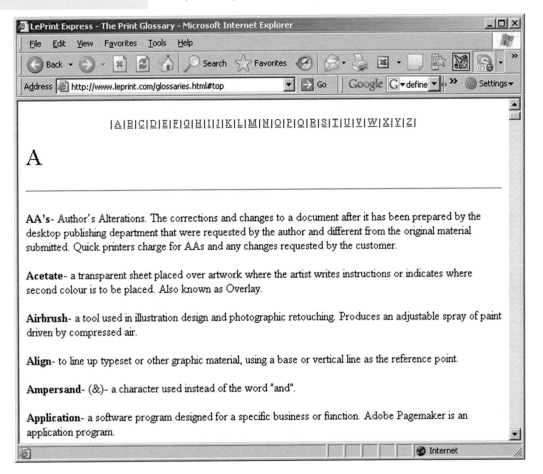

LePrint Express - The Print Glossary - Microsoft Internet Explorer

File   Edit   View   Favorites   Tools   Help

Back   Search   Favorites

Address http://www.leprint.com/glossaries.html#top   Go   Google define   Settings

|A|B|C|D|E|F|G|H|I|J|K|L|M|N|O|P|Q|R|S|T|U|V|W|X|Y|Z|

A

AA's- Author's Alterations. The corrections and changes to a document after it has been prepared by the desktop publishing department that were requested by the author and different from the original material submitted. Quick printers charge for AAs and any changes requested by the customer.

Acetate- a transparent sheet placed over artwork where the artist writes instructions or indicates where second colour is to be placed. Also known as Overlay.

Airbrush- a tool used in illustration design and photographic retouching. Produces an adjustable spray of paint driven by compressed air.

Align- to line up typeset or other graphic material, using a base or vertical line as the reference point.

Ampersand- (&)- a character used instead of the word "and".

Application- a software program designed for a specific business or function. Adobe Pagemaker is an application program.

Internet

E-mail links

In Dreamweaver, to insert a link that loads an e-mail client, in the **Insert** menu select **E-mail Link**. Enter the text to be displayed and the address the e-mail will be sent to. Click on **OK**.

The HTML code for this is, for example:

<a href="mailto:customerservices@pearsoned.com">Contact Customer Services</a>

The text displayed is Contact Customer Services and this opens an e-mail which is automatically addressed to **customerservices@pearsoned.com**.

Thumbnails

Thumbnails are very small versions of a picture that link to a full-sized copy of the same picture. You can display several thumbnails on a web page; the user clicks on a thumbnail if they want to see a bigger copy of the picture.

To do this in DreamWeaver, in the **Insert** menu, select **Image**. Choose the picture file you want to insert. Next select the image in Design View and make it much smaller by resizing it. While the image is selected, right-click and select **Make Link**. Choose the same picture file.

This is the easiest way to create a thumbnail. However, your web page will load faster if you create two copies of the picture file: one should contain a small version of the picture to be used as a thumbnail and the other a larger version for a full-screen display.

Tables

Tables are very useful for controlling the layout of a web page, because the position of blocks of text and images can be easily controlled.

To insert a table, in Dreamweaver, in Design View position the cursor where the table is to be placed. In the **Insert** menu select **Table**. The **Table** dialog box appears (see Figure 8.21). Set the features of the table and click on **OK**. The table outline appears in Design View. Click in a cell and enter text. You can also insert images in a cell.

The features of a table that you can set in the **Table** dialog box in Dreamweaver are as follows:

- **The number of rows.** Enter the number of rows in the **Rows** box.

- **The number of columns.** Enter the number of columns in the **Columns** box.

- **Table width.** This can be a fixed width stated in pixels and your table will always be the same size on screen. It can also be a variable width stated as a percentage of the screen width: 100% would be across the entire screen, whereas 50% would occupy half the screen width.

- **Border thickness.** Enter a number of pixels. If this is set at zero, the border will not be visible.

- **Cell padding.** This is the amount of space between the cell border and the cell content.

DID YOU KNOW?

Some people choose not to use **mailto** links because of the increased risk of receiving spam. Instead, they may choose one of the following techniques to hide their e-mail addresses from spambots:

- using javascript programming code to generate the link when the page is loaded
- using an image instead of text to show the e-mail address
- using a feedback form instead of publicising their e-mail address.

```
<table width="50%"
border="1" cellspacing="2"
cellpadding="3">

  <caption>The table's title</
caption>

  <tr>

    <th
scope="col"> </th>
<!--these are the table header
tags -->

    <th
scope="col"> </th>

  </tr>

  <tr>

    <td> </td>

    <td> </td>

  </tr>
```

 DID YOU KNOW?

The code ** ** means to insert a non-breaking space. This is used as a placeholder in table cells that would otherwise be empty, because older browsers were unreliable when drawing the borders of empty cells.

- **Cell spacing.** This is the amount of space between the cells in a table.
- **The position of the row or column headers.** Select an appropriate graphic.
- **Caption.** This will appear above the table. Enter the title of the table.

If you look in Code View, you will see HTML code similar to that on the left-hand side of this page at the top of the table. The code can be edited to alter the initial values set in the **Table** dialog box.

Cell content can be edited either in Design View, or in Code View by replacing ** ** with meaningful text.

Two columns are shown and this can be edited by changing the number of pairs of **<td>** and **</td>** tags between the **<tr>** and **</tr>** tags.

The number of rows can be edited by changing the number of pairs of **<tr>** and **</tr>** tags.

You can merge adjoining cells on the same row using **Colspan**. The code below is equivalent to two pairs of **<td>** and **</td>** tags. If you want the table to have the same shape then reduce the number of pairs of these tags.

<td colspan="2"> </td>

You can also merge two adjoining cells in the same column using **<th rowspan="2">**.

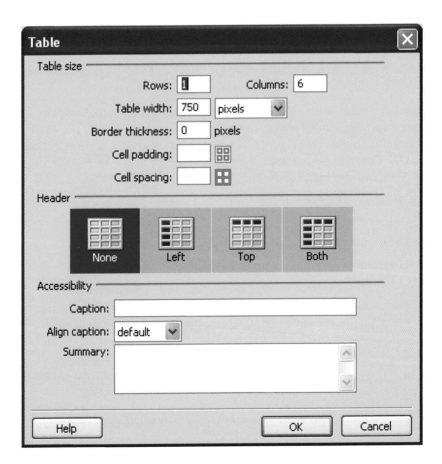

Figure 8.21 ▶
The Table dialog box

Styles

Styles are used to control the appearance of text and can help with consistency. They can be applied to the text in specific heading tags, throughout a web page, or throughout a website.

Inline style declarations

An **inline style declaration** will affect only the text in the tag. For example, to change the colour of the text to red and the background to silver for the second largest heading tag, insert this HTML statement:

<h2 style="color: red; background-color: silver">write your text here</h2>

Embedded style declarations

An **embedded style declaration** will affect all the relevant tags within a web page. However, an inline style declaration will override an embedded style declaration.

For example, to ensure that all second-level headings in a web page are blue, insert this HTML between the **<head>** and **</head>** tags in the header section of an HTML file:

```
<style>
   h2 {color: blue}
</style>
```

You can add more than one style declaration. These are added between the same **<style>** and **</style>** tags.

For example, to ensure that all level-one headings are in the Arial font, green, large, centred and bold, insert this HTML statement between the same **<style>** and **</style>** tags:

h1 {color: green; font-family: arial; text-align: center; font-size: 48pt; font-weight: bold}

Similarly, if you also wanted to set the appearance of the text between all the **<p>** and **</p>** paragraph tags to font Arial, size 12 pixels, background colour red and font colour white, then insert this HTML between the same **<style>** and **</style>** tags.

p {font-family: Arial; font-size: 12px; background-color: red; color: white}

External stylesheets

An **external stylesheet** can be used to create a consistent appearance on several web pages. To do this, set up a stylesheet and link each web page to it. This applies the styles defined in the stylesheet to each linked web page. However, inline or embedded style declarations will override the external stylesheet.

227

Set up an external stylesheet by creating a text file called **style.css**, for example, with these or similar statements in it:

> **h2 {color: red}**
>
> **p {font-family:Arial; font-size: 20; background-color: cyan; color: white}**

Save this file in the same folder as the web pages that will use it.

Every web page in your website will have a consistent style if you link them all to the external stylesheet. You can link a web page to the external stylesheet by inserting this HTML code between its **<head>** and **</head>** tags:

<link rel="stylesheet" type="text/css" href="style.css">

Inheritance rules

The browser first loads the external stylesheet and applies it to the page. Next it applies any embedded style declarations, leaving unchanged external styles that have not been affected by these. The browser finally applies inline style declarations. Again, unchanged styles are not affected.

Uploading a website

You have to copy your website to a web server before it is available over the Internet. Many Internet Service Providers (ISPs) offer hosting on their web servers and the tools to move your website to their web server.

Promoting a website

Because there are so many websites, search engines may not find your website or rate it very highly. You can improve visibility on the web as follows:

- Use meta tags

For example, the following tag provides the short description that is displayed when you point at search results.

<meta name="description" content="Hazel Cottage 2 for holidays in Settle, Yorkshire">

This tag provides keywords so that search engines can relate the web page to a search.

<meta name="keywords" content="Yorkshire, holiday, accommodation, self catering">

- Submit your website to search engines

Submit the address of your website to individual search engines. For example, to submit to Google go to **http://www.google.com/addurl**.

Submit the address of your website to multiple search engines. For example, go to **http://www.addpro.com/submit30.htm**.

DID YOU KNOW?

CSS stands for cascading style sheet.

HINT!

Before uploading, make sure that your home page is named **index.html** and all filenames are in lower case with no spaces and use the **.html** extension.

was much higher just before it was recorded at midday and much lower just before it was recorded at 6.00 a.m. You would get a clearer picture of the temperature in the greenhouse if you sampled it more frequently. In this case, sampling the information every half hour might be satisfactory, as it is unusual for the temperature to change so rapidly that damage would be done to the plants in a greenhouse before the change was sensed.

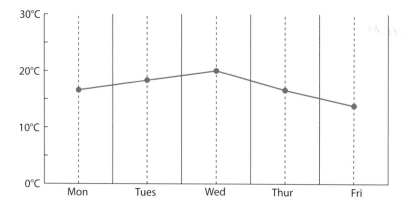

Figure 9.2
What the temperature appears to be if it is only sampled at midday

QUICK QUESTION

- Draw a graph similar to Figure 9.2 that shows what the temperature appears to be if it is only sampled at midnight.
- Consider whether the graph you have drawn gives a more accurate picture of the temperature in the greenhouse throughout the day.
- Decide what frequency of sampling would give the best picture of the temperature in the greenhouse throughout the day.

Cooling curves

One application of data logging is in generating cooling curves (see Figure 9.3). A cooling curve can be produced by placing a temperature sensor in a substance that has been heated. As the substance cools, the computer automatically collects and records its temperature. The time between samples may be very short where the substance is expected to cool very quickly. In contrast, it may be relatively long where the substance is expected to take a long time to cool. Using a computer for data logging means that the time between samples can be easily adjusted to suit the substance being monitored. Once the data has been collected, it can be used to generate cooling curves or analysed in other ways. The computer may be able to display cooling curves for different substances simultaneously so that comparisons can be made.

You may have done experiments in science to create cooling curves. These do not have to be done using a computer but could be done manually with a thermometer. However, a computer would not forget to take measurements and if a substance cooled very slowly or very quickly, a computer could probably take more accurate measurements.

Figure 9.3 ▶
Generating a cooling curve

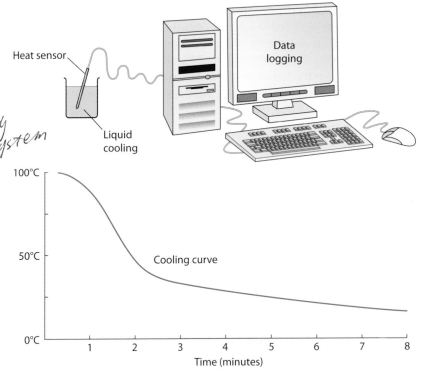

cooling curves
weather station
weather forecasting
dedicated control system
computer control

Science experiments done in school often measure the rate of cooling of substances that cool in the time available in a lesson. If you take measurements manually, you will have to save the data and draw the cooling curve yourself.

Weather stations

Weather stations (see Figure 9.4) are used to collect information about the weather. They may have sensors that measure, for example, the temperature, wind speed, wind direction, whether it is raining, and how much rain has fallen. This information may be collected from a weather station by a computer communicating with it using the telephone network. The computer will automatically collect the information and record it on backing storage. This is an example of data logging. The information collected can be useful in many ways; for example, for weather forecasting.

Local councils may find it useful to have weather stations. These will tell them if the temperature is likely to fall below freezing point so that they know when and where to grit the roads. Using weather stations spread throughout the district helps them save money because grit may not be needed everywhere. Having reliable records of past usage helps them predict future demand.

Local radio stations often provide information to car drivers commuting to work. Weather stations can give them information about driving conditions; for example, whether it is foggy; if there are high winds; whether it is raining or snowing; and if the roads are likely to be icy.

▲ **Figure 9.4**
A roadside weather station

234

Traffic can sometimes avoid these hazards if they are localised. For example, Queensbury is on the top of the hills overlooking Bradford and Halifax in Yorkshire in the UK. It is often very foggy when surrounding areas have good visibility. Some commuters find it convenient to drive through Queensbury on their way to work. However, many would choose to take a different route when it is foggy. The local radio station could use the information from a weather station to find out if it is foggy and let drivers know.

The data provided by a weather station could be collected by a computer communicating with it over the telephone network. The computer could automatically contact a number of weather stations spread over a wide area. It might contact them in rotation, collecting the information as often as possible. Alternatively, it might contact each weather station at particular times each day. The frequency of sampling might be designed so that a good illustration of the weather conditions throughout the day was recorded but data collection by the computer was kept to a minimum. This would provide useful information while keeping costs as low as possible.

If up-to-date information was not needed immediately, details of the current weather conditions could be recorded on backing storage at the weather station. The computer might communicate with the weather station very infrequently, perhaps only once or twice a year. When the weather station and the computer were in contact, the information recorded on backing storage at the weather station would be transmitted to the computer.

Weather stations are simply groups of sensors that provide useful information about the weather. They are only one of many data logging applications where information is collected and recorded automatically from remote, widely dispersed or dangerous locations. Other groupings of sensors can provide information about different environmental conditions. Here are some examples:

- sensors on icebergs can provide scientists with information that helps them understand how they formed and what becomes of them

- sensors underground can record information about earthquakes

- sensors on space vehicles can provide information about the atmospheres on different planets.

Weather forecasting

Weather forecasting tries to predict what the weather conditions will be by measuring and observing the current weather around the world and supplying the data collected to a supercomputer. Weather forecasting on a global scale uses highly developed methods for collecting data, such as the following:

- **Weather balloons at many locations around the world**. The instruments in weather balloons are similar to those in weather stations but are more complex and varied.

- **Satellites orbiting high above the earth.** These allow meteorologists to observe clouds across the entire globe.

Figure 9.5 ▶
The inside of a weather room, with
the computer showing different feeds
from a satellite

A supercomputer uses mathematical models of the atmosphere to make its predictions. Computer models are programs that contain complex mathematical equations and that try to predict what weather conditions will be like, based on historical data. However, even with the fastest computers, meteorologists cannot forecast day-to-day weather for more than about a week ahead. The models used are constantly being improved and new models are developed. Some of these will help to forecast tropical features such as hurricanes. Other models will help to forecast smaller-scale features such as thunderstorms and other outbreaks of severe weather. As these models become more developed, forecasters are able to issue more accurate and timely warnings. In the United States, the National Weather Service's National Center for Environmental Predictions (NCEP) runs computer models of the weather. All weather forecasters in the US rely on these models.

Control systems

Dedicated control systems

Control systems may be dedicated or computer controlled. **Dedicated control systems** are designed specifically for the task to be done and will use electronic components. Dedicated control systems are used in, for example, washing machines, microwave ovens and DVD players.

Figure 9.6 shows a typical dedicated control system used to control traffic lights. This can be built using logic gates embedded in microchips, which are widely available. Traffic lights work in different ways. The system shown relies entirely on inputs from a timer. A timer is another standard electronic component. However, some traffic light control systems may need to respond to the presence or volume of traffic and pedestrians, which would lead to much more complex control systems. Dedicated control systems built into equipment are compact but tend to be inflexible as the physical system is more likely to require rebuilding if the control logic needs to be changed.

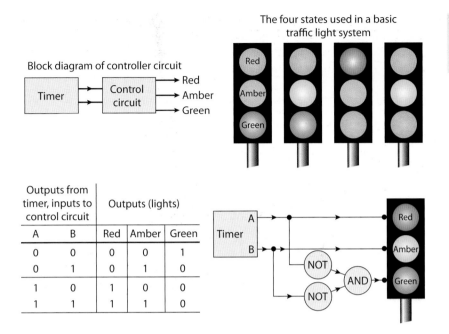

Block diagram of controller circuit

The four states used in a basic traffic light system

◀ **Figure 9.6**
A dedicated control system for traffic lights

Outputs from timer, inputs to control circuit		Outputs (lights)		
A	B	Red	Amber	Green
0	0	0	0	1
0	1	0	1	0
1	0	1	0	0
1	1	1	1	0

Computer control systems

Computers may replace dedicated logic circuits in larger and more complex control applications because they are more flexible.

Here are some important components of computer control systems:

- sensors
- actuators
- a control interface
- feedback loops.

Computer control systems have sensors so that they can measure environmental variables, such as the temperature. The computer will look at the environmental variables and adjust them using a range of actuators. An **actuator** is a hardware device that can perform actions to modify the environment; for example, heaters and motors.

A **control interface** is hardware that provides the interface between the computer and the sensors and actuators of the control system. The control interface translates the signals from the sensors so that the computer can understand them. It also translates the signals from the computer that tell the actuators what to do.

The advantage of a computer control system is that it can be reprogrammed so that the environmental variables and the logic controlling the system can be changed without rebuilding the physical system. For example, at a road junction controlled by traffic lights, you might want to vary the time the lights are on green throughout the day, on different days and for special occasions, such as when the local football match ends. It would be easier to make adjustments if the traffic lights were computer controlled. If all the traffic lights on the same road were connected to same computer, it could coordinate them so that you could drive through all lights, on green, without having to stop. The computer could regulate the speed of the traffic by regulating all the traffic lights. The speed would usually be the same from day to day, but might change occasionally, for example, if there were road works. The computer could easily be reprogrammed to make these changes.

Control logic

You can describe the logic of a control system by writing a paragraph explaining how the system works, by writing a pseudocode procedure or by drawing a flow chart. The example that follows is for a simple control system to heat a room by turning a heater on and off.

A temperature sensor in the room gives information to the computer about the temperature. The computer is programmed to maintain different temperatures at different times of the day. It inputs the information from the temperature sensor and decides if the temperature in the room is at the right level. If the room temperature is too low, the computer turns on the heating. Next, the temperature sensor tells the computer the temperature is higher. When the temperature is at or above the right level, the computer turns off the heating. The feedback loop is a cycle of finding out the room temperature, deciding if it is at the right level and taking action to get the temperature to the right level.

This process can be described in **pseudocode** as follows:

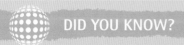

Start

Repeat indefinitely:

       Get the set temperature for this time of day

       Sense the temperature in the room

       If the temperature is too cold then turn on the heater

       If the temperature is just right or too hot then turn off heater

End repeat

End

The logic can also be described using a flow chart (see Figure 9.7).

Figure 9.7 ▶
A flow chart that shows the logic of a simple control system to heat a room

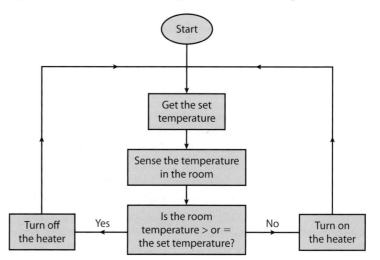

The bit pattern used by the computer to communicate with and control such robots can be very complex. Here is an example:

Bit	Device	Bit setting
10	Waist motor	1=on; 0=off
9	Waist motor	1=clockwise; 0=anticlockwise
8	Shoulder motor	1=on; 0=off
7	Shoulder motor	1=up; 0=down
6	Elbow motor	1=on; 0=off
5	Elbow motor	1=up; 0=down
4	Wrist motor	1=on; 0=off
3	Wrist motor	1=clockwise; 0=anticlockwise
2	Gripper motor	1=on; 0=off
1	Gripper motor	1=in; 0=out

For example, the bit pattern **11 11 11 00 00** would mean that the robot was rotating clockwise at the waist and raising the grippers at the shoulder and elbow. The wrist is not rotating and the grippers are stationary.

Robots with simple control systems that do simple tasks cost less than those with more complex control systems. A simple robot may have a dedicated control system or may be programmed through a key pad built into it; whereas more complex robots may be controlled by a computer. Such robots can be controlled using simple programming languages that are related to the tasks they do. For example, a simple robot may be instructed to pick up an object and raise it to a height of 15 cm by a program much like this:

QUICK QUESTION

Interpret this bit pattern:
00 00 00 10 11.

```
Start
Open grippers
Repeat until object is between grippers
        Down
End repeat
Close grippers until object is held
Up 15
Stop
```

▼ Figure 9.10
A computer-controlled robotic arm

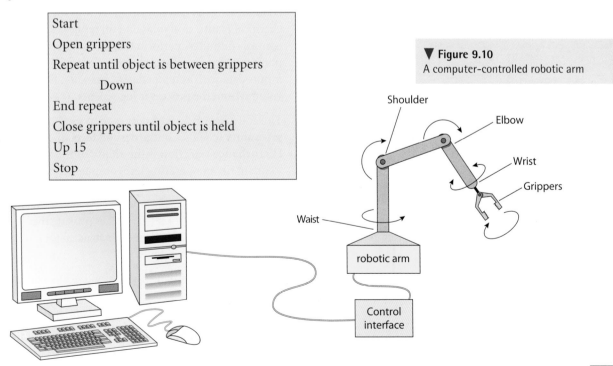

QUICK QUESTION

The pseudocode on the previous page describes how a simple robot could pick up an object and raise it to a height of 15 cm. Write the pseudocode so that the robot then turns through 180 degrees and places the object on a shelf 12 cm above the ground.

Robots can also be programmed to do tasks using a variety of **teach and learn** methods. You can program the robot under the control of the computer one instruction at a time. You watch what the robot does as it performs the instruction. If it is what you want the robot to do, you can save the instruction. If not, you can try again. In this way you can build up a complete program to control the robot. You can also program a robot by physically moving it through the actions you want it to do; the computer converts these actions into a program and saves it.

Computer-controlled robots may not have a feedback system built into them; in this case it is not possible to know exactly what the robot is doing. Such a robot cannot respond to its actual environment and it may be dangerous for humans to work with them. As the robot cannot sense and react to the presence of a person, it may continue doing its task, for example, welding, even when a human is in the way or when there is no panel to weld. More intelligent robots have built in feedback systems that tell the computer what the robot is doing. These help the robot detect and avoid humans and alert them to unusual situations.

If people are asked to do the same task over and over again, they may become bored or fail to concentrate. This could affect the quality of their work. Robots can do repetitive tasks with no loss of quality. They can also operate in dirty, dangerous, hot, radioactive environments where people would find it very difficult to work. However, it is time-consuming to set a robot up to do a particular task. If the task is only going to be done once, it could take longer to set up a robot to do it than to get a human to do the task. People are more flexible and creative than robots and can do a wider range and variety of tasks.

▲ **Figure 9.11**
A computerised control room showing the control board and an operator

Process control

Process control refers to the use of digital computers to monitor external processes closely and take corrective action if necessary, in industrial settings such as chemical plants, steel mills and oil refineries. Process control computers perform two main functions: set-point tracking and disturbance rejection. The computer inputs data such as temperature, pressure, flow and volume from the process using sensors.

The collected or derived data is then used to calculate **set-points** (changes in the desired level of operation). **Disturbance rejection** is the ability of the system to maintain an operating level despite varying conditions. Changes in conditions may be caused by equipment malfunction, unexpected variations in conditions and changes in set-points. If a set-point lies outside the acceptable range, the process computer sends signals to actuators to make adjustments, so that the process remains stable.

Process control systems still require human supervision because unusual or unforeseen developments might not be adequately managed by a computer-controlled system. Even so, there are many advantages:

- Data from the process can be stored and displayed. This is useful if there has been an industrial accident and investigators are trying to and so it is important to design output that can be customised by them. For example, partially sighted people may find it helpful to be able to enlarge the text on the screen, whereas this might not be very useful to people who are deaf.

Encoding data

When data is input to a computer it is often encoded. **Encoding** is using a brief **code** to represent a more detailed and lengthy description. This is something that we do frequently when we communicate. For example, when sending text messages on a mobile phone, words and phrases are often abbreviated. The code 'lol' could be used to mean 'laughing out loud'.

The American Speech-Language-Hearing Association (ASHA) describes on its website at **www.asha.org** how disabled people who find it difficult to communicate encode their language to make communication easier.

Codes can be used to represent lengthy snippets of language. For example:

- '1' could mean 'Can you switch the television on?'
- '2' could mean 'Which channel would you like to watch?'
- '3' could mean 'I'd like to have pasta for dinner'

Computers encode the language we use. You type the letter 'A' on your keyboard but it may be represented as a binary code in ASCII (see Figure 2.10) so that the computer can store and process it. The binary code is decoded before it is displayed for you to read.

Some codes are well known and widely used. Gender can be encoded as 'M' for 'Male' and 'F' for 'Female'. Many people would recognise this without the code being interpreted for them. This encoding is often used on data capture forms as it speeds up input by reducing the number of characters that have to be typed in, and less space is needed to store the information on backing storage. There is very little loss of meaning if this code is used in printed output or on a screen display. If you type 'F' instead of 'Female', you notice immediately how much faster and easier this is. If you had to do this several thousand times this would be a considerable saving of time and effort!

Validation checks on codes are often much easier. You could easily set up a validation check to make sure that only 'F' or 'M' were entered. Similarly, 'Male' and 'Female' could easily be validated if this was being entered in an interactive form on a website. You would most likely find that there would be a drop-down list that would not allow you to choose other alternatives. On a paper-based questionnaire, if you did not code gender, you might get a wide variety of different responses. Some people would write 'boy' or 'girl' and many responses would spelt incorrectly. If these responses were accurately copied from the form when they were input, it would be very difficult for a computer to know what was a reasonable response, particularly where words are misspelt.

Codes are widely used in ICT systems. Another example would be a database for a school library where books are classified as 'fiction', 'non-fiction' or 'reference', and there are other resources such as 'CDs', 'DVDs' and 'magazines' that can be borrowed. Coding these as 'F', 'N', 'R', 'C', 'D' and 'M' would speed up data input, reduce the space needed on backing storage and make output more concise. Library staff would understand these codes because they would use them frequently. There would be some loss of meaning for borrowers and other library users; however, they may not need to use the codes. Validating the codes would be much easier. If you were allowed to type in text rather than a code, some people might enter 'computer magazine' or the name of a magazine, such as 'Autotrader', and there would be many misspellings. It would be much more difficult for a computer to know what was a reasonable response than if it was told to accept one of 'F', 'N', 'R', 'C', 'D' and 'M' and no others.

Sometimes, having to select a code helps clarify what data needs to be entered. For example, in Figure 10.2, when you fill in the tick list this is effectively coding the data. The different ranges of annual income could be entered as '1' meaning 'less than £10,000', '2' meaning '£10,000 to £20,000' and so on. You could find it easier to estimate your income within a given range, and this groups the data for later statistical analysis and also helps preserve your privacy. If you are asked to tick a box instead of entering your annual income in full, this is much easier and faster. Validating these codes would be much easier. A computer could easily be set up to validate a '1', but if you were asked to enter your actual income, setting up a validation check (for example, for '£9,000', '9000', '£9000.00', '£8943.45') would be much more difficult. Less space would be needed to save a '1' on backing storage.

Codes should be meaningful and as brief as possible. They are used because:

- data entry is easier
- data entry is faster
- less space is needed to store the data on backing storage
- setting up validation checks is easier
- privacy can be preserved
- output can be more concise.

Exercise 10.2

1. A newspaper shop prints a list of customers' names and addresses and the amount they owe for papers that have been delivered to their homes.

   This is some of the data:
   Fran Jones of 3 Main Street owes £4.50; Simon Gower who lives at 237 Allerton Road owes £6.72; David Wilson — 78 Poplar Avenue owes £8.50; Manish Patel of 16 Greystones Drive owes £6.90.

If possible, other ICT systems that solve the problem in different ways will be looked at to see if they suggest approaches or features that could be included in the new ICT system.

During analysis, the proposal for the new ICT system is developed in great detail. Where possible the proposed system will be based on existing practice in order to minimise the eventual disruption and retraining of staff when it is introduced.

The proposed design criteria will be clearly stated. **Design criteria** or **task requirements** are statements of the tasks that the new system will carry out. These should include the original objectives of improved performance in the processing and delivery of orders and the accurate charging of customers. However, analysis may have suggested additional features that could be included in the new system and these will be described.

Existing and new data inputs needed to provide improved performance and the additional features are stated. Where possible, measures of success in meeting the design criteria should be stated. For example, orders will be posted to customers within one day of receiving them.

As the new ICT system is being designed for others to use, it is important that those who will use the new system agree with the design criteria. Users are consulted and the design criteria are modified to meet user requirements.

Which user requirements can be developed may be modified by constraints, especially by the availability of time and money. The development of the new system may be affected by the need to have a working system implemented by a deadline, or there may be only a limited amount of money to pay for it. These constraints will affect what can be done.

Design

Design is a detailed description of how the proposed ICT system will work. This could be illustrated using, for example, flow charts (see Figure 11.2), structure diagrams, tables or pseudocode. The processing to be carried out is shown, the data structures and input, output formats are clearly described, and the software and hardware needed are specified. Reasons should be given for the choices made.

First, the **output** required from the system will be specified so that it meets the design criteria and user requirements. In the case of the order processing system this will include:

- Invoices to be posted to customers and sent to the warehouse. An invoice is a printed confirmation of a customer's order, and this is posted to the customer. The invoice lists what the customer has ordered and gives the price of each item and the total cost. A copy of the invoice is sent to the warehouse where it is used to select the items the customer has ordered. The invoice is then sent to the customer with the order. The customer uses the invoice to check that the order

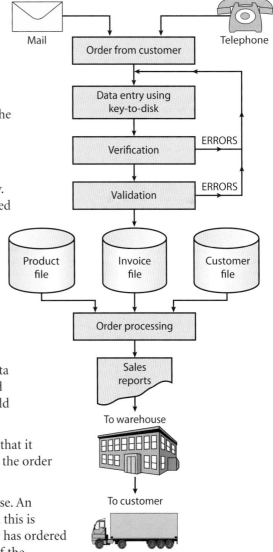

▲ Figure 11.2
An ICT system for order processing

is correct and that the company has delivered everything that was ordered. The company will need to store the information shown on the invoice so that it knows what has been sold and how much is owed by the customer.

- Internal reports and statistics. Management reports and statistical summaries of performance will be needed by senior management to help them improve the performance of the company. The total sales of every item stocked can be summarised using the stored information from each invoice, either for all items stocked or for a selection of items.

The layout of all printed reports and screen displays will be shown in detail. They must be presented in a way which is clear and easy to understand. An example of what each looks like will be drawn in sufficient detail to allow the actual screen display to be produced.

The demand for specific data displays implies a need for the corresponding hardware. The output devices needed could be simply monitor screens and printers but may also be more specialised output devices, such as graph plotters.

Next, the **input** to the system is looked at in greater detail. All the output from the system is produced by processing the input. It is important to be sure at an early stage that all the data needed will be captured. If this is not already the case as part of the existing system then arrangements will have to be made to get the new data that is required. The way in which data is input to the system should be designed so that it helps data preparation staff and others to work quickly and easily. **Data preparation** staff process and input data into the computer; for example, they type in the information written on questionnaires, and make sure the input of OMR forms is done carefully and effectively. The data input is usually recorded on backing storage and processed at a later date. If OMR forms are used, then an OMR reader must be available.

In the case of the order processing system, it is likely that most, but not all, of the input needed for the new system is already being generated by the old one. However, it is possible that a manual system would work without customer numbers if the orders are filed using customers' names. However, an ICT-based system must have customer numbers, to be used as a key field (or **primary key**) on the customer file to identify customers. If the existing order processing system does not use customer numbers, then arrangements will have to be made to generate these. Similarly, in a manual system the invoice containing details of the order can be identified using the date of the order. In the case of two or more orders on the same day, the actual items ordered could be used to identify the invoice. This is easy for a person but cumbersome for an ICT-based system. Consequently, each invoice is given an invoice number which the customer and the order processing department can refer to in case of enquiries about the order. The invoice number is the key field on the invoice file.

The way in which the data is input must also be considered. A working ICT system will use some method of **data capture**. If the data cannot be read directly by the computer it may be collected on a written form and then transferred to a computer-readable medium such as magnetic disk.

During testing, the test data is input and the actual outcome is recorded. This is compared with the expected outcome and, if there are differences, the action that needs to be taken is decided so that the new ICT system will work in the future.

The purpose of testing is to ensure the ICT system is robust and can deal with any input data, either processing it or reporting errors. If the test data causes unexpected output, or crashes the software due to an inability to process the input data, then the system should be amended. The cycle of testing, amending and retesting continues until the whole of the new ICT system works.

Implementation

Implementation is the putting into practice of the proposed ICT system. It includes the following:

- The purchase and installation of any new hardware, software or networks that will be used.
- Converting existing data files for use in the new system, if this is necessary.
- Putting the system into practice using an appropriate means of introducing it. For example, a parallel run.
- Training users to use the ICT system.

Even so, a working system is of little benefit if users are not happy with it. **User acceptance testing** is carried out to make sure that the ICT system works in a way that is easy to use and understandable to users. User acceptance testing can be done by:

- observing users operate the new ICT system
- interviewing users
- sending users a simple questionnaire asking them about their experience of using the system.

When it appears that the system is working, it is put into practice. However, there will still be a possibility that the system will not work as intended. Different methods of system implementation may be used:

- **Direct changeover**. At a specific date and time, the old ICT system is completely abandoned and the new ICT system is put into use. This avoids the confusion that could happen if both the old and the new system are used at the same time. However, if the new ICT system does not work satisfactorily then there is no possibility of using the old system while the new system is amended. This may lead to the new ICT system being in use and working satisfactorily much quicker as the computing staff developing the new ICT system will be under considerable pressure to make it work.
- **Parallel running** (see Figure 11.3). Both the new ICT system and the old system are used at the same time with real input data and the results from the old and the new system checked against each other. If there are differences in the output, the reasons are found and the new system is amended if necessary. When the new system can be relied on to work correctly it 'goes live' and the old system is no longer used. This avoids situations where business processes cannot be carried out: if the new ICT system does not work the old system is used.

- **Phased implementation**. The new system is implemented step by step. Parts of the old system are used until they are replaced by the corresponding part of the new system. The part of the new system is checked against the old, and when it is clear that the part of the new system works, the old part is abandoned. This is done in several steps so that each part of the new system is checked before the corresponding part of the old one is abandoned.

- **Pilot running**. The new ICT system and the old system are run at the same time but the new system only processes a part of the input data. The results from the old and the new system are checked against each other. This method is essentially a live test and could be used with any other method.

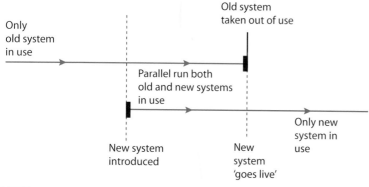

Old system taken out of use

Only old system in use

Parallel run both old and new systems in use

New system introduced

New system 'goes live'

Only new system in use

▲ Figure 11.3
A parallel run

Parallel running, phased implementation and pilot running are attempts to avoid the data loss and system downtime which may happen if there is a direct changeover and the new ICT system, despite thorough testing, cannot handle all the situations encountered when it goes live.

Implementation also involves **training** users to use the new ICT system. There may be changes in practice which staff using the system (for example, the order processing department) have to understand. If the change is from an entirely manual system to an ICT system, staff will need to gain confidence in using ICT.

Implementation can be an extremely complex process and mistakes will occur. It is important that these are seen simply as problems to be overcome rather than the personal faults of particular employees. The implementation of an ICT system demands personal change and adjustment of all employees. This should be recognised in a considerate way if the new system is to be implemented smoothly.

Documentation

Documentation describes how to use the new ICT system and records the details of its design. The purpose of documentation is to provide all the detail needed to understand what the ICT system does and how it does it. User documentation will be useful to those unfamiliar with the system, such as new employees, and technical documentation will be helpful to those who maintain it. Documentation is written throughout the development, testing and implementation of a new ICT system.

User documentation is instructions to users on how to run the ICT system. It could be a printed manual, help within the software or a website. User documentation may include the following:

- Help to get users started using the software.

- An indication of the purpose of the ICT system, a description of what it can do and instructions showing how to do it.

- A description of the hardware and software needed.

- Examples of how different tasks would be done using the ICT system, including descriptions of the inputs and outputs relevant to each task.

- A description of the limitations of the system.

- A list of error messages produced by the ICT system, and a trouble-shooting guide with suggestions on what to do if an error message or some other problem is encountered.

- A list of **frequently asked questions (FAQs)** with answers, so that the problems most users have are dealt with.

- Contact details to get further help.

User documentation is written for users to help them make use of the ICT system. Users should have quick and easy access to user documentation as it is likely to be referred to fairly frequently when the system is in use. Technical problems beyond the ability of users to resolve will be passed on to ICT technical support.

Technical documentation is complete and detailed documentation of the entire ICT system and its component parts, written for technical support. This may include everything that is in user documentation but fully described in depth using, for example, flow charts, tables, sketches, diagrams, pseudocode and source code listings. There is a complete description of the entire ICT system. Technical documentation will also include descriptions of the following:

- How to customise the software.

- Annotated printouts of program code, the related program flow charts; and a list of the names and formats of all variables used in a program.

- System flow charts.

- The data and file structures used and the validation carried out.

- Arrangements for verifying input data.

- Details of all testing carried out and the results of testing.

Technical documentation is written to help ICT technical support run and maintain the system, and it is referred to when necessary. If there is a need to extend the ICT system so that it can do additional tasks, documentation will make it easier to build extra processing capability.

Evaluation

When the system was first thought of it was hoped that it would solve certain difficulties in running the business. In the case of the order processing department, the system was expected to ensure the processing and delivery of the correct order within a stated period and the accurate charging of customers. On implementation, the new ICT system should achieve these objectives and should be efficient and easy to use. However, in due course the same problems could arise again as the volume of orders increases once more.

The purpose of **evaluation** is to check that the new ICT system is effective in doing the job it was designed to do and that it remains effective. Evaluation is against the design criteria or task requirements derived during analysis, and should clearly state whether these have been met, and if not, why not. During the development of the ICT system, useful additions may have been identified but not implemented. Possible future development of the system should be described.

Any ICT system, however well designed and tested, is likely to go wrong at some time. For example, there may be errors due to faulty logic in the design of the system which was not detected during testing, or circumstances may change in ways that were not anticipated. **Monitoring** is the process of detecting such errors and **maintenance** is the process of correcting them so that the system functions correctly. Maintenance of the system may involve changes to any of the components of the system. The technical and user documentation will need to be updated as the system changes.

It is easier to deal with problems if they are anticipated. Instead of waiting for angry customers to draw the attention of management to the breakdown of the system as it becomes overloaded again, constant evaluation of its effectiveness will identify problems before they result in customer dissatisfaction and lost business. If problems are known to exist, they can be avoided by either increasing the effectiveness of the existing system or developing a new system. At some point, all ICT systems become less effective or obsolete and are replaced by new systems. Even reliable, well-designed systems will become obsolete at some time, if only because the hardware and software used is superseded. Very often, users are the first to know that there are difficulties using an ICT system. The same methods that are used for user acceptance testing are often used to evaluate the continuing usefulness of the ICT system.

Exercise 11.1

1. a) Explain what is meant by an **ICT system**.
    b) Explain what is meant by a **manual system**.
    c) Discuss the advantages and disadvantages of using an ICT system rather than a manual system.

2. List the stages of the ICT system life cycle.

3. Match the words in this list to the descriptions:
    - Design criteria
    - Problem identification
    - Testing
    - Implementation
    - Technical documentation
    - User documentation

Description	Words from the list
Typical, extreme and invalid data are used to make sure the ICT system works	
Where you look for instructions on how to get started	
Starting to use a new ICT system which replaces an older manual or computer-based system	
Clear statements of the tasks that the new ICT system will carry out	

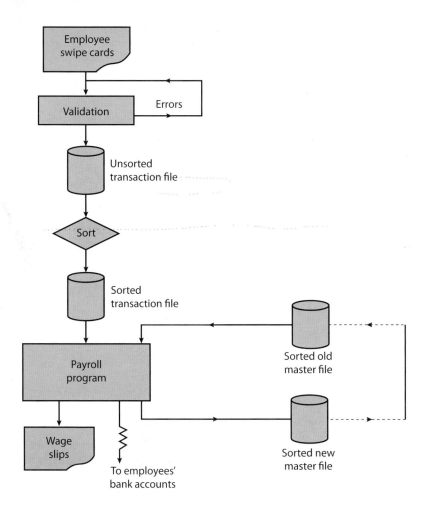

◀ Figure 12.2
An ICT system for payroll processing

Workers are paid a week in arrears; that is, they are paid for the week before the one they have just worked. This means that there is one week in which to process the payroll data.

Validation checks are made on all the data input to the ICT system. Employee numbers can be checked against a table of known employee numbers (table look-up); the clock in time and clock out times can be checked to see if they are in a reasonable range (range check) – for example, between 7.00 hours and 19.00 hours. The clock in time should be less than the clock out time; the hours worked each day should usually not exceed 10 hours; the total hours worked each week should usually be less than 45.

Invalid data must be corrected before further processing but data that has been successfully validated is written to the unsorted transaction file. The **unsorted transaction file** contains only the data saved on it day by day. This is the data about employees that changes daily.

The data that does not change so frequently is saved on the **old master file**. There is one record on the old master file for each employee. The records are sorted and stored in employee number order. A record on the old master file contains the following:

- employee number
- employee name
- address and other contact details

- hourly rate of pay
- details of the tax to be paid
- cumulative totals of the tax paid during the current tax year
- employee's bank account details.

For each employee, the record on the transaction file and the record on the old master file must be quickly matched so that all the data for an employee is available when the payroll program is run. For this reason the unsorted transaction file is next sorted into the same order as the old master file. Both files are sorted into ascending order on the employee number. It is important to have both files in the same order because they are **serial files**; that is, records are read in order from the beginning of the file to the end. More accurately, the sorted transaction file and the old master file are **sequential files** because, in addition to being serial files, the records are stored in order on the key field. If the sorted transaction file and the old master file were not in the same order, matching the corresponding records for an employee would be much slower. For this application, it is likely that serial files will lead to a faster processing time than any other form of file organisation.

Now that the data to be processed has been captured, validated and sorted, it can be input to the payroll program. In the **payroll program** each sorted transaction file record will be matched with the corresponding old master file record. The hours worked will be calculated from the clock in and clock out times on the sorted transaction file. The hourly rate of pay is found on the old master file so that gross pay can be calculated. Tax details on the old master file are used to calculate deductions from the gross pay to arrive at net pay. The cumulative totals on the master file will be **amended** (updated); for example, the tax paid will be added to the total tax paid this year. These cumulative totals change each week so a **new master file** record is created containing the amended totals. The payroll program prints a wage slip to give to each employee so that they have all the information they need about how their pay is calculated (see Figure 12.3), and the payroll program pays each employee directly into their bank account.

DID YOU KNOW?

Gross pay is the amount earned before deductions.
Net pay is the actual amount paid to an employee after deductions.

Figure 12.3 ▶
A wage slip printed by the payroll system

RADIO U.K. LTD. ⍓

Name: A. Jones	Employee number: 86502		Date: 10/07/92
Hours worked: 45	Hourly rate of pay: £3.50		
Gross pay:	£157.50		
Tax:	£26.25	Tax paid this year:	£240.75
National insurance:	£17.40	National insurance paid this year:	£136.14
Net pay:	£113.85		

It will also be necessary to **add** records for new employees to the new master file and **delete** the records of those who have left the company. This is done by adding extra records to the transaction file indicating which records are to be inserted and deleted. These extra records will be prepared by the personnel department and **merged** with (that is, added to) the transaction file before it is sorted. When the payroll program is run, an extra record is added to the new master file for each new employee, and the records of those employees that have left are deleted by not copying them across from the old master file to the new master file.

Backups of files for security purposes can be generated as a consequence of the need to create a new master file each time the payroll program is run. The **ancestral backup system** (see Figure 12.4) normally provides three levels of backup (see below); however, this could be extended to four or more levels.

Son	New master file — will become the old master file the next time the payroll program is run
Father	Old master file — stored securely but accessibly, possibly on site
Grandfather	Previous old master file — stored securely, probably off site

Corresponding copies of the sorted transaction file must also be kept so that if the current files are lost they can be recovered by repeating previous runs of the payroll program. Backup copies of the old master file and the transaction file can be used to restore the current file.

The system described above is a known as a **batch processing** system because the data captured can be divided into batches before processing. It is characteristic of batch processing that all the data to be processed is available before processing begins and that there is no need to process

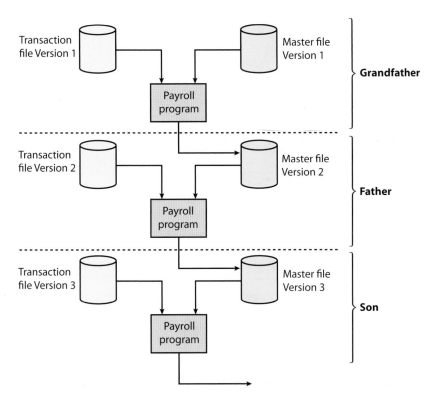

◀ **Figure 12.4**
The ancestral backup system

the data immediately. The system can be run off line; that is, it is not interactive. Once the data has been captured, there is no need for additional input from users while the payroll program is running.

The hardware needed to run the system will include:

- Swipe card readers – to read employees' swipe cards
- Printers – with the capability to print wage slips
- Disk drives – additional disk drives may be required.

Airline booking system

A large airline keeps details of flight schedules and passenger bookings on a **mainframe computer** (see Figure 12.5). Passengers may make enquires at travel agents anywhere in the world at any time to find out if a seat is free on any of the flights operated by the airline. Passengers require immediate up-to-date information. The travel agent can make online contact with the airline's computer via the telephone network using a desktop PC and a broadband connection. This gives the agent and the passenger immediate access to the flight information and booking file stored on hard disk on the airline's mainframe computer.

The airline's mainframe computer should support **multi-access** as there may be a large number of travel agents wanting to make enquiries at

Figure 12.5 ▶
An airline booking system

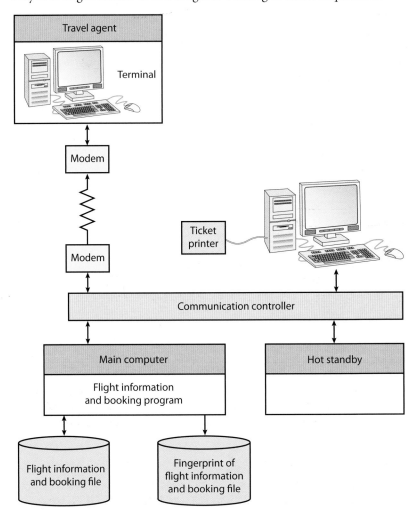

the same time. The flight information and booking file must be held on magnetic disk as data held on disk can be read by direct or random access. **Direct access** (or random access) means that any record on the file can be read without having to read previous records. Consequently, direct access to a record is usually much faster than serial access. Access to the flight information and booking file must be made using direct access for high-speed data retrieval so that the information requested can be displayed instantaneously and kept up to date while displayed on the screen.

The passenger may decide to book a seat on a flight. The travel agent books the seat online (see Figure 12.6). Once a seat has been booked the flight information and booking file must be updated immediately so that further enquiries show the seat as already booked. When the flight information and booking file is being accessed to book a flight, to avoid double booking, all other attempts to book the seat must be locked out. Tickets for booked seats may be printed out on the spot or may be sent to customers at a later date. Payment may be made in cash at the travel agents, online using a credit card, or passengers may be sent the bill by mail some days later. There should also be a facility for cancellation and refund of payments online. Security of access to the system is maintained by giving each travel agent a unique username and password.

▲ **Figure 12.6**
Booking a flight

Since the ICT system needs to be online 24 hours a day, it is very important that the computer is not out of action for any time due to mechanical breakdown. This is avoided by having two identical computers: the main one in use and an additional computer available as a **hot standby** to be used if the main computer breaks down. This helps the airline make its booking system available 24 hours each day.

As the ICT system is in constant use, file **backups** cannot be done in the usual way by copying all the files onto a backup disk at regular intervals; for example, each evening. This would mean halting the flight information and booking program while the backups are done. Instead two disks are used, both having copies of the flight information and booking file on them. Any changes that are made to the file are made on both disks at the same time. This technique is known as **finger printing**. It ensures that if one disk becomes faulty there is an exact copy of the file immediately available on the other disk.

This is a highly specialised ICT system. The computer hardware and software involved are only used for running the airline booking system. Any other data processing required must be done on other ICT systems.

An online booking system such as the one described above is an example of a **real-time** processing system. It is so called because processing is in real time; that is, as data is input it is processed, before any further input can be processed. A real-time ICT system must be fast enough to ensure that input data is processed immediately so that the results can influence any further input. Typically, data can be input to a real-time ICT system at any time, from a variety of sources. Even so, processing must be instantaneous and immediate.

The hardware needed to run the system will include:

- Terminals – networked PCs and dedicated thin client terminals. These will be needed throughout the world in order to access the booking system. Dedicated terminals will be needed in locations where there is a high volume of bookings. Elsewhere, the booking system may run on travel agents' computers as one of many networked applications.

- Mainframe computers – two are needed: one to operate as the main computer and one as a hot standby. These need to be sufficiently fast to handle high volumes of booking requests immediately.

- Disk drives – two are needed: one to store the main flight information and booking file and the other as fingerprint backup. The capacity of these disk drives depends on the volume of data being handled.

- Communication – a specialised computer will act as a communication controller.

Supermarket stock control

A large modern supermarket will have an ICT system similar to that shown in Figure 12.7. At the checkout, the **point of sale (POS)** terminal has a laser scanner which is used to read the bar code printed on items

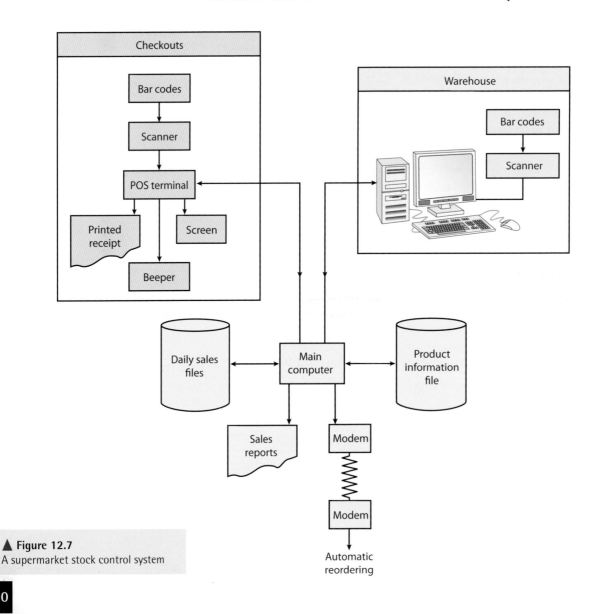

▲ **Figure 12.7**
A supermarket stock control system

sold by the supermarket. The POS terminal also has a keyboard for entering the product details of the few items that do not have bar codes printed on them. A small screen is used to display messages sent from the central computer to the POS terminal, and a small dot matrix printer built into the terminal is used to print receipts for customers.

There will be several checkouts in the supermarket, all connected to the supermarket's main computer located in the store. This computer also has terminals in the warehouse and elsewhere. There are disk drives, a printer and a broadband link to other computers via the telephone network. This is a **general purpose** ICT system and is used for all the data processing done by the supermarket, including payroll; however, we are only going to look at its use for stock control.

Most products sold by the supermarket have on them a bar code. The data held on a bar code identifies the product and includes a product code and a check digit. When an item is sold, the bar code is read by the laser scanner and the data on it is transmitted to the main computer. Here the **check digit** is recalculated from the product code and then checked against the check digit received from the POS terminal. If these are not the same, the bar code must be re-entered. If both check digits are the same, the product code is checked against the product information file. A record on this file contains the following fields for each product:

- Product code, e.g. 152907
- Name of product, e.g. baked beans 570g
- Price.

If the bar code received from the POS terminal is not on the product information file, it may have been entered incorrectly. In this case, the bar code must be re-entered. When it is necessary to re-enter a bar code an error message is displayed on the screen of the POS terminal. If the bar code has been damaged and cannot be read, the checkout operator can type in the number printed under the bar code. The entry of valid bar codes is indicated by a loud beep.

The product code that is input from the bar code is used to find the corresponding record in the product information file. The name of the product and the price contained in this record are sent to the POS terminal from the main computer and these are printed on the customer's receipt.

For every item sold, the price is added to the total for the customer and this is printed on the receipt when all the customer's purchases have been processed. Access to the product information file must be fast enough so that customers are not kept waiting and, in consequence, it must be a direct access file on disk.

The sales made at each checkout are recorded in the daily sales file as the goods are sold. It is sufficient to record the product code and quantity sold. At the end of each day the individual product codes are read from this file, the total quantity of each item sold is calculated and a report printed showing the product code, name of product and the total number of each product sold. An extract from this report follows:

DID YOU KNOW?

It is a very common belief that the bar code contains the name of the product and its price. This is not so. These are kept in the product information file and transferred to the POS terminal when required.

Sales Report Wed 23rd March		
Product code	Name of product	Total number sold
152907	baked beans 570g	500
923673	pea soup 300g	258
025993	peaches 420g	367
300609	pasta 500g	124
007085	tomato puree 50g	356

This information is also used to update the stock control file. The stock control file contains a record for each product with fields as follows:

- Product code, e.g. 152907
- Number in stock, e.g. 1200
- Reorder level, e.g. 1000
- Reorder quantity, e.g. 800.

For each product, the total number sold that day is subtracted from the number in stock, which is updated. In the above example, the total number of baked beans 570g sold on Wed 23rd March is 500. The number in stock is 1200 so the updated number in stock is 1200 less 500, i.e. 700.

The supermarket has to be careful that it does not run out of stock because this will annoy customers and sales and profits will be lost. Periodically a stock report will be printed showing existing stock levels as recorded on the stock control file. Those products that have a lower number in stock than their reorder level will be emphasised in the report. The supermarket manager will go through the report and reorder those products that are needed. If the manager wishes, items can be reordered automatically when the stock control file is updated. For these products, if they have a lower number in stock than their reorder level, the manufacturer is contacted and asked to send more of the product. This is done automatically using e-mail sent by the supermarket's computer to the manufacturer's computer. In the example, 800 (the reorder quantity) baked beans 570g should be reordered because the number in stock (700) has fallen below the reorder level (1000).

When items that have been ordered arrive at the supermarket they are received by the local warehouse. At the warehouse the goods are checked as they arrive and stored until they are moved into the supermarket to be sold. As they arrive, the warehouse manager enters the quantity of each product that is delivered at the terminal in the warehouse. This data is used to update the stock control file. For example, if 800 cans of baked beans 570g are delivered then the number in stock is updated to 700 plus 800, i.e. 1500, bringing the number in stock above the reorder level. Using this system the manager can control the flow of stock into the supermarket in response to sales of stock to customers.

The above description focuses on one basic aspect of a stock control system. In practice, the same system would be used to do a range of additional tasks. For example:

- the number of items sold and the takings at each till could be recorded and used to monitor the performance of checkout operators

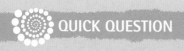

QUICK QUESTION

What other tasks could a stock control system be used for?

- the rate of sales of each product could be calculated and used to increase the choice of popular goods or to reduce stocks of unpopular items
- the pattern of sales of every product could be recorded so that stocks are not held at times of the year when they are unlikely to sell
- the effectiveness of sales promotions (see Figure 12.8) could be monitored
- goods that have high profit margins could be stocked in preference to those with lower profit margins.

To keep business expenses to a minimum, stocks of goods should be kept as low as possible. If a maximum stock level is recorded for each product on the stock control file then the quantity reordered can be adjusted so that this level is not exceeded when new supplies arrive at the warehouse. This maximum stock level can be adjusted so that the extra costs involved in frequent reordering are balanced against the expense of storing larger quantities of a product in the warehouse.

The system can be also be used to determine the extent of theft from the supermarket and improve security. If the actual number of each product in stock is counted and found to be less than the number in stock on the stock control file then this difference is due to loss of stock. Loss of stock can be due to damage or theft. If damages are recorded as they occur then loss due to theft can be calculated. This information can also be used to identify high-risk products so that security can be improved.

▲ **Figure 12.8**
A sales promotion in a supermarket

ICT systems for stock control allow managers to monitor stock levels very closely and to exercise greater control over the business. This allows the manager to increase the profitability of the business and improve customer service. Prices can be kept lower and customer service is quicker due to the speed of the POS terminals. The customer's receipt is itemised and fewer mistakes occur at the checkout. However, the purchase cost of the ICT system is high and it will be necessary to train employees to use it. Because the productivity of checkout employees is increased, there may be a reduced number of employees at the supermarket.

The stock control system described above is an online interactive multiprocessing ICT system. Online systems use checkouts and other terminals connected to a computer. These interact with the ICT system, sending data to it and receiving data from it. A real-time system is an online interactive system but not all such systems are real-time. The stock control system described here is not real time.

In order to print an itemised receipt showing the description and price of every item sold, this data must be found in the product information file, using the product code contained in the bar code input by the laser scanner at the checkout. As a result, interactive processing is necessary as an interchange of data takes place. However, there is no need to immediately update the stock control file at the moment goods are sold. It is quite acceptable for recorded stock levels to be an hour or so out of date as this is unlikely to significantly affect the business. The expense of a specialised real-time system cannot be justified in these circumstances.

Only simple outlines of the payroll, airline booking and supermarket stock control ICT systems have been described above. In reality these ICT systems are much more complex than described. For example, the hardware, networks and data structures will be more extensive than can reasonably be described in this textbook. It is also most likely that, in practice, an ICT system will be a hybrid involving some batch and online interactive processing with links to a real-time system where one is in use. For example, both payroll and stock control could be run by the supermarket on the same mainframe computer.

The hardware needed to run the system will include:

- POS terminals – at every supermarket checkout. These are used to record sales and to collect payment. They are likely to include a bar code scanner, small screen, receipt printer, beeper, smart card reader and arrangements for handling cash.

- Mobile terminals – for use in the warehouse and elsewhere for recording deliveries and stock taking. These will be built to be robust and are likely to incorporate a bar code scanner, touch screen and stylus.

- Communications – an internal network based on the main computer and external access to the Internet for general e-mail, etc. and automatic re-ordering.

- Main computer – this might be a general computer used for a range of applications. Even so, it must have sufficient capacity to handle communications from all the POS terminals and sufficient storage to record details about all the products for sale.

Banking

ICT systems are used throughout banking. Banks use ICT for storing customer information, processing transactions and in almost all aspects of banking operations. This improves the competitiveness and efficiency of the banking industry and provides greater convenience for customers. Many banks also offer home or Internet banking. A customer has to be able to connect to the Internet to use this (see Chapter 7 for more details).

Cheque processing

Every day millions of cheques are written worldwide. This method of payment, though decreasing in use, is still an important way of paying for goods and services.

- An individual or organisation receiving a cheque deposits it at the bank. The amount of money to be paid has already been written on the cheque and this is now typed on the cheque using a **magnetic ink character recognition (MICR)** font.

- If the cheque is presented at the bank where the cheque originated, payment can be received immediately. If both parties have accounts at the same branch, the cheque is cashed and the accounts of both parties are updated.

- However, a cheque originating from a different bank is sent to a central clearing house. The information at the bottom of the cheque is read using a MICR reader and the cheque is sorted according to its bank of origin. Payments between the different banks are made according to the value of cheques received. The cheques are then sent to the originating banks so that customers' accounts can be updated.

Automatic teller machines (ATMs)

ATMs or cashpoints are electronic terminals (see Figure 12.9) that allow routine banking transactions at almost any time. They are situated in the walls of banks, in shopping malls, supermarkets, bus stations and other suitable locations. Most ATMs can be used by customers of any bank to access their accounts and carry out transactions, although a fee may be charged.

ATMs can be used to:

- Withdraw cash
- Make deposits
- Transfer funds between accounts
- Obtain account balances
- Pay bills.

▲ **Figure 12.9**
An ATM

Using an ATM

To use an ATM, a customer must have an **ATM card** issued by a bank. This card stores the customer's account number. Debit and credit cards can be used in ATMs.

- When a customer inserts a card, the ATM reads the information from the card and communicates with a central computer to access the customer's account. The information may be recorded on the card on a magnetic stripe or on a microchip embedded in the card.

- A message appears on the ATM's screen asking for a personal identification number (PIN).

- The customer enters the PIN using the ATM's numeric keypad.

- If the PIN does not match the one stored in the computer's memory, the customer is given several chances to enter the information again. If the correct PIN is still not entered, the ATM keeps the card and the customer cannot carry out any further transactions.

- If a match is made, the customer is asked to select a transaction from a list displayed on the screen. In the case of a withdrawal or transfer of funds, the computer checks the customer's account to determine if sufficient funds are available for the transaction.

- If there are sufficient funds, the account will be updated immediately to reflect the transaction. The customer can be issued with a receipt showing the date, time, amount and type of transaction, and the transaction will be shown on the customer's bank account statement. Otherwise the customer will get a message saying that the transaction has failed.

Electronic Funds Transfer (EFT)

Many supermarkets, gas stations, hotels and other businesses use **electronic funds transfer** (**EFT**) as a means of transacting business. EFT is the movement of funds from one account to another electronically. Typically, funds are transferred from a customer's account to the retailer's account when the customer pays using a debit or credit card. When this occurs at the point of sale or checkout, the process is known as **electronic funds transfer at point of sale** (**EFTPOS**).

The use of **debit and credit cards** and EFT is a step towards the 'cashless society'. Debit and credit cards are issued by banks or by independent companies such as Visa, MasterCard or American Express, and are fast becoming one of the most frequently used methods of payment for goods and services. These cards usually contain a magnetic stripe at the back or a microchip that holds the customer's account number, which is also stored by the bank or the credit card centre.

When a customer pays for goods or services using a debit or credit card, this process takes place:

- The customer gives the merchant the card and this is read by the merchant's EFT machine (see Figure 12.10). The account number stored on the card is input and used to access the customer's bank or credit account.
- The merchant enters the amount of money to be paid.
- The customer enters the PIN used with the card, or signs a receipt.
- If the account has sufficient funds to pay for the transaction (if a debit card is being used), or a sufficiently high credit limit (if a credit card is being used), the money is deducted from the customer's account immediately using EFT and deposited into the merchant's account. The customer is issued with a receipt as proof of the transaction.
- If the customer fails to enter the correct PIN or has insufficient funds, a 'failed transaction' message will be displayed.

Smart cards are predicted to be the means by which most payments will be made in the near future. Smart cards are more technologically advanced versions of debit and credit cards. Whereas debit and credit cards usually have magnetic stripes on them, smart cards have a microchip built into them. While a magnetic stripe can be altered or forged, it is more difficult to tamper with the microchip in a smart card. As a result, smart cards can provide better security. Microchips also have a larger memory capacity than magnetic stripes do. Eventually microchips on smart cards will store biometric data such as voiceprints, fingerprints and retinal scans, and it may be possible to have one card per person rather than the variety of cards which people currently have.

▲ **Figure 12.10**
An EFT machine

Engineering and Manufacturing
Computer-aided design (CAD)

A CAD system uses computer hardware and software in the drawing of engineering or architectural designs. A CAD package is designed to make it easier to produce detailed plans and accurate technical drawings. It contains software that provides a set of standard components and basic elements such as points, lines, circles, shapes and solids, from which CAD drawings can be constructed. CAD programs can produce three-dimensional drawings that can be rotated and viewed on screen from many different angles. In addition, the computer keeps track of design dependencies, so that when a value is changed all other dependent values are automatically changed.

A CAD package can be run on most PCs but a high-resolution graphics monitor is needed to show sufficient detail. The input devices required for a CAD system include a light pen or digitising tablet for drawing. A special printer or plotter is required for printing detailed design specifications on large sheets of paper.

CAD has considerable advantages:

- Designs can be produced faster, reducing cost.
- It is easier to make changes to the original design.
- It is easier to make duplicates.
- Documentation is generated with the design.
- Standard components can be used, which reduces construction time and costs.

There are many types of CAD software that are used to design products, buildings and parts in the automotive, aerospace and consumer electronics industries. They include CATIA® (developed jointly by Dassault Systemes and IBM) which is a general purpose CAD, testing and manufacturing system used in the automobile and aerospace industries; and CADdy® (now owned by the German company DataSolid) which is used in areas such as architecture, electronics, engineering and manufacturing.

Computer-aided manufacture (CAM)

Computer-aided manufacture (CAM) refers to the use of a computer to control manufacturing plant and equipment in a production system. It is used in applications where precision and accuracy are important, including processes such as welding, paint spraying, cutting and polishing (see Figure 12.11).

CAM software generates instructions for the computerised control of machines. These **CNC (Computerised Numerical Control)** machines include computerised lathes for turning and drilling and machines for cutting and polishing large stones for building purposes.

The advantages of CAM include:

- Faster production of parts and products
- Production of a more consistent product
- The ability to better control and maintain the quality of a product
- Production of more complex designs and mouldings.

▲ **Figure 12.11**
Computers are used in the steel industry

CAD/CAM systems

CAD/CAM systems are used to integrate design and manufacturing. Engineers use the system to create product designs, and then to control the manufacturing process. Two CAD/CAM software packages currently available are SolidWorks® and MasterCAM®. They can create drawings, model trajectories (develop and work out the movement) of cutting tools, and develop numeric control programs. They support 3D modelling, sheet metal punching and bending, and plasma and laser cutting.

Computer-aided engineering (CAE)

Computer-aided engineering (CAE) systems analyse engineering designs produced by CAD systems, and simulate a variety of conditions to see if the design actually works. CAE features are found in most CAD packages. One CAD/CAM/CAE package is hyperMILL®.

Education

ICT is widely used in schools, colleges and universities, both to help students learn and for management of the institution.

Many students now learn how to use ICT at school or college, and use ICT to learn about other subjects. Perhaps because of the widespread use of ICT in education, there has been a shift to a more student-centred approach. Some teachers have changed their focus from being dispensers of knowledge to being facilitators of learning. Many teachers now use ICT to support teaching and learning.

The Internet and the Web are invaluable tools for researching and gathering data. Students can search remote databases and the Web, and choose what they need from millions of pages of information. Students can also communicate and collaborate with other students by e-mail or through chat sites.

The Web is a very useful tool for finding information but schools often wish to structure students' learning so that it is more focused. **Virtual learning environments (VLEs)** help students access a range of specific learning resources in school, college, university and at home and in other places where there is web access, and **computer-aided learning (CAL)** software helps students learn specific skills.

Virtual learning environments (VLEs), such as Blackboard (see Figure 12.12) and Moodle, have a range of different functions that help teachers teach and support students with their studies. These are a few examples of what may be done using a VLE:

- **Learning resources can be made easily available** anywhere there is Web access; for example, in class at school and at home. This makes access much easier. Students who are ill can keep up with schoolwork and homework can be done online.

- Students can **study at any time**, at their own pace and for as long as they wish.

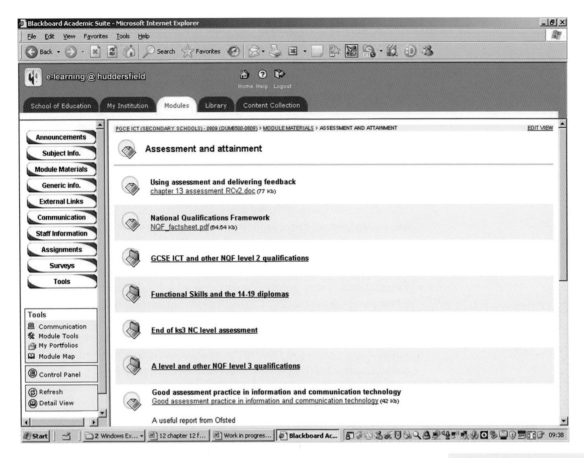

▲ Figure 12.12
A page from the Blackboard VLE

- Students can **break off their studies and return to them** at any time.

- **Learning resources can be well organised** so that students can find worksheets, help sheets, task sheets, homework, simulation programs, and any other materials the teacher makes available to help students.

- Students can have access to **wikis, blogs, podcasts, web links** and **glossaries** that are especially relevant to their studies and they can contribute to them.

- **Digital drop boxes** can be used to store work and to submit it by uploading it.

- Students can find out their **grades** for assessed work as these can be viewed online when the teacher has assessed their work. There is no need to wait until the next class.

- Teachers and students may look at **grade profiles** for the student and the class and see what progress they are making.

- There are online surveys to help students and teachers with their research.

Computer-assisted learning (**CAL**), also known as **computer-aided instruction** (**CAI**), can be generally described as the use of ICT to help students to further their skills, knowledge and understanding of a specific part of a subject. CAL programs are usually designed to develop a very narrow range of skills, knowledge and understanding.

Most CAL programs fall into three categories:

- **Drill and practice.** This type of CAL is used to complement a teacher's instruction – to reinforce old lessons rather than teach new ones. Most drill and practice programs enable individual students to practise skills and knowledge. This has been found to be a useful approach where material has to be memorised, such as when learning vocabulary work. The computer generates questions in a random order chosen from a stored set, and the student is required to answer them. Some programs keep scores and enable the student's progress to be tracked.

- **Tutorials.** These are self-instructional programs designed to introduce and teach new material to students. The computer acts like a tutor and allows students to move at their own pace. Many tutorial programs can assess a student's competence level and adjust the course accordingly. They are very useful for introducing and reviewing new topics.

- **Simulations.** These predict the outcome of a real-life situation by using a computer-based model of the situation. Simulation is one of the most effective CAL tools available for teaching students, since it provides the opportunity to vary situations in order to see different outcomes without any risk to the students or wastage of materials. Simulation packages are available in subject areas like physics, chemistry, biology and geography. Simulation software is sometimes used to prepare learner drivers for their first trip in a car.

CAL has many advantages:

- CAL can provide immediate feedback to students, who are able to tell immediately whether they understand the topics.

- CAL enables students to recognise their own weaknesses, and provides the opportunity to work on strengthening them.

- Most CAL courseware encourages students by displaying a congratulatory message for each correct response. This helps to motivate students to continue studying and move on to more complex material.

- CAL may be embedded in a learning programme accessible using a VLE.

School information management systems (SIMS) are widely used to help with the day-to-day running of schools. They can be used for various purposes: to store students' records, to produce class lists, to register students, to produce reports, to manage book loans from the school library, to construct the school timetable and for many other tasks.

The advantages of SIMS are as follows:

- They support automatic reporting. For example, attendance at school can be tracked and the SIMS can automatically inform parents of the absence of their son or daughter using e-mail, letter or telephone. Similarly, school library systems can automatically inform students that books are overdue.

▲ **Figure 12.13**
Students at work using a CAL package

- Communication with parents can be personalised using, for example, mail merge.
- The quality of communications with parents can be monitored. For example, standard forms and letters can be used, and school reports can be compiled using statement banks which have been vetted for appropriate language and content and accuracy of spelling and grammar.
- Access to information is faster.
- Statistics and accounting information can be generated automatically and quickly.

The disadvantages of SIMS are as follows:

- The data stored on the system must be kept up to date and this can be expensive. For example, office staff are needed to ensure that students' records are accurate. This is essential so that, for example, students' progress can be tracked and accurate progress reports sent to their carers. Another alternative is to allow carers or students to keep their personal information up to date using a web-based system with password protection; however, in this case, the school cannot be sure the information is up to date.

The law
Law enforcement

ICT systems are an important tool for the police and law enforcement officers in their fight against crime. National databases have been set up to hold information such as criminal records, profiles of wanted persons, data on stolen cars, DNA patterns and fingerprints of convicted individuals, and drivers who have had their licences suspended or revoked. These databases, such as the National Crime Information Center (NCIC) in the United States and the Police National Computer (PNC) in the United Kingdom, can be accessed by law enforcement officers throughout the country.

Police and other law enforcement officers also use the computers available in local police departments for a wide range of functions such as the following:

- Preparing reports.
- Tracking the history of telephone calls from a particular address.
- Managing cases.
- Identifying trends and patterns of criminal behaviour, and carrying out statistical analysis.
- Tracking parolees (criminals who have been released before the end of their jail term because of good conduct).
- Posting surveillance photos of wanted criminals and missing persons.
- Developing contacts with other police organisations, including transmitting, exchanging and obtaining information from other police officers in other departments or other countries.

▲ **Figure 12.14**
The control room at a police station

- If a witness sees but cannot identify a criminal, the police can use appropriate software to compose a picture of the alleged criminal, based on the witness's description. This is called *profiling*. This picture can then be compared with one that is stored in the national database.
- A device attached to a computer is used to digitise and store an individual's fingerprint. The computer can then compare it with those stored in national or local databases. If a match is found, the individual's record is then retrieved.
- Holding equipment inventories.

In some countries, police officers can use laptop computers from their patrol cars to make online enquiries about vehicle registrations and drivers' licences from national and local police databases. The laptops are mounted in police cars and there is a wireless network link to a central computer in the police department headquarters. This enables officers to access information quickly, and has been instrumental in many arrests.

More recently, some police forces are using video glasses. A pair of spectacles has a very small video camera or webcam built into them and communicates wirelessly with the local police station. A high proportion of what a police officer sees is videoed and recorded for later use in prosecutions. Also, a police officer dealing with difficult circumstances can be advised by remote experts.

Law firms

Law firms have found that the productivity both of attorneys and of other staff increases with the use of ICT. Tasks such as reviewing case status and deadlines and preparing legal documents can be very time-consuming if ICT is not used.

ICT usage in law firms falls into two main categories: business management and practice management.

In the area of **business management**, ICT can be used for:
- Word processing — typing legal documents and other documents. Detailed templates of legal documents can be set up and quickly adapted for specific clients.
- Data storage and retrieval — storing information about clients.
- Spreadsheets — for accounting purposes such as billing, income and expenses.

Practice management software helps lawyers practise law. It includes:
- Software that offers expertise in a substantive area of law such as bankruptcy, family law or personal injury.
- Software to help with case management and document assembly. This can enable lawyers to find information easily on past cases and judgements to use as precedents in their arguments in cases with which they are currently dealing.
- Legal research websites, such as Westlaw and Quicklaw, help lawyers and law students obtain comprehensive information about case law and legislation from many countries around the world.

Some websites help members of the public prepare their own legal documents. This reduces the cost of legal assistance.

Healthcare and medicine

The use of ICT in healthcare and medicine is becoming more prevalent as ICT systems are developed that help doctors provide better medical care for their patients.

Computerised patient records

Many hospitals and doctors' offices still use paper-based systems for storing patients' medical records. A doctor writes notes (symptoms, diagnosis and drugs prescribed) on a patient's card while attending to the patient, with the card being filed away until the next visit. The same procedure takes place in the hospital. This can be very inefficient and cumbersome. It is not uncommon for hospital clerks to tell patients that their files cannot be found or that information from a file is missing. Manual files only enable doctors in one institution at a time to view patient information. This method of storing patient information may not lead doctors to make the best diagnoses, since they may not have all the information at hand.

To alleviate some of the problems of manual patient files, some institutions in the United States have introduced ICT systems to handle patient records. One such system allows doctors at over 120 different locations simultaneous access to patients' records stored on a central database. Each patient has a card with an ID number, which doctors can use to access a lifetime record that contains the notes from all the doctors and institutions that the patient has attended. This system enables doctors to easily find and send reminder notices to patients who may need follow up treatment. It also gives them a way of comparing methods of treating illnesses and, based on responses from many patients, deciding which is the best method of treatment in a particular case. It can also be used to identify patients taking a particular drug that new research has shown could be dangerous.

Patient monitoring

Patient monitoring systems help doctors treat patients by providing a twenty-four hour service and reducing false alarms. Some surgery patients and very ill patients must be continuously monitored in an intensive care unit. These patients are fitted with sensors connected to a computer, which record vital signs such as blood pressure, heart rate, temperature and blood oxygen levels. If a particular vital sign goes below or above the preset range, an alarm is sounded to alert nurses and doctors. The information obtained during the monitoring can also be stored on hard disk and analysed later.

Magnetic resonance imaging (MRI)

Magnetic resonance imaging (MRI) machines scan the body using very large magnets. A patient on a table is moved into a large magnetic machine, which scans a small area at a time and sends the image (also called a *slice*) to a MRI computer. This reconstructs the image in a two- or three-dimensional form so that it can be viewed.

MRI images are excellent for showing abnormalities of the brain such as strokes, tumours, infections and haemorrhages, and can be used to detect diseases of the neck and spine.

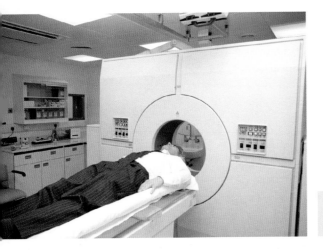

Computer axial tomography (CAT) scanning

The CAT scan machine is basically an X-ray tube that rotates in a circle around the patient, taking as many as 30 pictures in a few seconds as it rotates. The multiple X-ray pictures are reconstructed by a computer in three-dimensional axial slice images. Each slice can then be examined separately. It is very useful in detecting brain tumours.

◀ **Figure 12.15**
A CAT machine

Medical expert systems

An **expert system** or **knowledge-based system** is a program that analyses questions input by a practitioner and provides answers at the level of an expert in a particular field. An expert system is useful in providing support for making decisions and can also 'suggest' alternatives or other issues to be considered. It consists of two parts: the **knowledge base** and the **inference engine**. The knowledge base contains a large volume of information in a particular field — for example, the different types of diseases, symptoms and possible treatments. The inference engine of an expert system analyses the input data using *reasoning* methods and the knowledge base to arrive at a conclusion. It also provides the user with an explanation of how it arrived at its conclusion.

The Quick Medical Reference (QMR) system (available from the Camdat Corporation) is a medical expert system that performs differential diagnosis in many areas of internal medicine. Other examples of expert systems are Mycin and Dendral.

A medical expert system has the following advantages:

- It can indicate the range of possible health problems based on the known symptoms.
- It gives support in making decisions about which a doctor may be doubtful because of a lack of knowledge or lack of experience.
- It can help experts arrive at an accurate solution much faster.
- It can be developed and kept up to date as new discoveries are made and knowledge is advanced.
- It can show the concepts it used to arrive at its conclusions.

A medical expert system has the following disadvantages:

- It lacks judgement and intuition, which are sometimes vital in diagnosis.
- It cannot learn from mistakes.

Telemedicine

Computers and the Internet are being used to allow scarce and expensive human and other medical resources to be shared around the world. Many rural residents in large countries such as the United States and Australia have difficulties in obtaining proper healthcare services because they live in very remote areas where there is a lack of medical facilities. Patients can visit a doctor online and doctors can treat their patients at a distance. Doctors are able to send X-rays to radiologists hundreds of miles away, and transmit video images of patients to specialists for instant consultations. Doctors can match their patients' radiographic information with data in a distant laboratory to help determine diagnosis and treatment.

Besides giving invaluable help to patients, the Internet also allows doctors to search for Internet sites that help them stay informed and involved with healthcare topics.

Libraries

Libraries use ICT systems to keep track of books and other resources they lend to borrowers (see Figure 12.16). Using an ICT system for a library, it may be possible to do these tasks:

- Store and access the personal details of borrowers.
- Store and access a catalogue of books owned by the library.
- Search the catalogue to see if the library has a book in stock.
- Reserve a book either from the library's stock or from another library.
- Keep track of which borrowers have which books. This is usually done by scanning the borrower's identification number on a membership card and the identification number of the book being borrowed.
- Send reminders to borrowers who have not returned books.
- Keep track of fines paid by borrowers.

Such an ICT system is commonly used in school, college and university libraries, public libraries and other types of library. Database software can be used to produce such an ICT system. At its simplest, there are likely to be three tables in a relational database:

▲ **Figure 12.16**
ICT system for a library

Borrowers table	Book catalogue table	Books borrowed table
Borrower identification number	Book identification number	Borrower identification number
Name	Title	Book identification number
Address and other contact details	Author	Date borrowed
Other details	Location	Other details
	Reviews and other details	

The records in the **books borrowed** table are produced by reading the borrower's identification number off the membership card and the identification number of the book as it is borrowed. When the book is returned, it is only necessary to find the record in the **books borrowed** table and delete it, so only the identification number of the book is needed. This is why when you borrow a book you have to take your membership card and the books to the library desk so they can be issued. In contrast, in some libraries, when you return a book, it is possible to put the book into a post box when the library is closed, because your membership card is not needed to identify the record in the books borrowed table and delete it.

1. An ICT system is used to print pay slips and pay workers.
   a) Explain why payroll is a common application.
   b) Explain what is meant by a **transaction file**.
   c) Explain why the transaction file must be sorted into the same order as the new master file.
   d) Describe what is meant by **merging** two or more files.
   e) Describe how backups can be done using the **ancestral backup system**.
   f) Give reasons why payroll files can be serial files.
   g) Describe what is meant by **batch processing**.
   h) Explain why batch processing is appropriate for payroll.

2. An ICT system is used to book airline tickets.
   a) Describe how you could book an airline ticket.
   b) Explain why an ICT system for airline booking should be multi-access.
   c) Describe what is meant by real-time processing.
   d) Explain why real-time processing is appropriate for an airline booking system.
   e) Explain how backups can be done on a real-time ICT system.

3. An ICT system is used for stock control in a supermarket.
   a) List the hardware used at a POS checkout in a supermarket.
   b) State the information input at a supermarket checkout from a bar code.
   c) Describe how the name and price of each item purchased can be printed on an itemised receipt for each customer.
   d) Explain how the ICT system knows when to reorder goods.
   e) Describe the advantages of using an ICT system for stock control.
   f) Describe three other tasks that could be done using the information generated by an ICT system for stock control.

4. a) Describe what is meant by **computer–aided design (CAD)**.
   b) Give two examples of where CAD would be used.
   c) Describe three benefits of using CAD.
   d) Name three peripheral devices that are used with a CAD ICT system.

5. a) Explain what is meant by **computer–aided manufacturing (CAM).**
   b) Describe two benefits of using CAM.
   c) List two industries where CAM systems are used.

6. Banks issue customers with plastic bank cards that have magnetic stripes or microchips on them. These can be used to withdraw cash from an automatic teller machine (ATM).
   a) State one item of information that is stored on the magnetic stripe.

b) Explain how a customer would use a bank card to draw money from an ATM.

c) Explain why a customer has to enter a PIN when withdrawing money from an ATM.

d) Describe how the bank could prevent customers from withdrawing more money than they have in their account.

7. a) Describe what is meant by **electronic funds transfer (EFT)**.
    b) Explain how EFT is used when purchasing goods and services.
    c) Discuss the advantages and disadvantages of smart cards in comparison with magnetic stripe cards.

8. a) Explain what is meant by a **VLE**.
    b) Describe an example of a VLE that you are familiar with.
    c) List two advantages of a VLE for a student.
    d) List two advantages of a VLE for a teacher.
    e) Give two reasons why a teacher may not use a VLE in the classroom.
    f) Describe how the Internet can be used to assist teaching and learning in the classroom.

9. ICT systems are useful tools for law enforcement officers in their fight against crime.
    a) Describe how ICT systems can be used by police officers to fight crime.
    b) Describe how ICT is used by law firms to manage the firm itself and to practise law.

10. ICT systems are used in healthcare and medicine.
    a) Describe the information about patients that would be stored in an ICT system for keeping medical records.
    b) Describe three advantages to doctors of using an ICT system for patients' records.
    c) State three measures you would put in place to prevent unauthorised users from accessing patients' records.
    d) Explain what is meant by a **medical expert system**.
    e) Describe two advantages and two disadvantages to doctors of using a medical expert system.
    f) State three other ways ICT can be used in healthcare and medicine.

The social impact of ICT

The widespread use of ICT systems has had a significant impact on society. As governments, companies and other organisations increasingly introduce and rely on ICT systems, important social issues arise. ICT has had an impact on employment and workers' health. Individual privacy is threatened and computer crime has increased. One response to this is to increase the security surrounding access to ICT systems.

The effects of ICT on employment

Job losses

The introduction of ICT systems has resulted in the loss of jobs in many companies. Heavy job losses in the automobile industry came with the introduction of automated assembly lines when robots were installed to do jobs previously done by humans.

ICT systems for process control have also resulted in the loss of many jobs. Chemical plants and oil refineries use ICT systems to monitor and adjust plant and machinery to control processes. Workers previously did these jobs.

Changes in job skills

With the introduction of computers in the workplace, many workers have had to acquire new skills or upgrade existing ones. A secretary who once used a typewriter now has to become proficient in the use of word processing packages and other applications. Designers and architects are now required to be able to use CAD packages. Even workers in the computer industry have been affected because of the rapid introduction of new technologies which require new skills. Workers in almost every industry at almost every level have to keep up with technological developments or face unemployment.

Job creation

The introduction of ICT systems has directly and indirectly been responsible for many new jobs. Jobs created directly in the ICT industry are in areas such as research, design, manufacturing, sales, training, programming, communications, education and consultancy. Jobs created indirectly include those in the areas of video and CD production, and the production of magazines and books.

Changes in work patterns

ICT has changed the way people do their jobs. For example:

- A journalist can work from home, or sit in a train or on a bus and complete an article using a laptop while on the way to work, instead of having to be at a desk in the newspaper's offices.

- A teacher can have an entire class work on a VLE or CAL software and provide very little input during the session, although considerably more planning and preparation may be needed prior to the lesson.

- A police officer can access information on criminals and stolen vehicles from a police car, instead of having to go back to the police station to do this.

- Workers can telecommute (see below) instead of having travel to work every day.

Telecommuting

Many office workers spend much of their time at the office using ICT. However, computers are relatively cheap and can be found in many homes, so that instead of going to the office, many workers now work at home some or all of the time, and communicate with the office using a network such as the Internet. This is called **telecommuting** (see Figure 12.17). Many companies use this method of employment, and there are many benefits for the worker and for the company.

Advantages for workers include:

- Reduced stress – no need to drive long distances to work or get up early to avoid congestion on the way to work
- The time that would have been spent on commuting can be spent working or relaxing
- Reduced expenses for travel and clothing
- Flexibility – you can work at your own convenience
- Working in the comfort of your own home
- Supervising a babysitter and working at the same time.

Disadvantages for workers include:

- Distractions from family members, neighbours and household chores
- Lack of social interaction with other workers
- Lack of access to specialist facilities and advice that may only be available at the office
- A feeling that you might be overlooked for promotion.

Advantages for the company include:

- A perk to attract and retain good workers
- The ability to employ workers who live a long way away, perhaps in another country
- Reduced sick leave – many telecommuters continue to work despite illnesses such as colds
- Increased productivity – employees are more relaxed at home and therefore work more effectively
- No stoppage of work because of floods or snowstorms
- Less expensive overheads in areas such as the purchase or rental of floor space and equipment.

Disadvantages for the company include:

- Management of the task rather than the worker may be more complex and time-consuming
- Managers may feel they do not have sufficient control over what workers are doing during working hours
- Workers may not be available when the company tries to contact them.

▲ **Figure 12.17**
An employee telecommuting

Effects on employees' health

As employees spend more time at work using ICT, there is a greater likelihood that this will affect their health. This has some associated health risks:

- Repetitive strain injury (RSI) to the hands and arms. RSI is a painful condition that occurs because of damage to tendons, nerves, muscles and soft body tissue, and can be caused by the repetitive use of keyboards and a mouse. It can be avoided and its effects reduced by taking regular breaks, using specially adapted keyboards and using wrist supports (see Figure 12.18).

- Eye problems such as soreness, lack of focus and eye dryness can arise from staring at a monitor all day. Potential problems can be avoided by taking regular breaks, having regular eye examinations by an optician and using antistatic and other screen filters. Using a larger screen can also help.

- Backache and similar problems can arise through sitting in an inappropriate posture for long periods of time. The solution is to use a purpose-designed operator's chair and a footrest, and to take regular breaks.

- Other complaints that can be caused by the prolonged use of computers include fatigue and headaches. Again, part of the solution is to take regular breaks.

▲ **Figure 12.18**
A wrist support can help to prevent RSI

Privacy

Many businesses, organisations and governments hold personal information about individuals. This personal information is stored on ICT systems, and could be easily copied and transferred around the world across international networks from one organisation to another. Different countries have different laws and so the ways in which personal data can be legally processed will vary around the world. These developments raise questions about how to ensure the individual's right to privacy. **Privacy** refers to the right of individuals to determine what information is stored about them and how that information will be used.

In the United Kingdom, the **Data Protection Acts** (**1984** and **1998**) set out principles to make sure that personal information is handled appropriately. Organisations in the UK that store personal information must, by law, keep to these principles. These principles include:

- data must be fairly and lawfully processed
- data must be used only for its intended purpose
- the data collected must be adequate for its intended purpose, relevant to it and should not be excessive
- the accuracy of the data must be maintained — it must be kept up to date and complete
- the data must not be kept for longer than is necessary
- the data must be processed in line with your rights — for example, unauthorised people should not be given access to it

- the data must be stored securely and protected from unauthorised access and use
- personal data must not be transferred to countries that do not have similar rules to protect personal privacy.

Many other countries have recognised the need for such legislation.

Computer crime

Computer crime — that is, crime that is only possible because of the widespread use of ICT systems and networks — has increased in variety and extent. In this section, some computer crimes are briefly described.

Software piracy

Software piracy is the unauthorised copying, using or selling of software without an appropriate licence. It includes copying CDs with software or music on them, and downloading software or music without paying for it. These activities are effectively software theft.

Copyright violation

Using the Web you can download music, pictures, animated graphics, videos and books, as well as software. The copyright to some of this material is restricted to its owners. They may sell you the right to copy it, but if you copy it without permission this is effectively theft. The profitability of the music industry has been badly affected by music being freely copied and downloaded over the Web.

DID YOU KNOW?

After a number of years, copyright expires and anyone is free to copy the work.

Hacking

Hacking means gaining unauthorised access to an ICT system, and an individual who does this is referred to as a **hacker**. Many hackers break into ICT systems just for the challenge or as a prank. This might seem harmless, but it can cause considerable damage and is illegal in many countries.

The reasons why criminally minded hackers gain unauthorised access to ICT systems include:

- To steal data — this may have a security classification or could be commercially sensitive.
- To alter data or destroy data, by deletion or by installing a virus to destroy or corrupt it. This may be done in order to disrupt legitimate commercial or governmental activities.
- To steal money by transferring it from one account to another using EFT.

Hackers who break into ICT systems across external networks are relatively rare. Most fraud carried out using ICT occurs when a person within an organisation makes changes to information in a computer without authorisation, for personal benefits or for malicious reasons. For example, someone working in a company and who has access to payroll files, changes details on these to increase his or her salary, or when bank employees make fraudulent changes to bank accounts.

Identity theft

When you are connected to the Web, **spyware** may be installed on your computer without your knowledge. This could send information about your computer to others who may have malicious intent. For example, they may want to know when your computer is online so they can use it to send spam without your knowledge, or they might collect information about you and your online bank accounts so that they can steal your identity, pretend to be you and steal your money or buy goods in your name. Such **identity theft** is an increasing problem.

Anti-spyware software, such as *Spybot – Search & Destroy*, can be used to remove spyware but information about you may not only be stolen when you are online. Thieves sometimes collect addressed envelopes, bank statements and credit card receipts in household rubbish and, consequently, it is advisable to shred these. The information on them can be used to commit thefts online.

Figure 12.19 ▲
Shred anything with your address on before putting it in the rubbish.

Phishing

A **phishing** attack is when you receive an unsolicited e-mail inviting you to a response which involves you entering your username, password and other personal details. For example, a phishing e-mail may direct you to a website for online shopping. This might be a website criminals have set up for a bogus company. Users can view items on this website that are apparently on sale. In order to pay for goods being purchased, the customer fills in a form with information such as name, address, telephone number, e-mail address and the item number and quantity desired. The customer then enters a credit card number and other details to pay for the item. Internet fraud occurs when the bogus company bills the unsuspecting customer for the purchase, collects the money and does not deliver the items purchased. More seriously, the bogus company may have been set up to lure individuals into giving their credit card numbers in order to steal even more of their money.

A variety of this scam is when you receive an e-mail which appears to be from your bank asking you to access a particular website and to enter your bank account details so that the bank can confirm that these are correct. When you do this, the criminals operating the scam will steal money from your bank account. To help avoid this type of scam, do not access your bank's website using the link in the e-mail. Always open your browser and access your bank's website independently. This breaks the link with the fraudulent website.

The Nigerian scam

You receive an e-mail which looks something like Figure 12.20. The senders of this e-mail, who may or may not be Nigerian, are making you think that you are going to scam the Nigerian Government when in fact they are going to scam you. They hope you will be so interested in earning US$4 million that you fail to notice that this is a scam. If you give them your bank account details, they will transfer money out of it. If you meet them in Lagos, there will be a delay, and then a requirement that you pay additional money to clear up the delay, and then another delay and more money, and so on until your money is exhausted, or you give up and leave.

FROM: Mr. Ben Ahore
Central Bank of Nigeria
Lagos, Nigeria

Dear Sir:

I have been requested by the Nigerian National Petroleum Company to contact you for assistance in resolving a matter. The Nigerian National Petroleum Company has recently concluded a large number of contracts for oil exploration in the sub-Sahara region. The contracts have immediately produced moneys of US$40,000,000. The Nigerian National Petroleum Company is desirous of oil exploration in other parts of the world; however, because of certain regulations of the Nigerian Government, it is unable to move these funds to another region.

You assistance is requested as a non-Nigerian citizen to assist the Nigerian National Petroleum Company in moving these funds out of Nigeria. If the funds can be transferred to your name, in your United States account, then you can forward the funds as directed by the Nigerian National Petroleum Company. In exchange for your services, the Nigerian National Petroleum Company would agree to allow you to retain 10%, or US$4 million of this amount.

However, to be a legitimate transferee of these moneys according to Nigerian law, you must presently be a depositor of at least US$100,000 in a Nigerian bank which is regulated by the Central Bank of Nigeria.

If it will be possible for you to assist us, we would be most grateful. We suggest that you meet with us in person in Lagos, and that during your visit I introduce you to the representatives of the Nigerian National Petroleum Company, as well as with certain officials of the Central Bank of Nigeria. If this is not possible, could you send me details of your US bank account so an account can be set up for you at the Nigerian National Bank.

Please call me at your earliest convenience at [Phone Number]. Time is of the essence in this matter; very quickly the Nigerian Government will realize that the Central Bank is maintaining this amount on deposit, and attempt to levy certain depository taxes on it.

Yours truly, etc.

Ben Ahore

▲ **Figure 12.20**
A Nigerian scam e-mail

Security

Security is important in ensuring privacy, data integrity and preventing computer crime. Such crime would not exist if ICT systems were not used and could not be exploited for financial gain. Security precautions are needed to prevent physical access and access via software and networks.

Physical safeguards

Physical safeguards deal with the protection of hardware and software from accidental or malicious damage or destruction. For example:

- **Access control** to ICT rooms using locks that are opened using entry codes, swipe cards, or biometrics such as fingerprints and retinal scans. Security guards can ensure that those entering using entry codes and swipe cards are actually those who are allowed entry.
- **Access monitoring** using CCTV cameras so that those entering and leaving ICT rooms can be recorded.

- **Data security** can be ensured by taking regular backups and storing these in a fireproof safe in another location.

- **Protect hardware from fire, floods, theft and malicious damage** by locating it in buildings and areas where such problems can be reduced. For example, in a concrete underground bunker on top of a hill that is accessible only through a well guarded and narrow passage. Or more usually, not on the ground floor of a building where hardware is accessible to thieves.

- Further precautions to **protect hardware from theft** involve clamping individual computers to desks or securing them to walls; installing burglar alarms attached to individual computers in addition to those already used for the building; and using CCTV cameras in ICT rooms to discourage inappropriate use of computer equipment and to allow any such use to be traced and the culprits identified.

- Make detailed **contingency plans** and **disaster recovery** arrangements so that ICT systems continue operating with a minimum of disruption and recovery is swift. For example, make arrangements with an organisation with similar ICT facilities that is located at a distance so that their ICT facilities can be used should your own be destroyed.

Software safeguards

Software safeguards can protect data from theft or damage by hackers and other unauthorised persons accessing the software to steal or damage it. For example:

- Use of ICT systems and networks is restricted to those who have valid **usernames and passwords**.

- **Access permissions** that allow access to the data to the minimum number of people who need it. Others are blocked from accessing the data.

- **File-level passwords** that restrict access to individual files to those who have appropriate access permissions and passwords.

- Use a **virus scanner** to prevent viruses entering the system. The intention of some viruses is to damage software recorded on the ICT system or steal it by copying it and e-mailing it to unauthorised persons.

- Use a **firewall**. This is a program or hardware device or combination of both that filters the information coming through the Internet connection into a computer or network, to prevent unauthorised users from gaining access. Some firewalls also block cookies, pop-up adverts and spam (electronic junk mail). Popular firewall software packages are BlackICE Defender, ZoneAlarm and Freedom.

- Establish **transaction logs** to automatically track alterations to ICT systems, including the identity of those who access data and all the changes made.

- **Data encryption** is used so that if data is access by unauthorised persons it cannot be understood. Encrypted data is scrambled during storage and transmission so that it cannot be understood by someone without the encryption key to unscramble it.

▲ **Figure 12.21**
Logging on to a networked computer

Paper 1

Paper 1 is a written examination which is 2 hours in length and there is no choice of questions. Questions mainly require a short response — that is, a word, phrase or one or two sentences – although there will be some questions where you will be asked to write more extended answers. You will not be asked to write long essays. There will be space below each question for you to write your answer and the marks that can be awarded for each question are printed on the examination paper.

Paper 1 tests Assessment Objective AO2 and sections 1–8 of the curriculum content and you are advised to download the syllabus and read these. Sections 1–8 of the curriculum content covers:

1. types and components of computer systems

2. input and output devices

3. storage devices and media

4. computer networks

5. data types

6. the effects of using ICT

7. the ways in which ICT is used

8. systems analysis and design

Paper 2

Paper 2 is a practical test which is 2 hours and 30 minutes long and assesses Sections 9–16 of the curriculum content which cover:

9. communication

10. document production

11. data manipulation

12. integration

13. output data

14. data analysis

15. website authoring

16. presentation authoring

Paper 3

Paper 3 is also a practical test which is 2 hours and 30 minutes long and it also assesses Sections 9–16 of the curriculum content.

Papers 2 and 3 will require you to carry out a range of practical tasks rather than explain the theory of how the tasks can be completed. You can use any hardware, operating system or application software to do the tasks but you need to check that these will allow you to show that you have all the skills described in sections 9–16 of the syllabus. You will be asked to print out your work so that it can be submitted for assessment.

Preparing for assessment
During your course

Why is achieving a good grade important to you? If you know why you need a good grade you may work harder and do better. Students often find ICT interesting and enjoyable, and it may be a useful preparation for work or further study. Many jobs in ICT are well paid, and knowledge of ICT will help you in your studies in other subjects. Convince yourself it is important to succeed. Always do your best work. If you have a clear idea of why you are studying ICT you may find it easier to put in the effort required to do well. If you are well motivated you are already on the road to success. However, to do well, you also need to pay careful attention to preparing yourself for the assessments.

The purpose of assessment is to test your knowledge and understanding. If you do not know your subject then you cannot expect to do well. Preparation for the examination begins on the first day of the course.

- Try not to miss lessons. If you do, catch up with the work quickly.

- Keep all the notes you write and the work you do.

- Do all your homework to your best standard.

- Learn your work as you progress. If you have any spare time, go back over the course and revise the work. Make sure you understand all the work you do.

- Use the library to look up topics you are unsure of.

- If you have problems, ask your teacher.

You can enrich your knowledge and understanding in a variety of ways:

- Discuss your work with a friend who is doing the same course.

- Read computer magazines.

- Go to local shops that sell computers and ask the sales staff about the computers they sell.

- Go on trips to computer exhibitions.

- Talk to someone who works with ICT systems and ask them about their job.

- Arrange a visit to an office or factory where ICT systems are used.

- Get your own computer and learn to use it.

- Use the Web for research and keep notes about what you discover.

Revision

Start revising in good time and plan your revision carefully. Try to allocate set times each week when you will revise for Cambridge IGCSE ICT. Make sure you allow time to revise all the subjects you are taking, and build in periods for rest and relaxation. Expect to work very hard in the weeks leading up to your IGCSE papers but leave some time to enjoy yourself. Overwork and worry can be as bad as not doing anything.

When you are revising, this is the time to make sure you have learnt all you need to know. Read the Cambridge IGCSE ICT syllabus, and be clear about what you have to learn. Make a list of all the topics you should cover.

A useful revision technique is to repeatedly *revise, condense and learn.* Read through your notes and all the work you have done and, as you revise your knowledge, take a brief note of all the topics. These brief notes should cover all the important points in enough detail to refresh your memory of them at a later date. Try to learn these brief notes. If there is still too much material to learn, then condense these brief notes yet again. You should end up with condensed notes which summarise the whole course. These can be learnt and revised frequently. You can carry them with you and revise on the bus, in the queue for the cinema, or when taking the dog for a walk!

Practise for the papers by doing questions of the kind you will meet in them. You can download specimen papers with answers and a mark scheme from the CIE website. Work through them carefully. Your teacher may give you a 'mock' examination and may have papers from previous years that you can practise on. Check your answers to these practice papers and, if you have made a mistake, make sure that you understand why you have made it. It is likely that similar questions will appear on the papers you will take. You can find out what examiners are looking for when they mark your work by checking your answers against the mark scheme.

Revise those topics where you have weaknesses again. You can make extra notes on them if you need to. Do more practice questions in these topic areas until you are confident you understand what is required. You could identify those topics you understand, and answer questions on these in the examination papers. Perhaps you will be able to avoid questions on topics you are not so familiar with.

Try to complete some of the specimen papers under examination conditions in the time allowed for them. This will give you some idea of how fast you will have to work in the actual papers. If you find you are short of time, plan ahead and use your time effectively.

Before the examinations

However much you know, you will perform better if you are wide awake, healthy and relaxed. Look after yourself! You are likely to do your best work if you are alert. Alertness depends on good health, plenty of sleep and a calm determination to do well.

- Make sure you get plenty of sleep in the days before the examination. Go to bed reasonably early and you will be more alert and cope with the examination much better.

- You are also likely to perform better if you are fit and healthy. A bad cold, hay fever, headaches, broken bones, sprained ankles and other maladies can distract you from your work in the examination. The best remedy is to avoid accidents and situations that could make you ill. For example, the day before the examination may not be the right time to go horse riding, skiing, sky diving, bungee jumping or motor cycle racing! If you have unavoidable medical problems, your doctor may be able to help.

- Many people find that examinations make them nervous. They get so nervous they make silly mistakes and are unable to do their best. Most people are affected by examination nerves to some extent. Being too nervous will probably have a bad effect on your work. On the other hand, some people are so relaxed they do sloppy, careless work. Being too relaxed is as inappropriate as being too nervous. Make sure you are keen to do well but keep calm.

The day of the examinations

- Pack your bag the night before the examination, and make sure you have any equipment you will need in the examination. You may require a pencil, a pencil sharpener, a rubber, a ruler and at least two pens, in case one runs out. A calculator might be useful. This equipment is essential for accurate, written communication. If you have to borrow a pen, for example, it may not suit you or it may not work properly and consequently you may work at a slower pace. It is possible that equipment may not be available to borrow and you will have to manage without it.

- Make sure you get up in time. You will need plenty of time to have breakfast and get to the examination centre early.

- Make sure you go to the lavatory just before the examination. You could waste five or ten minutes of valuable examination time if you have to go during the examination!

- Always arrive on time for an examination. If you are late it is very unlikely that you will be allowed extra time.

Examination techniques

Examination techniques are common-sense methods to help you communicate what you know more effectively. They are not magic, and using examination techniques will not make up for ignorance or lack of thorough preparation.

- Start work as soon as you are allowed to.

- Read the instructions at the start of the examination very carefully, and do what you are asked.

- In any examination, you should first make sure you know which questions you are expected to answer. Doing extra questions will not earn extra marks but if you leave questions out you will lose marks.

- Next, work out how much time you can spend on each question. It is often useful to work out how much time you can devote to each mark. This is the number of minutes per mark. You can use this to work out how long can be spent on questions that may not be worth the same amount of marks. For example, in a two-hour paper you have 120 minutes to earn perhaps 60 marks. This is 2 minutes per mark. This means that you can spend 4 minutes on a question worth 2 marks, and 12 minutes on a question worth 6 marks. Having worked out the time you can spend on a question, try to stick to it.

- Attempt all the questions you are expected to answer. This is very important. The first part of each question is often the easiest to answer and the first few marks on any question are often the easiest to obtain. You cannot be given marks for questions you haven't answered. Higher marks will almost certainly be given for correct answers to part of all the required questions than for complete answers to a very few questions.

- Make sure you read the question thoroughly. Many students lose marks because they read the question in a hurry and do not fully grasp what it means. They then answer the question they think they have read. This means their answer may not relate to the actual question. You will only be awarded marks for a correct answer to the actual question set. Read questions slowly and carefully.

- You should always give as much detail as possible in the space provided.

- If you give answers such as 'quicker', 'easier', 'cheaper' or 'more efficient', you are unlikely to be given marks unless you clearly say, for example, what is quicker or why it is quicker.

- You will only be given credit for relevant answers. For example, if the question asks you to give advantages to a customer, then you will only be awarded marks if the advantages are to the customer rather than to some other person or organisation. If you are asked to state what the letters DTP stand for then you will only be awarded marks for the answer 'Desk Top Publishing'.

- If you are asked to describe the difference between two methods (for example, inputting data using a keyboard and an Optical Mark Reader), to be awarded a mark you should make a clear statement for each method. For example, 'inputting data by typing it on a keyboard takes much longer than reading an OMR form that has been filled in correctly'.

- If necessary, give examples and draw diagrams to illustrate your answers. It is helpful to label diagrams so the examiner knows what you are illustrating. Communicate clearly and in full.

- If there are two marks for a question, you should make two separate points.

- If it is difficult to read your answers, you will probably lose marks. Handwriting should be neat and easy to read.

- Pay attention to your spelling, punctuation and grammar. If your answers cannot be understood by the examiner, you will not be awarded marks. Ensure you know how to spell the technical words used in ICT.

- Never leave an examination before the end. Spend all the time allowed to you to do the examination answering questions or checking your answers. Make sure that what you can do is correct and make a determined attempt at the more difficult questions. Marks are always given for correct answers but it is not often that marks are deducted if you are wrong. An important exception to this is in multiple choice questions where marks will be deducted if you select too many options.

Paper 1

- Paper 1 is 2 hours in length.
- Answer all questions.
- In the examination, you would write your answers on the paper in the space below each question.
- You should use a blue or black pen to write your answers, and use a pencil for diagrams.
- Do not use highlighters, correction fluid, paperclips, glue or staples.
- The marks that can be awarded are printed on the paper in brackets at the end of each question or part question.
- In total, there are 100 marks.

1. Name the devices using words from the list.

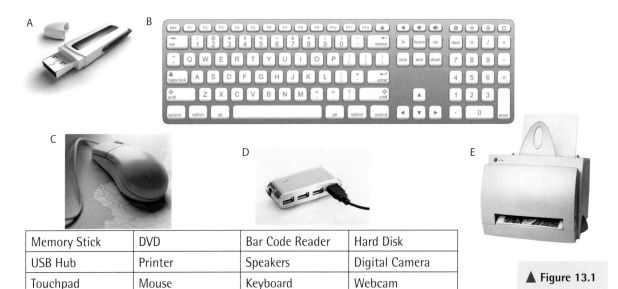

Memory Stick	DVD	Bar Code Reader	Hard Disk
USB Hub	Printer	Speakers	Digital Camera
Touchpad	Mouse	Keyboard	Webcam

▲ Figure 13.1

A ....

B ....

C ....

D ....

E ....

2. Tick **true** or **false** next to each of these statements.

	True	False
A word processor can be used to produce a business letter		
A search engine is usually used to monitor the environment in a computer-controlled greenhouse		
A spreadsheet can be used by a plumber to produce an estimate of the cost of fitting a new bathroom		
MICR (Magnetic Ink Character Recognition) is used to read the information on a bank cheque		
An operating system must not be running when a computer is being used		

3. Describe **three** features of spreadsheet.

    Feature 1 ....

    Feature 2 ....

    Feature 3 ....

4. Ring **three** items which are used to store computer files.

Speakers	Printer	DVD
Memory stick	Hard disk	Keyboard

5. Complete each sentence using **one** item from the list.

    - Keyboard
    - Bar code
    - DVD
    - Laser printer
    - Microchip
    - Monitor
    - Headphone
    - Magnetic tape
    - Pencil

    a) Animated output can be shown on a ....

    b) The identity number of a tin of beans is stored on the tin on a ....

    c) Bank account details are stored on a debit card on the embedded ....

    d) A backup of a 500 GB hard disk would be made using a ....

    e) A CD has a much smaller storage capacity than a ....

6. A desktop computer has a hard disk and RAM memory.

    a) Give **one** use of a hard disk.

    b) Give **one** use of RAM.

    c) Describe **two** differences between RAM and a hard disk.

7. A student does some coursework in ICT and wants to have a copy at home.
    The student can send the coursework by e-mail or copy it onto a 128 MB memory stick.

    a) Give **one** advantage of using e-mail.

    b) Give **one** disadvantage of using e-mail.

    c) Give **one** advantage of using the memory stick.

    d) Give **one** disadvantage of using the memory stick.

8. A fitter is using a computer-controlled cutter to cut a shape out of sheet metal.
    These are examples of instructions the fitter could use:

Instruction	Meaning
FORWARD 6	Move 6 mm forward
BACKWARD 4	Move 4 mm backward
LEFT 45	Turn 45 degrees to the left
RIGHT 60	Turn 60 degrees to the right
PENUP	Lift the cutting blade
PENDOWN	Lower the cutting blade

    Write down the instructions to cut out the shape.
    Each square has sides 10 mm long.

    You should start at **S** with the cutter pointing in the direction shown.

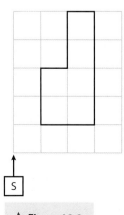

▲ Figure 13.2

9. Complete each sentence using **one** item from the list.

- Modem
- Graph plotter
- Laser printer
- Scanner
- Fax machine
- Telephone

a) An architect using A0 size paper to print house plans would use a...............

b) A student printing coursework would use a ....

c) A secretary listening to voicemail would use a ....

10. Office workers can access the company's intranet and the Internet.

a) Describe what is meant by an intranet.

b) Give **one** advantage to the company of having an intranet.

c) Give **one** disadvantage to the company of having an intranet.

d) Give **one** advantage to the company of giving workers access to the Internet.

e) Give **one** disadvantage to the company of giving workers access to the Internet.

11. Students have to log on to a college computer network they wish to use it.

a) State **two** items a student will need to type into a computer in order to log on to the network.

b) Give **one** reason why students have to log on before using the network.

c) The college has a VLE (Virtual Learning Environment). Give **one** advantage of a VLE.

12. A manufacturing company use a database to store personal information about their employees. This is part of the database.

Employee Number	Name	Job Title	Weekly Wage (£)
09134	Jacobs	Fitter	350
01834	Hodgson	Packer	300
08474	Harrison	Packer	300
17774	Casey	Supervisor	5000
03752	Patel	Electrician	350
18943	Casey	Packer	300

a) How many records are there in this part of the database?

b) How many fields are there in this part of the database?

c) The records shown are to be sorted into descending order on the *Name* field. What will be the *Employee Number* of the first record in this part of the database after it has been sorted?

d) Give the name of a field that contains text data.

e) Give the data type of the *Weekly Wage* field.

f) Which field would be the key field? Give **one** reason for your answer.

13. When a computer is connected to the Internet there are security threats. One security threat is virus infection.

a) Describe what is meant by a virus.

b) Describe **one** way a virus can infect a computer.

c) Give **two** ways to help prevent virus infection.

d) Name **one** other security threat and give **one** way to help prevent it.

6. Produce a report.
   - Show only the records where the Product is Bananas. ☐
   - Show only the fields Country, Code and Price. ☐
   - Produce the report in ascending order on the Country. ☐
   - Give the report the title 'Banana Producing Countries'. ☐

   Save the report. ☐

   Print the report. ☐

7. Produce another report.
   - The title of the report is 'Value of Stock of Rice'. ☐
   - The report should contain a new field called *Value* which is calculated at run-time. ☐
   - The Value field is the Stock multiplied by the Price. ☐
   - The Value field is formatted as currency with 2 decimal places. ☐
   - The report shows only rice and only the fields Product, Country, Code, Stock, Price and Value. ☐
   - The total value should be calculated and shown below the Value column formatted as currency with 2 decimal places. ☐
   - The report should be sorted into descending order on the Value. ☐
   - The report should fit on a single page. ☐

   Save the report. ☐

   Print the report. ☐

8. Produce another report.
   - The title of the report is 'Low Stock'. ☐
   - The report should show only the records where the Stock is less than the Reorder level. ☐
   - The report should show only the fields Product, Code and Stock. ☐
   - The report should be sorted into ascending order on the Code. ☐

   Save the report. ☐

   Print the report. ☐

9. Using the file **productchart.csv** (see Figure 13.6) create a comparative vertical bar chart (or column chart) to show the number of sales of each product each month.
   - Include data for March to June only. ☐
   - The horizontal axis should show the name of the month. ☐
   - The vertical axis should show the number of sales. ☐
   - The chart should have the title 'Sales from March to June'. ☐
   - Put appropriate labels on the horizontal and vertical axes. ☐
   - Show a legend that identifies the products. ☐

   Save the chart. ☐

   Print the chart. ☐

▼ Figure 13.6
The file productchart.csv

```
Sales
Product,January,February,March,April,May,June,July,August,September,October,November,December
Bananas,3100,1300,1350,13528,1360,1150,1150,1150,1300,1350,1100,1000
Rice,2800,2815,2850,2860,2850,2850,2800,2800,2850,1000,800,750
```

10. You are now going to edit a document about bananas and rice.
    - Using a suitable software package, open the file information.rtf (see Figure 13.2). ☐
    - Set the page size to A4. ☐
    - Set the page orientation to portrait. ☐
    - Set the top, bottom, left and right margins to 3 centimetres. ☐
    - Place the following in the header on every page: your name and candidate number left-aligned; and your centre number right-aligned. ☐
    - Place the following in the footer on every page: an automated file name left-aligned; an automated page number centre-aligned; and today's date right-aligned. ☐
    - Set all the text in a sans serif font, to 1.5 line spacing except in the table, left-aligned and to font size 11 point. ☐

11. Move the following bulleted list so that it is the second paragraph of the document. ☐

    Our principles of business are:
    - seek the finest products available
    - buy direct from known producers
    - buy in large quantities
    - ensure rapid transit of products from producer to consumer

    Change the bulleted list to a numbered list beginning with 1. ☐
    Indent this numbered list by at least 2 centimetres. ☐

12. Insert the heading 'Good-Food Bananas and Rice' at the beginning of the document.
    The heading should be:
    - Centre-aligned. ☐
    - In font size 18 point. ☐
    - In bold and italic. ☐

13. Insert the subheadings:
    - 'Bananas' after the second paragraph. ☐
    - 'Rice' in an appropriate position. ☐
    The subheadings should be:
    - In font size 16 point. ☐
    - Left-aligned. ☐
    - Underlined. ☐

14. Find the table at the end of the document.
    - Add a third column to the table. ☐
    - Give this column the heading 'Budget'. ☐
    - Enter the following data into the new column: ☐

Employee	Responsibility	Budget
John	Web Design	£10,000
Asif	Database Design	£15,000
Shirda	Online Security	£9,000
Julie	Project Management	£5,000

Block

1. A section of the screen display that has been highlighted.
2. A group of records on magnetic disk that is read or written together.

Boot sector

A reserved area on a disk that contains instructions for the computer as to where on the disk it will find the operating system.

Booting up

Loading the operating system into memory.

Bridge

A bridge is a hardware device that connects one LAN to another. The LANs are otherwise separate. See hub and switch.

Browser

A piece of software used to browse the information available on the Web. For example, Internet Explorer.

Buffer

Extra memory that acts as an intermediate store between a sending device and a receiving device. For example, a printer buffer is extra memory, usually built into the printer itself, which is used to hold output while it is waiting to be printed.

Bus network

A network in which a single line or cable with nodes at different points is used to connect servers, computers and other devices. Also known as a line network.

Button

Similar to an icon but usually part of a collection of similar buttons, such as the tool bar in Paint. When the button is clicked it appears to go in on the screen. See toolbox.

Byte

A byte is a set of bits used to represent one character. There are normally eight bits to the byte.

CAD (Computer-Aided Design)

CAD is the use of graphics software to help produce effective 2D and 3D designs. The graphics software used for CAD contains detail features not found in less powerful graphics software.

CAI (Computer-Aided Instruction)

The use of a computer to help learners acquire knowledge in a particular subject area. Also known as CAL.

CAL (Computer-Assisted Learning)

Using software to learn about another subject. For example, in Mathematics, using software to practise multiplication tables.

CAM (Computer-Aided Manufacture)

Using a computer to control the manufacture of a product.

CD-ROM

CD-ROMs are used for backing storage for computers. CD-ROMs can store text, sound, pictures, music and video. They are used with multimedia systems. They are very similar to audio CDs. Storage capacity is around 800 MB.

CD-RW

A CD that can have data written to it. The data can then be read many times.

Cell

The intersection of a row and a column in a spreadsheet, used to hold a label, value or formula

Cell range reference

Referring to a rectangular block of cells in a spreadsheet by giving the cell reference of the top left-hand and the bottom right-hand cells; e.g. **A4:G10**.

Cell reference

The cell's position described using the column and row; for example, **B7**.

Character

One of the symbols that can be represented by a computer. Characters include A to Z, 0 to 9, and punctuation marks.

Character code

A code used to represent characters; for example, ASCII.

Character set

All the characters that can be represented by a computer.

Chat

Communicating interactively in real time, probably using the Internet.

Check digit

A number or character placed after (or before) a string of numbers or characters to check that they have been correctly input, stored or transmitted.

Client

See server.

Client/server

A network with clients and at least one server. See server.

Clip art

Clip art means graphic images or pictures that have been prepared for importing into a word processor, DTP and other software. A wide range of clip art is available with illustrations for a range of different situations.

Clipboard

A temporary storage area used to hold information cut or copied from a document. Sometimes called the paste buffer.

Colour box

A palette of colours that are available for use.

Column break

The position in a column where the text ends and the next column starts.

Command line interface

A way of communicating commands to a computer by typing them in as text.

Computer

A computer is an automatic, electronic data processing machine which inputs, processes and outputs data under the control of a stored program.

Concept keyboard

A flat keyboard that can be programmed to correspond to overlays with pictures or simplified keys.

Control system

An ICT system used to monitor and control environmental conditions. For example, a control system to monitor the temperature and humidity in a greenhouse.

Control Unit (CU)

The part of the CPU that controls the running of programs and the input and output of data.

Copy

Copy selected material from a document to the clipboard. The copied material remains in the original document. See paste.

Corrupt data

Corrupt data is data that has been altered so that it is no longer meaningful. Data can be corrupted by accidental failure of the software or hardware being used. It may also be corrupted by malicious actions by hackers or by viruses.

CPU (Central Processing Unit)

The main part of the computer, where all the processing takes place. It consists of the Control Unit (CU), the Arithmetic and Logic Unit (ALU) and the memory (RAM and ROM). The processor box of a modern desk top computer usually contains the CPU, a hard disk and a floppy disk drive.

Crash

When a computer 'crashes', it stops working. Crashes can be associated with hardware failure, for example, a hard disk crash; or software failure, for example, a programming error.

Create

Set up for the first time.

Crop

To remove that part of an image outside the selected area.

Cursor

The pointer or other symbol on your screen that follows the movement of your mouse. It can be a pointer, or a vertical line that appears on a monitor screen. The cursor often flashes to attract attention.

Cursor control keys

The arrow keys on a keyboard used to control the movement of the cursor around the screen.

Cut

Remove selected material from a document and copy it to the clipboard. See paste.

Cyberspace

The mental visualisation or conceptualisation of the Internet and the Web.

Data

Data is numbers, characters and other input before it is interpreted and becomes information.

Data capture

Data capture is the collection of data for input to a computer. Data capture can be online (e.g. point of sale terminals at supermarket checkouts) or offline (e.g. questionnaires).

Data integrity

Ensuring the accuracy and completeness of data when it enters a system and throughout its subsequent processing.

Data item

An individual piece of information stored in a field.

Data logging

The use of sensors to measure environmental conditions. The sensors are connected to a computer which records the measurements.

Data preparation

Data preparation is the conversion of written or printed information into a form that can be processed by the computer. It usually involves the entry of data, using the keyboard, from a source document to a computer readable medium such as magnetic disk.

Data processing

Computers input, process and output data. In commerce this activity is sometimes called data processing.

Database

A means of storing and accessing information. The information is structured by subdividing it into tables, records and fields. The stored information can be searched, selected, sorted and reported.

DDE (Direct Data Entry)

DDE is data entry directly to the program that is processing the data. For example, using bar code readers.

Delete

Remove. For example, a file is deleted from a disk when it is removed from it.

Demonstration disk

A demonstration disk contains a demonstration version of software. Demonstration disks are often sent to intending purchasers so that they can evaluate software for themselves. The software on a demonstration disk may be complete but often there is some essential feature, such as printing, omitted. This is to encourage potential purchasers to buy a full copy of the software.

Dialog box

A temporary display window offering advice or information and asking you for a response.

Digital

The representation of data as binary codes made up of 1's and 0's. These can be stored in the computer as 5 volts and 0 volts, respectively, using two state, digital electronics.

Direct access

Direct access is the fastest method of accessing records in a file. The computer can store or retrieve the records without the need to read other records first. Direct access is used with magnetic disks but not with magnetic tape which use serial access.

Directory

A collection of files and subdirectories organised in a hierarchical tree structure. See root. A directory is also known as a folder.

Disk

Magnetic disks are a backing storage medium. There are floppy disks ($3\frac{1}{2}$") and hard disks. Hard disks may be exchangeable or fixed.

Documentation

Documentation for a piece of software should include a written description of how to install the software on a computer, what it does and how it is used. The manuals and help files supplied with a piece of software are its documentation.

Domain Name System (DNS)

A distributed database for translating a host computer name (such as **a.b.com**) to an IP address (such as **192.54.122.5**) or vice versa.

Download

Transfer a file from a web server to your computer over the Internet.

DTP (Desktop Publishing)

DTP combines graphics and word processing in a format typical of a newspaper or magazine with text in columns, varying character sizes, photographs and other illustrations.

Duplex

A transmission line that can simultaneously send and receive data.

DVD (Digital Versatile Disk)

A high-density disk for storing large amounts of data, especially high-resolution audiovisual material.

Dynaset

A group of records produced as an answer to a database query.

EDI (Electronic Data Interchange)

The exchange of information in electronic form over a network. For example, examination entries can be sent from schools to the GCSE examination boards using EDI over the national telephone network, and the examination results can be returned to schools in a similar manner.

Edit

Amend, delete or insert.

EFT (Electronic Funds Transfer)
A method of transferring money between bank accounts using a communications network.

EFTPOS
Electronic Funds Transfer at Point Of Sale. See Electronic funds transfer and Point of sale.

E-mail (electronic mail)
The sending and receiving of electronic messages (text, sound, video and graphics) using computers.

E-mail client
An e-mail client is the e-mail software on a client in a client/server network.

E-mail server
An email server is the file server that manages, distributes and stores e-mail.

Encryption
Encoding (scrambling) data during storage or transmission so that it cannot be understood by someone who does not have the encryption key.

Error message
A computer will occasionally detect an error when running software, and display an error message that tells you what has gone wrong.

Execute
To execute software (a program) is to run or use it.

Expert system
Software that allows users to recognise particular situations, providing help and advice on the appropriate action to be taken.

Extension
The part of a file name that follows the dot and identifies the kind of file it is. For example, a file called 'alpha.exe' has an extension of 'exe' which indicates that it is an executable program.

Feedback
Feedback occurs when a sensor senses information about a situation that requires the computer to take action by telling actuators to alter the situation. As this happens, the information sensed changes and there is a cycle of sensing and reaction until an equilibrium state is reached. For example, a central heating system uses feedback to maintain a constant temperature.

Fibre optics
The use of very thin fibre glass strands to transmit information encoded as pulses of light. The underground cabling used to distribute cable television is a fibre optic cable. Fibre optic cable can transmit very high volumes of information.

Field
A field is a data item within a record.

Field size
The maximum storage size allocated for a field.

File
A file is the envelope in which data is stored on backing storage. It may contain, for example, a word processed document.

File name
A unique name that identifies a file on backing storage.

File server
A computer attached to a network whose main function is to enable network stations to access shared files stored on one or more hard disks.

Firewall
Software used to prevent unauthorised users gaining access to a computer from the Internet.

Flip
To reflect an object in a line through its centre.

Flow chart
A diagram used to illustrate a sequence of operations.

Folder
A directory.

Font
A complete set of consistently shaped characters, for example, the Times New Roman font.

Foreground colour
The colour of the brush or other drawing tool being used.

Format
The format is the structure of the information, for example:
1. Formatting a floppy disk prepares its structure for use with a particular computer system. An unformatted floppy disk cannot be used.
2. The layout of a word processing document.

FTP (File Transmission Protocol)
A set of rules for **downloading** and **uploading** files from servers via the Internet.

Function
A predefined method of performing a specific task.

Gigabyte (GB)
Gigabytes are a measure of the storage capacity of a computer's memory or backing storage. 1 Gigabyte is 1024 Megabytes or 2^{30} bytes.

Graph plotter
An output peripheral that produces detailed pictures and diagrams on paper using one or more pens.

Graphics
Pictures or symbols which can be processed by a computer. They can be displayed on the screen, saved on disk, imported into applications software, etc.

Graphics pad
A graphics pad is a peripheral which allows the user to transfer line drawings to the computer by drawing on a sheet of paper that is resting on it.

GUI (Graphical User Interface)
A user interface that avoids the need to remember complex, text-based operating system commands by providing a visual interface that uses menus and icons. These can represent commands, processes or objects such as floppy disks. To make a selection from a menu or to activate an icon, the user points at it and clicks a button on the mouse.

Hacker
An unauthorised user of a computer system who has broken into the system, possibly by discovering a valid username and its associated password, or by bypassing them. Hacking is an illegal activity.

Half duplex
A transmission line that can send and receive data but not simultaneously.

Hard copy
Printed output from a computer.

Hard disk
A rigid disk used for storing data magnetically. Its construction allows for high storage densities and fast access times.

Hardware
The physical components of a computer system, such as the computer itself and input, output and storage devices.

Header
Text or graphics that appear at the top of every page of a document.

Help
Instructions showing how to use a piece of software that are accessible using the software when it is running. Also known as online help.

Help line
A telephone information service sometimes provided by hardware retailers, software vendors and others. Users who are having difficulty can ring the appropriate help line for immediate assistance in overcoming their particular problem. Many help lines are free to owners of a particular product; others are free during the guarantee period; some make a charge for their services.

HTML (Hypertext Markup Language)
A mark-up language used to create web pages.

Hub
A hub is a hardware device which connects a large number of computers to the rest of a LAN by means of one or more links to it.

Hyperlink
A link in a web page or other document which when clicked takes the user to another web page or document.

Icon
A picture that represents a command, function, process, device or tool.

ICT (Information and Communication Technology)
The use of computer-based technology to store, process and communicate information.

ICT system
The organisation of human and other resources, including ICT, into a coherent system for the purposeful processing of information.

ILS (Integrated Learning System)
A suite of computer-assisted learning programs that covers a wide range of studies, providing examples, demonstrations, explanations, exercises, assessment and other learning materials.

Immediate access storage
The memory immediately available to the CPU. Also known as the main memory or RAM.

Indent
Push a line or paragraph in or out from the left or right margin.

Index
A table containing two columns, one storing a sorted list of values in the field or fields being indexed, and the second storing pointers that give the location of each occurance of the data value.

Information
Information is data that is meaningful to us.

Inkjet printer
A printer that uses inkjet technology. A jet of ink is squirted onto the paper to form characters. There is no contact between the paper and the print head.

Input
Data entered into a computer system.

Insert
To insert means to put into.

Interactive processing
Interactive processing takes place when the user and the computer are in active two-way communication.

Interface
The interconnection between two different systems or devices, for example a computer and a printer. Also see Graphic User Interface.

Internet
The Internet is a global network that consists of a collection of smaller interconnected networks. There is no central organisation or ownership.

Intranet
A version of the Internet within a company or organisation.

IP address
The unique address that identifies a computer on the Internet.

ISP (Internet Service Provider)
A company that is directly connected to the Internet and gives you access to it, usually for a fee.

Joystick
A lever used to move a pointer or other image around a monitor screen. A joystick is often used with computer games.

Justify
Align text to the left, centre or right of the page or margin.

Kilobyte (KB)
Kilobytes are a measure of the storage capacity of a computer's memory or backing storage. A kilobyte is 1024 or 2^{10} bytes.

Key field
Every record in a database table should have a unique key field which identifies the record. Another name for a key field is the **primary key**.

Key-to-disk
A method of data preparation where data is entered at a keyboard and saved on disk.

Knowledge-based system
An expert system.

LAN (Local Area Network)
A collection of computers in a building, department or school that can share peripherals, share information and communicate with each other on the network.

Laptop
A portable computer that is small enough and light enough to be carried around.

Laser printer
Laser printers are expensive to buy but cheap to run and produce very high-quality printing. A wide variety of fonts and graphics can be printed. Laser printers are fast in comparison with inkjet printers.

Laser scanner
A hardware device that inputs bar codes by scanning the pattern of light reflected off the bar code by a laser beam.

LCD (Liquid Crystal Display)
A technology used to provide screen displays.

Light pen
A hardware device shaped like a pen that inputs bar codes by scanning the pattern of light reflected off a bar code.

Load (or Open)
To retrieve from backing storage.

Logic operation
For example, AND, OR and NOT.

Magnetic stripe reader
A device that reads the data contained in magnetic stripes, such as those on the back of credit cards.

Magnetic tape
A data storage medium consisting of a thin, flexible plastic strip of tape covered with magnetic material on one side.

Mail merge
The merging of a data file and a standard letter to produce personalised mail. Mail merge is a common function of word processing software.

Mail server
A computer on the Internet that receives incoming messages and delivers outgoing messages.

Mailing list
A group of people using e-mail to communicate their views on common issues or interests.

Main memory
The part of the CPU that is used to store programs while they are running and data while it is being processed. Also called RAM or the IAS.

Mainframe computer
A large, fast computer, probably having a variety of peripherals, including a high-capacity backing store and terminals, and telecommunications links.

Manual system
A manual system is paper based, and in contrast to an ICT system, it does not involve the use of ICT in any way.

Master file
A data file which is used to store most of the data for a particular application. It is updated by the transaction file.

Megabyte (MB)
Megabytes are a measure of the storage capacity of a computer's memory or backing storage. A megabyte is 1024 kilobytes or 2^{20} bytes.

Menu
A list of tasks which can be carried out by a computer program. The user selects a task from the menu.

Menu bar
An area, usually horizontal and near the top of a window, containing the names of menus relevant to the program's operation.

Merge
To combine two or more files into a single file.

Merge field
The name of the data that will be stored in the data source and later be merged into the main document as part of a mail merge.

MICR (Magnetic Ink Character Recognition)
A method of input where characters printed in magnetic ink are read directly into a computer. This method of input is used to process cheques.

Microfiche
An output medium consisting of microfilm sheets. Highly compressed storage can be achieved using this method.

Microprocessor
A single microchip containing all the elements of the CPU.

MIDI (Musical Instrument Digital Interface)
A standard for playing and representing sounds electronically, including their volume, pitch and other qualities.

MIS (Management Information System)
A comprehensive, integrated ICT system for management and administration.

Model
A representation of a real or an imagined system. Computer-based models can be constructed using a spreadsheet. For example, a model of predator/prey relationships or a financial model.

Modem
A modulator/demodulator. Used to convert digital data output by a computer to analogue signals that can be transmitted along a telephone line and vice versa.

Monitor
A screen used to display the output from a computer.

Mouse
A hand-held input device having one or more buttons on top and a ball or optical system underneath to detect movement over a flat surface. When the mouse is moved, a pointer on the screen moves in a corresponding direction.

Multi-access
When many users are connected to, and in simultaneous communication with, a single computer using terminals, this is multi-access computing.

Multimedia
The combination of text, sound, pictures, music and video. Often based on CD-ROM backing storage technology.

Multitasking
When one user, on one computer, is apparently running more than one program at the same time, this is multitasking.

Narrowband
Narrowband is used to refer to data transmission over a telephone line using an analogue modem which can transmit data at speeds up to 56 Kbps or 56 Kbaud. Narrowband is much slower than broadband.

Network
A network is a system of connecting cables. For example, networks can be used to connect computers; the telephone network connects telephone users.

Network station
A computer connected to a network.

Newsgroup
A group of people with common interests who communicate by posting messages and replies on the Internet.

NIC (Network Interface Card)
A card that is installed in a computer to enable it to communication with a network.

Non-volatile
ROM memory is non-volatile; that is, its contents are permanent. They are retained when the computer is switched off. Information stored on backing storage is also non-volatile.

NOT
A logic operation that is true if the condition is false.

Notebook
A smaller version of a laptop computer. Usually A4 size.

OCR (Optical Character Recognition)
The use of software and a scanner to read and recognise characters that are printed or written.

Offline
Not connected to a network, or connected but not in communication with it.

OMR (Optical Mark Recognition)
An input method where pencil marks on paper are detected. The position of the mark is interpreted as information. For example, it is used for the input of National Lottery numbers.

Online
Connected to the network and in communication with it.

Opaque
Unable to be seen through.

Open (or Load)
To retrieve from backing storage.

Operating system
An OS is software that controls and monitors the resources of a computer and acts as an interface between the user and the computer. An operating system is always present when a computer is used. Microsoft Windows is an example of an OS.

OR
A logical operation that is true when at least one of the conditions is true.

Packet
A group of bits transmitted as part of a data stream across the Internet. Packets are numbered so that the data stream can be reassembled when it arrives at the destination computer.

Parity bit
An extra bit used to check for data transmission errors. It is appended to a character to make the total number of 1s odd (**odd parity**) or even (**even parity**).

Password
A code that restricts access to a computer system. Usually associated with the username.

Paste
Copy material from the clipboard into a document. See cut.

PDA (Personal Digital Assistant)
A pocket-sized computer that has similar functions to a paper-based personal organiser. They can often read handwriting.

Peer-to-peer
A network in which each computer can communicate directly with every other computer attached to the network.

Peripheral
A peripheral is a hardware device that is connected to a computer system but is not a part of the computer itself. For example, a printer is a peripheral.

Phishing
Phishing is done by sending a fraudulent e-mail that pretends to be from a bank or another reliable source. In the e-mail you are asked to send personal information, e.g. usernames and passwords. These are used for identity theft and fraud.

PIR (Passive Infra Red detector)
A device attached to a burglar alarm system that uses infra red radiation to detect the presence of intruders.

Pixel
The smallest area of a screen that can be used in building up a picture. That is, a dot on the screen.

Plotter
A device that draws by moving a pen, and is especially suited for line drawings and charts in conjunction with CAD software.

Pointer
A pointer is an arrow or similar symbol which appears on the monitor screen. Its form depends on the operation being used. The position of the pointer is controlled by the mouse, and it is effectively the on-screen representation of the mouse.

Port
A connector used to link peripherals to a computer.

POS (Point Of Sale) terminal
A supermarket checkout or other point of sale. Often incorporates a laser scanner to read bar codes and a dot matrix printer to print receipts.

Primary key
A key field in a table that uniquely identifies a record.

Printout
The output from a printer.

Process control
The use of digital computers to monitor external processes closely and take corrective action if necessary, in industries such as chemical plants, steel mills and oil refineries.

Processor
See microprocessor.

Processor box
See system unit.

Program
A set of instructions used to control the operation of a computer.

Programming language
A language that allows a computer user to control the computer. For example: Logo, BASIC, Pascal, and COBOL.

Prompt
A displayed symbol or message indicating that the computer is waiting for your input.

Protocol
A set of rules and procedures, for example, to control the transmission and reception of data so that different devices or computers can communicate with each other.

Proxy Server
A proxy server is installed between a client and a web server. It regulates data communication between the client and the web server, speeding up web access, and acting as a firewall or filter protecting the LAN. The user thinks that they are accessing pages on the actual web server but they are accessing the proxy server. Pages from the web server have been downloaded and cached (stored) on the proxy server.
Similarly, the web server connects to the proxy server and not to the clients' computers on the LAN. The web server only identifies the proxy server and not the computers on the LAN. This can improve security by hiding the organisation of the LAN from the Internet.

Pseudocode
A method of representing an algorithm, using words and sentences, in a structure similar to an actual computer program.

Pull-down menu
A feature of a GUI where a hidden menu can be revealed (pulled down) by pointing at it.

Query
A method of searching for information in a database. See search condition.

Radio button
A circular button in a form that you can select using a mouse. Its function is the same as that of a tick list.

RAM (Random Access Memory)
Read/write memory within the computer's memory. RAM is volatile. RAM is used to store programs while they are being executed and data while it is being processed.

Random access
See direct access.

Range check
A validation check that checks that a data value is within realistic limits. For example, the number of months in a year must lie in the range 1 to 12 inclusive.

Range of cells
A group of continuous cells that forms a rectangle and is treated as a unit. See cell range reference.

Real-time processing
The processing of data being input which takes place so fast that when more data is input the results of the processing are already available. Real-time processing occurs in real time, i.e. as it happens.

Record
A record is a collection of related fields about a specific subject.

Relative cell reference
A reference to a cell in a spreadsheet that changes with respect to its current position when the formula is moved or copied; for example, **A5**.

Report
A screen display or printout of the information in a database table or query.

Resolution
The number of dots horizontally (w) and vertically (d) specified in the form 'w × d'. Resolution is specified for screen displays and printers.

Robot
An electro-mechanical device that can be programmed to a follow a sequence of commands in order to perform specified tasks. Robots include functions such as locomotion, mobility, grasping and recognition.

ROM (Read-Only Memory)
Memory within the computer's memory that can only be read. ROM is non-volatile.

Root
The top directory in a file system which is organised as an hierarchical tree. See directory.

Rotate
To turn an object around a point.

Router
A router is specialised hardware that receives data and redirects it between networks. The router can receive data from several computers connected to one network and redirect it to another network; for example, between a home network and the Internet. Data from the Internet is redirected to the appropriate computer on the home network. Routers may have a built-in firewall.

Run
To run a piece of software is to use it. See also execute.

Run time error
An error detected during the running of software.

Save
Store a document on a storage device so that it can be retrieved at a later date.

Scanner
A peripheral used to input photographs, line art, pictures and printed text into a computer.

Scroll
The display on a monitor screen is said to 'scroll' when it moves off the screen at the top and onto the screen at the bottom, automatically, at the same time. More accurately, this is known as 'vertical scrolling'.

Scroll bar
A control at the side or bottom of a window that you can use in conjunction with a mouse to show part of a document that is too big to fit on the screen.

Search
Look for. Query.

Search condition
A search condition is used to determine which records are selected when searching or querying a database table.

Search engine
A website that enables you to find information on the Web by typing in keywords or phrases.

Sensor
An input device that measures physical quantities such as temperature and humidity.

Sequential access
Similar to serial access but the data records are stored in the file in some known order.

Serial access
A method of accessing data records. In order to access a data record in a serial access file, it is necessary to start at the beginning of the file and read all the preceding records. The records are not stored in any particular order.

Server
On a network, a computer running software that allows resources to be shared with the other computers (called **clients**).

Simplex
A transmission line that can send or receive data in one direction only.

Simulation
The use of the computer to predict the outcome of a real-life situation by using a model of that situation.

Skew
To move the edge of an object either horizontally or vertically, leaving the other edges in their original positions.

Smart card
A card similar in shape and size to a credit card, but with an embedded microprocessor and storage capacity.

Software
Computer programs.

Software package
A complete set of programs and documentation.

Software piracy
The unauthorised copying, using or selling of software that is copyrighted.

Sort
To put into order.

Source document
A document or questionnaire used for data capture. It is the source of the data input to the computer.

Spam
The e-mail equivalent of junk mail.

Speech recognition
A method of input to a computer by speaking to it. Computers have limited ability to recognise speech. Consequently, commands are likely to be spoken in a strictly defined and restricted language. Normal spoken conversation is not usually recognised.

Speech synthesis
Sounds generated by a computer which synthesise human speech. A wide variety of words can be spoken but synthesised speech often lacks fluidity.

Spider
A program that searches the Web looking for new pages to add to a search engine's database.

Spreadsheet
Spreadsheets are used to calculate and display financial and other numerical information in columns and rows. Graphs can be generated, numerical models constructed and 'what if?' scenarios explored.

Standalone
A computer that is not connected to any other computer is being used in standalone mode; that is, it stands alone.

Status bar
A bar which displays a message relating to the processes being carried out using the software. This is often along the bottom of the window.

Stretch
To enlarge an object along the X-axis leaving the distances from the X-axis unchanged. Also to enlarge along the Y-axis leaving the distances from the Y-axis unchanged.

Stripe card
A plastic card containing a magnetic stripe which stores a limited amount of data. For example, a credit card.

Surfing
Surfing is the act of browsing through information on web servers throughout the world by wandering from server to server by selecting hyperlinks.

Swipe card
A card, usually the size of a credit card, that is swiped through an input device. It usually has a magnetic stripe on it.

Switch
Network switches perform similar functions to hubs and bridges. Switches use less bandwidth and so perform better than hubs. Switches transmit data faster, have more ports and cost less than bridges.

System unit
The cabinet containing the CPU, the hard disk and the other electronic components of your computer. Peripheral devices are attached to the system unit. Sometimes referred to as the processor box.

Systems analysis and design
The in-depth analysis of the software and hardware requirements of an ICT system and its detailed design.

Systems lifecycle
Investigation; analysis; design; implementation; monitoring and maintenance; evaluation.

Table
A list of information in a database shown in rows and columns. A database file may have several tables within it.

Tapes
Magnetic tapes are a backing storage medium. Tape cartridges are often used for backup.

TCP/IP
Transmission Control Protocol/Internet Protocol. A set of protocols used during the transfer of data from one computer to another over the Internet.

Technical documentation
Documentation written for technical specialists, such as ICT technicians. Technical documentation contains, for example, the detailed design of the system, program listings and error code listings.

Telecommuting
Working at home using a computer instead of at the office, and transmitting work over a communication network to the computer at the office.

Terminal
A peripheral device used to communicate over a network. Dumb terminals consist of a keyboard and monitor combination with no processing power of their own, and are often connected to mainframe computers. Desktop PCs can be used as 'intelligent' terminals as they have their own onboard processing power, and can be connected when the requirement arises.

Test data
Data used to test a piece of software for functional errors.

Toolbar
A rectangular area, often positioned near the edge of the screen or window, containing icons that represent tools relevant to the operation of the software. See toolbox.

Toolbox
A collection of buttons performing related tasks such as editing graphics. See toolbar.

Topology
The way in which computers in a particular network are connected together. Also known as network configuration.

Touch screen
A screen that enables you to input data by touching it with a stylus or your finger or another object.

Track
A track is the path on a magnetic disk on which data is stored.

Tracker ball
A hardware device with the same function as a mouse. A tracker ball has a ball and buttons accessible on its upper surface. Instead of moving the mouse to control the screen pointer, the ball is turned while the tracker ball unit remains stationary.

Transaction file
A file used to store recent data captured since the last master file update. The transaction file is used to update the master file.

Transparent
Able to be seen through.

Turnaround
Output which has data entered on it and is returned to the originating organisation so that the data can be input.

Turtle
A programmable robot with wheels. A turtle is used to learn how to control the movement of mobile robots on a flat surface. It is often controlled using Logo or a similar programming language.

Update
To bring a file or document up to date by amending, editing, inserting or deleting data.

Upload
Transfer a file from your computer to a web server over the Internet.

URL (Uniform Resource Locator)
The address of a web server; for example, the URL for Huddersfield University is **http://www.hud.ac.uk**.

User documentation
Documentation written for users. User documentation should be user-friendly. It should help users install software on a computer and explain how to use it.

User-friendly
Easy for users to operate and understand.

User interface
The way in which a computer system communicates with users. For example, a graphical user interface (GUI) such as Windows.

Username
A unique username is given to every user of an ICT system so that it can recognise each user. Each username is associated with a password, and this helps to prevent unauthorised access to the system.

Utility
Software that may be a part of the operating system and is used to do a task that is useful only in relation to the organisation of the computer system. For example, format a disk.

Validation
A check that data is realistic. For example, a range check.

Verification (visual)
A visual check comparing what is on the screen with what is written on a source document.

Verification (purpose)
A check on the accuracy of the input process. That is, a check that what is written on a source document is accurately transferred to a computer-readable medium.

Verification (double entry)
What is written on the source document is typed into the computer by one person, and then typed in again by another person. The computer compares both versions to see if they are the same, and if not, an error report is produced so that mistakes can be corrected.

Virtual reality
A model world constructed using ICT. The rules governing relationships in a virtual reality model may be very unreal.

Virus
A virus is a computer program that infects a computer system, usually without the user's knowledge. Viruses may be benign but more often they cause damage.

Voice recognition
The indentification of a person by recognising their voice.

Voice synthesis
The ability of a computer to produce sounds resembling human speech.

Volatile memory
Volatile memory loses its contents when the power is switched off. RAM memory is volatile.

WAN (Wide Area Network)
A network spread over a wide area, possibly international, making use of, for example, permanent cable connections and satellite communications.

Web
The Web is a multimedia information service accessible using the Internet. It consists of Web pages written in HTML and software to display these, for example, a browser.

Web page
A hypertext or hypermedia document on the World Wide Web.

Web ring
A web ring is a way of interlinking a group of websites that have information on related topics or themes. The websites are linked so that you can visit each site one after the other, eventually (if you keep going) returning to the first website. Users can go backwards or forwards through the web ring.

Website
A server (or part of a server) on the World Wide Web, containing one or more web pages and other files.

Window
A rectangular subdivision of the screen which enables the user to look at the output from a program. There may be more than one window open on the screen at the same time.

Wireless access point
A device attached to a LAN that can receive and broadcast wireless signals. It communicates with wireless Network Interface Cards (NICs) in computers, allowing them to connect to the network.

Wizard
Guidance provided by an application that takes you through a task a step at a time.

Word wrap
A feature of a word processor. When typing beyond the right-hand margin, the word automatically carries over to the next line. This is word wrap.

Word processing
The preparation of letters and other documents using a computer in a manner similar to a typewriter but with additional features.

WYSIWYG (What You See Is What You Get)
What is displayed on the screen is what will be printed on the printer. This phrase is particularly used in connection with word processors.

Zoom in
To view an object as if you were closer to it.

Zoom out
To view an object as if you were further away from it.

Index